More Acclaim for Bill Cummings'

Starting Small and Making It Big:
An Entrepreneur's Journey to Billion-Dollar Philanthropist

"Across his career, whenever the world zigged, Bill had the great instincts and confidence to zag. That's what makes *Starting Small* required reading for anyone wanting to understand entrepreneurialism. Even more important are the vital lessons Bill and Joyce offer for how to share wealth in such a smart and meaningful way."
—NEIL SWIDEY, Author of *Trapped Under the Sea* and *The Assist*

"There are so many life lessons in this book. I thank Bill for taking the time to document and summarize the many life and business lessons he has to share."
—ADELE FLEET BACOW, President, **Community Partners Consultants** and First Lady of **Harvard University**

"A fascinating account, full of valuable lessons for readers ranging from aspiring entrepreneurs to experienced managers. Yet the book's appeal reaches far beyond the business world. In Bill's reflections about relationships, principles, and the nature of success, he offers wisdom that will benefit people in all walks of life. I have recommended this memoir to our faculty for discussion with our students, particularly our management students."
—SISTER JANET EISNER, SND, President, **Emmanuel College**

"A really fun and thought-provoking read. There are countless lessons in this book—including having some perspective about making a difference in your community and having a sense of place."
—DR. JOHN McARDLE, Faculty Director,
Salem State University Center for Entrepreneurship

"*Starting Small and Making It Big* shares a remarkable American story—culminating in business success and a profound impact on the greater good. A deeply personal book, it is also filled with insights into entrepreneurship and leadership that will be valuable for those seeking to shape and grow organizations, whether they are fresh out of college or seasoned professionals. Bill Cummings has led a truly exemplary life, and his book makes clear why he has become a valued friend and advisor to so many individuals and in so many communities."

—Dr. ANTHONY MONACO, President, **Tufts University**

"Given *Starting Small's* many business and life lessons, I am not at all surprised that it has been selected as required reading at so many colleges. It is a worthwhile read—and a fun one—for students and seasoned professionals alike."

—RICHARD C. OCKERBLOOM, Retired President, *The Boston Globe*

"Bill Cummings grew up poor, but through a series of highly successful business ventures became one of the wealthiest individuals in Massachusetts. He has committed to donate more than 90 percent of his wealth to charity."

—SUSAN SALISBURY, *Palm Beach Post*

"His narrative isn't a slick Silicon Valley story; nor is it a story of someone born into a family with wealth and prestige. It is a story of Everyman and Everywoman. And that is most inspiring of all."

—DEIRDRE SARTORELLI,
Angle Center for Entrepreneurship, Endicott College

"It is all the proof one could ever want that 'good guys can finish first'—a fascinating story sprinkled throughout with business tips that will prove especially helpful to any young person just starting out on a career."

—NILS SHAPIRO, *Palm City Spotlight*

"It is interesting to hear Bill's rags to riches story and his unbelievable drive and entrepreneurial spirit that have helped create his company. The book provides not only history about the commercial real estate industry but also an inside look at one of the most entrepreneurial people I've encountered."

—TAMARA SMALL, CEO,
National Association of Industrial and Office Properties (NAIOP)

STARTING SMALL
— *AND* —
MAKING IT BIG

An Entrepreneur's Journey to
Billion-Dollar Philanthropist

by BILL CUMMINGS

Published by Cummings Foundation, Inc.

Fifth Edition

Cummings, Bill.
Starting Small and Making It Big: An Entrepreneur's Journey to Billion-Dollar Philanthropist/Bill Cummings
Library of Congress Control Number: 2018941733
ISBN: 978-0-692-99546-4 (trade pbk.)
ISBN: 978-0-692-06407-8 (hardcover)
ISBN: 978-0-9998951-1-5 (digital)

100% of all sales for charitable purposes.
Enjoy FREE domestic shipping on all orders.

Pricing
Individual: $16.95 paperback / $24.95 hardcover
Three-pack: $40.00 paperback / $60.00 hardcover
Case: $265.00 for 26 paperbacks / $210.00 for 14 hardcovers

For larger bulk purchases and book stores, contact:
Book Marketing Manager, Cummings Foundation
200 West Cummings Park
Woburn, MA 01801, 781-935-8000

Order direct via **Cummings.com/book** or **Amazon.com**

Set in Adobe Caslon Pro / Printed in USA by King Printing Company, Inc., Lowell, MA.
Designed by Sarah Coelho-Rivera, cover design by Mike Lamothe

About the Author

My autobiography is not a Horatio Alger story, or maybe it is a little bit. Born during the Great Depression, I grew up poor but first tried my hand at being an entrepreneur at six or seven years old. I sold bottles of soda pop each afternoon at a neighborhood construction site, and there are still so many similar opportunities today.

A decade later, I talked my way into college and was able to pay all of my tuition and expenses by always working and by being forever frugal. Soon after graduation, I made a point of paying back a single $50 scholarship award with a 1958 contribution and have continued giving to my alma mater ever since.

I became a serial entrepreneur in earnest after first working all over the country with two national consumer products firms. In 1964, I spent $4,000 to purchase my first real business, a hundred-year-old manufacturer of concentrated fruit-juice-beverage bases, which I quickly expanded by providing refrigerated dispensers and drinks to several hundred colleges and universities.

With the proceeds from the sale of that once tiny business in 1970, I founded a suburban-Boston commercial real estate firm. Cummings Properties quickly grew from one small building to a portfolio of more than 11 million square feet today. Along the way, we accumulated uncommon wealth, which my wife, Joyce, and I have begun actively disbursing through Cummings Foundation, which we established together in 1986.

Joyce and I were the first Massachusetts couple to join the Giving Pledge, an international philanthropic organization founded by Bill and Melinda Gates and Warren Buffett. We have been honored to receive dozens of community accolades, from organizations as varied as the Irish International Immigrant Center, the Archdiocese of Boston, Friends of Israel, and NAIOP, the association for the commercial real estate development industry. We have both received several honorary doctoral degrees and have three of those times served together as joint college commencement speakers.

In 2012, *The Boston Globe* named us runners-up as Greater Bostonians of the Year. More recently, the Greater Boston Chamber of Commerce named Joyce and me to its Academy of Distinguished Bostonians. We have lived together in Winchester, Massachusetts, for fifty years.

Dedication

Joyce Cummings

To Joyce, with my everlasting love,

You have quietly made me look good for more than half a century. Supporting me and our wonderful family, you have always been there and have always done whatever was needed, and so much more.

Thank you eternally for being my only true love, and for so carefully tempering and moderating our now fifty-two years together. You and our family have been the greatest blessing of my life.

Special Remembrance

James "Jamie" McKeown   Douglas Stephens   David Leland

This linear memoir is also dedicated to the memory of three of my closest colleagues and best friends with whom I worked with such admiration for a combined total of ninety years. All three died so prematurely as they approached the apexes of their professional careers. Jamie, Doug, and David were integral to the ultimate success of Cummings Properties and Cummings Foundation. Our total organization would not be anything like what it is today without their wisdom, dedication, and guidance. Sorely missed every day, all three were wonderful human beings who left us far too soon.

Contents

Prologue

MY WIFE, JOYCE, hesitated in May 2011 as she packed her suitcase for our early summer trip to the great Southwest. The event's registration materials stated that attire would be "casual," but what did that mean when we would be meeting with a large group described as the top 1 percent of the world's wealthiest people? We had just joined the Giving Pledge, the philanthropic organization founded by Melinda and Bill Gates and Warren Buffett to encourage the world's most affluent people to donate at least half of their assets to charitable causes, either during their lifetime or upon their deaths.

Giving Pledge members submit written pledges to this effect. The complete, updated versions of our and other Giving Pledge members' letters are maintained within a philanthropy exhibit at the Smithsonian Institution. They can also be found on the Smithsonian's website and the Giving Pledge website.

For us, the donating part of the decision was easy. The issue with which we wrestled was revealing publicly, for the first time, that we had reached the prescribed billion-dollar net worth. The fact is, we never had a goal to attain any certain level of affluence, and over time we accumulated much more than we ever paid any attention to. As appears to be the case with many of the early Giving Pledge members, the decision to use our earnings philanthropically during our lifetimes came well before this association's formation.

The past few weeks had been a whirlwind in our otherwise relatively ordinary lives. Shortly after Joyce and I submitted our written pledge, a front-page, above-the-fold story in *The Boston Globe* "outed" us as billionaires, much to the surprise of many who knew us. Close friends and acquaintances were aware that we were well-off financially, but none had any idea that our assets placed us in this league. After all, I still delighted in finding golf balls in the rough, and Joyce still regularly used coupons at the supermarket. We had much the same lifestyle, habits, and friends as we'd had for decades, since well before we had the means to establish Cummings Foundation in 1986.

For the most part, our foundation's giving had been focused in northeastern Massachusetts—extremely local. We took it slowly, gradually increasing our gifts over a good many years until we decided to join the Giving Pledge. During its first year, the new group grew to a total of about seventy individuals and couples, all of whom acknowledge being billionaires—including at least one other member who, like Joyce and me, would still be a billionaire if he hadn't already given away the large majority of his assets for philanthropic purposes.

Member Chuck Feeney, founder of the huge Duty Free Shops chain, went so far as to write in his autobiography with Conor O'Clery, "I am giving it all away right now, and I want my last check to bounce."

Then came the *Boston Globe* article, highlighting this major turning point in our lives—the switch in our primary focus from making money to giving it away. This change did not mean that I had stopped building. During a long and highly successful career in commercial real estate development, I had built the Boston area company known as Cummings Properties and, together with a truly phenomenal team, we grew its portfolio to now 11 million debt-free square feet. Now my new job, after four decades, was to help others build the foundation's capacity to feed the hungry, assist immigrants, support solid educational programs for young people, create homes for the elderly, and so many other things.

After many successful years building and leasing commercial real estate in Greater Boston, Joyce and I came to recognize and believe that no one can truly "own" anything. With our ever-so-brief stays upon this earth, how can we possibly think of ourselves as *owning* land? How can we ever be anything more than caretakers of the ground that lies beneath whatever we might develop on a site? It was easy thereafter to start giving away much more.

At about the time we established Cummings Foundation, we pledged to donate 10 percent of all our income each year to it. Gradually, as it became clear that our four children and any future grandchildren were well provided for, we also began donating many of our commercial properties to the foundation. We donated about 60 percent of the total family assets, giving Cummings Foundation sufficient resources to become a meaningful philanthropic factor.

Having already pledged privately years ago to donate the large majority of our wealth to charity, we publicly signed the Giving Pledge in 2011 in the hope that, with every new member, the association would gain momentum and provide encouragement to others who have the capacity to give more. We gave most of our assets first to Cummings Foundation. Now, with an enormous amount of volunteer assistance from an extremely diverse group of community leaders throughout northeastern Massachusetts, we have disbursed $200 million of the foundation's earnings to deserving nonprofits.

We never particularly liked the expression "Give until it hurts." We thought the better goal would be "Give until it feels good." The Giving Pledge feels really good to us, and we applaud the vision and leadership of its three founders: Warren Buffett and Bill and Melinda Gates. Although there are many references to the Giving Pledge within these pages, including some details from members' own biographies, this book is not *about* the Giving Pledge. In fact, I have sometimes described *Starting Small* as a book about business, entrepreneurship and philanthropy, but *disguised as* an autobiography.

BY ANY STANDARD, our story of a young couple from working- and middle-class American homes who has already given away so much to a thousand Boston-area charities is unusual. Noteworthy, too, is the story of what took place during the sixty-plus years spent building up to this level of philanthropic ability. Beyond the narrative, this autobiography is full of ideas about entrepreneurship.

Although some people may be predisposed to an entrepreneurial lifestyle, I believe that highly effective entrepreneurship is something that can absolutely be taught and learned, if one has the right role models and teachers, and most important, a strong desire. Then, once success has been achieved, an entrepreneur must assume the mantle of mentor, passing on key business philosophies to others who will carry on and build upon his or her success.

Given the right environment, entrepreneurship can begin at a young age, as it did for me. From the classic lemonade stand to my days and months spent washing store windows, or buying, rehabbing, and reselling small boats, there are myriad ways that ambitious youth can gain basic business experience while earning their first dollars. Most children today may be missing out on these valuable pursuits simply because they lack discretionary time. American society seems to be denying young people the opportunity to develop the skills to enrich themselves, which they likely would do if given the time and freedom to explore and take risks. The number of students interested in after-school jobs, for instance, seems to have dramatically decreased.

Another significant difference from the time I started my career is technology. So many entrepreneurs today are focused on creating a smarter phone, a smaller electronic device, or the next great app. These are all worthy goals, but aspiring entrepreneurs should also be aware that the more mundane opportunities are still there, perhaps now more than ever before. In fact, today's obsession with technology might have created greater opportunity for young adults, especially those willing to invest sweat equity in buying, improving, and reselling fixer-up real estate. This career that I effectively began fifty years ago still offers great promise today.

Regardless of the type of business one engages in, many of the philosophies captured in this book can be readily applied. Being an opportunist, planning for succession, buying "right," and many of the other principles I discuss can contribute so much to one's personal and professional growth, and increase the chances of success and profitability. Anyone trying to open, build, or grow any kind of new business may be either encouraged or discouraged by the contents of this book. If the reader is a businessperson looking for guidance, and he or she is not geared for and ready to take on the workload, he or she should absolutely consider going in another direction. After all is said and done, anyone who wants to be a business success will likely never make it if the workload itself is not fun or fulfilling in some way.

Some of these entrepreneurial ideas and philosophies are reflected in the early stories I relate about selling things as a preteen and about a collection of self-initiated part-time moneymaking activities that closely parallel some of the early part-time work described in the 1995 Warren Buffett biography I read decades ago. My accomplishments thereafter pale by any and every comparison with Buffett—one of my few personal heroes.

One key concept of this book concerns the necessity of monitoring costs and buying things "right." How foolish is it to talk about buying substantial quantities of products or services based only on the silly notion of getting three bids first? How lazy is the buyer who does not work with prospective sellers to at least try to get them to give up their lowest effective price? Getting three quotes is fine, but start first with one quote, and then learn whatever you can learn from the first bidder to let each subsequent bidder know where it needs to be in order to stay in the game.

People who repeatedly purchase the same or similar things or services need to occasionally disappoint their low bidders by awarding a contract to a second-lowest bidder, making it at least appear that the "regular" low bidder has some competition.

Entrepreneurs must first work at distinguishing their product from others, so that they can then tout these differences in such a way as to make their product better, or at least worth more. In real estate, think of this as assiduous estate management. For instance, people with whom I work have heard so much over the years about the importance of cleanliness and housekeeping details such as keeping litter out of the parking lots, or pruning bushes or low-growing tree branches so that they are not even slightly blocking sidewalks or signage. Think how off-putting it is to enter a restaurant when the front glass entrance door looks like no one has even thought about cleaning it all day. How about frayed or soiled carpet just inside the same door?

It's a question always of looking out for the details that might reflect negatively on how anyone's property looks and feels, though the principle certainly applies far beyond real estate.

Bill Cummings

[1]

Early Lessons of Cost and Value

MY DAD, Gus Cummings, was considered too old for military service during World War II. He spent the war years working for Bethlehem Steel Company at Fore River Shipyard in Quincy, Massachusetts, and took great personal pride in his work: painting the interiors of destroyers and light cruisers.

Sometimes he would spend a week just painting the intricate interior of a major gun turret, and he always stressed to me how important it was that he did his job correctly—even when his work couldn't be seen. Dad abhorred the waste, theft, and inefficiency he saw daily at the shipyard, and I remember him frequently telling my

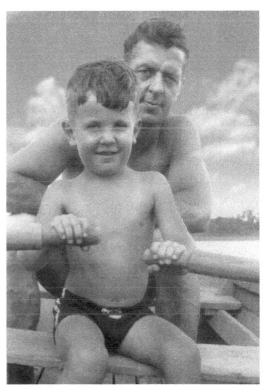

Bill and his dad in the "family boat," 1942, in the Fore River, in Weymouth, Massachusetts

mother how lax the company was about workers repeatedly stealing tools and supplies by carrying them out under their coats or in their lunch boxes at the end of the day.

Although Dad was not highly paid, he took full advantage of the many opportunities to work overtime, especially at a double-time rate on weekends, to help alleviate his Depression-era debt. His steady work afforded our family some relief, but by no means any sort of affluence.

I *Bill and his mother, Dorothy Cummings, 1939*

As a young man, Dad had served as a seaman in the U.S. Merchant Marine, sailing mostly between East Coast ports and South America. Unlike with his experiences at "The Yard," I rarely heard him talk about his seagoing days, probably because I did not know enough to ask. He never talked much about pool halls either, but I knew there were a couple of them he especially liked, and the opportunity to gamble was a big part of the appeal. He made out pretty well, hustling bets on his own abilities with the expectation of supplementing his otherwise meager income.

Augustus William Cummings, Jr., was born in Somerville, Massachusetts, in January 1899, and he left school after ninth grade. He spent most of his younger years around Davis Square in Somerville, and, from the stories I occasionally heard, he worked on his conditioning at a local boxing club, where he sometimes fought for prize money.

Throughout the 1930s, long before the days of electric refrigerators, Dad drove one of several milk delivery wagons for his father's modest milk company. He did this seven days a week. Since his horse knew the route by heart, Dad could frequently doze between his early-morning stops. The only time he couldn't chance a nap, he told me, was after the last stop, when the horse, if not fully controlled, would take off dangerously fast on its return to the barn. Even at the end of World War II, with no new motor vehicles available, Seven Oaks Dairy, Happy Home Bakery, and Metropolitan Ice Company all had daily horse-drawn deliveries in my Salem Street neighborhood in Medford, where we moved just prior to my entering first grade.

My mother, Dorothy Purington Cummings, was born in 1904 in Sunapee, New Hampshire, but she graduated from Somerville High School after she had moved there with her family as a child. Grandpa Purington once told me that driving to Boston from their home in Goffstown, New Hampshire, now little more than an hour's ride, used to be a real adventure. It was a half-day drive, and the trip often included repairing a flat tire or two along the way. There were so few cars on the road at the time that drivers were pretty much expected to wave to each other in passing.

My mother's parents, John and Mary (Clarke) Purington, came to Massachusetts from Ireland in 1898, as best I can determine. Grandfather Purington, who became a skilled auto mechanic from about as early on as automobiles were invented, died when I was quite young, as did both paternal grandparents. My grandmother Purington suffered greatly during much of her early life from the virulent anti-Irish sentiment she encountered as a recent immigrant.

Grandma adamantly refused to talk with me about Ireland. "I am an American, Billy," she would say, when I asked about her earlier circumstances. Sometimes she would say just a bit more: "I am an American, Billy, and that's all you need to know." She would never admit in any way, even to me, that she was Irish. Until the day she died, she was afraid someone would "find out" she was Irish. As her mind weakened near the end of her earthly journey, Grandma feared she would be thrown out of the nursing home in her final days if "they" learned about her Irish heritage.

The first time I ever told that story was fifty years after her death, during a talk I gave in 2013 at the annual meeting of the Irish International Immigrant Center in Boston. The comments were met with ready and complete understanding from many of those present.

We know infinitely more about my father's side. One of my considerably older first cousins, Leonard Cummings, was the first person to tell me anything about our Yankee roots, going all the way back to the founding of the First Parish Church in Salem, Massachusetts. Dad's first-known North American ancestor, Isaac Cummings, landed in Salem in 1638, and Leonard told me Isaac lived briefly in Salem and in Watertown before eventually settling in the part of Ipswich that is now Danvers, Massachusetts. Isaac Cummings' memory is kept alive through the work of the Isaac Cummings Family Association.

Leonard and his brother Whitley were the first family members to graduate college. Soon after their discharges from the U.S. Army and the Marine Corps, following World War II, they returned to Harvard University and Boston University, respectively. Both went on to lifetime careers with national insurance companies. Their father, Whitley Cummings, who was himself quite successful, would keep my dad posted on his boys' progress, and Dad would always hold them up to me as the great role models they were.

I came into the world at Somerville Hospital on March 11, 1937, and then lived briefly on Milton Street, in Arlington, Massachusetts. Although my earliest years coincided with the end of the Depression, I recall nothing but

Dorothy Cummings

| *Bill and his father, Gus Cummings*

a simple, happy childhood, even if it was with only the barest necessities. I then grew up a few miles north of Boston, in Medford, a lower middle-class, blue-collar community on the Mystic River.

In 1942, we lived on Adams Street on Medford Hillside, three blocks behind the campus of Tufts University, which was known as Tufts College until 1955. U.S. involvement in World War II had begun, and my only real memory from the Adams Street days was of finding my way with a slightly older friend to see the anti-aircraft guns being installed at the four corners of a small, rectangular reservoir, almost exactly where Tufts' Carmichael Hall dormitory is today. At five years old, I enjoyed rolling down the steep bank around the reservoir—until one day I slid off the lower edge and into the water. My friend helped me out, but it was to my great chagrin as police arrived to make a big move on me.

COST AND VALUE—I heard those themes repeatedly throughout my upbringing. Mom never wanted me to hear Depression tales, but my sister, Marian, nine years my senior, still told me her stories and those of her friends who formerly seemed to have everything and then suddenly had virtually nothing in the meanest of times. During one winter, Marian's chores included picking up coal at the railroad tracks that ran along nearby Boston Avenue to help heat our rented apartment. Those were the days when coal-fired steam locomotives pulled the trains, and each train had a "fireman" shoveling coal into the firebox to keep the steam pressure high. One particular train worker on his daily run into North Station became Marian's friend. They would exchange waves, and then he would "accidentally" spill a shovelful of coal that she would pick up from the tracks to fill her bucket.

> *Frugality was a family theme. Always saving and never wasting money were constant parts of our life.*

Frugality was a family theme. Always saving and never wasting money were constant parts of our life. Developed during the Depression, my parents' passion for frugal living was then strongly reinforced by wartime shortages, when "making do with what we had" was an absolute necessity. "A penny saved is a penny earned" was a regular reminder. So many things were rationed during the war: fresh meat, canned meats, butter, sugar, chocolate, gasoline...

Automobiles were not rationed, but there were simply none available. Everything was directed toward the war effort. Yet I remember that the auto companies' radio commercials persisted. One jingle I especially recall: "There's a Ford in your future / but the Ford in your past / is the Ford you have now / so you'd better make it last."

As more and more resources were diverted to the war effort, the community came to know when local stores received fresh stock of scarce items, and it often meant long lines on those days. Sometimes, my mother would ask her five- or six-year-old

> *If we are honest with ourselves in setting achievement goals, our individual work will likely be far more satisfying.*

"Billy" to get into the neighborhood A&P market early and set aside certain things. She would then take quiet delight in arriving at the cash register, much later in the day, with her mayonnaise, corned beef hash, and canned salmon, all of which I would have hidden for her behind the Scott toilet paper. Perhaps that was Mom teaching me from my youngest years how to be an opportunist.

Mom earned five stars running the family finances, with great emphasis on the importance of "putting something away." She also preached about the necessity of hard work and ambition, "like Daddy." Mom and Dad's passionate financial goal was to own their own home. Saving enough money to purchase a two-family home, and then to secure a mortgage, was our whole family's dream during the war years.

What constitutes success in life is as individual as our lifestyles. I have always believed that learning to honestly assess our shortcomings as well as our strengths is vitally important in helping us know when we are aspiring to more than we should expect to attain. If we are honest with ourselves in setting achievement goals, our individual work will likely be far more satisfying.

To me, financial success means reaching a certain stage in life when one can feel adequately assured of living out one's days in a reasonably comfortable and happy lifestyle. I find it quite sad when intelligent people with limited resources get close to retirement before they begin making practical adjustments in their living and spending habits. So often they fail to act in a timely manner because they have become trapped in "keeping up with the Joneses," or they are just too intent on enjoying today's pleasures with no thought of tomorrow.

I also find it extremely puzzling that so many of today's young people seem to have no money sense whatsoever. Frequently, they do nothing to set money aside and out of reach. They often pay outrageous prices for clothes, concerts, fancy food and wines, sporting events, cars, and so on, and they can never figure out why they run out of money so quickly.

Saving money, economizing, and investing must be essential elements for everyone, from their teenage years through retirement age. While still in elementary school, I started to make (and save) money in all sorts of ways. My allowance was twenty-five cents a week, which was the first thing I deposited in my savings account at Medford Savings Bank at six years old. I still routinely had more pocket-cash than my friends and classmates seemed to have, even though most of my money went quickly in the bank. Such a savings account today would be a terrible investment for anyone with real income, but there are so many investment opportunities available now. For those with access to a company IRA and/or a 401(k) plan, it is usually financially foolish not to take maximum advantage of such accounts, and certainly so when a company offers meaningful matches. Regularly investing a set amount or percentage of every paycheck will do wonders for younger workers. This type of thinking seems not to come naturally, however, if parents do not set examples and actively teach their kids how important it is to develop early saving habits and prepare for the future.

For three years during the war, we lived at 456 Salem Street in Medford. Our Salem Street home was a one-bedroom apartment in an old three-story wooden tenement above a liquor store, a coin laundry, and a taxi stand. My sister and I shared the apartment's only bedroom, and our parents slept in the living room, often struggling to pay the $10 or $12 monthly rent.

For the warmer months during the last two years of World War II, my parents also owned a modest summer cottage on Holbrook Road in North Weymouth. The cottage was close to my father's work at the shipyard. This kept him from having to make the rush-hour commute from and to Medford (before there was any expressway from Boston to Quincy), saving him more than an hour each way. Because of his long commute during the rest of the year, however, Dad received rationing coupons for gasoline and tires year-round. As a result, the Cummings family entertainment frequently consisted of taking rides to interesting places in Dad's old Model A Ford.

Mark Anderson was the only other child my age who lived around our busy Medford block in the middle of Haines Square. Indeed, except for Mark and for David Jackson, who lived just on the other side of Route 28, there were no other children in my neighborhood. It was hardly a family setting, lacking any hint of lawns, trees, or flowers, and with me at only six years old, people paid me little attention. I would dart in and around traffic, including dozens of streetcars. Each morning the streetcars set out in three directions from the car barns of what was then the Boston Elevated Street Railway, directly across the wide cobblestone street from our apartment.

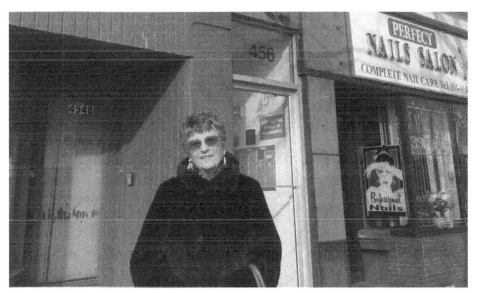

| *Joyce Cummings, in front of the modernized entrance to the Cummings home of 1942-1945*

I had enrolled in first grade at Medford's Curtis Elementary School on Paris Street at five and a half, but then I promptly missed the first three weeks of classes with whooping cough. At the end of the school year, I developed measles and missed more class time. From the looks of that year's report card, I was off to a less-than-auspicious start. Fortunately, the "Promotion Prospect: Doubtful" designation on my first-grade report card did not doom my academic career.

By age seven or eight, my friends and I frequently hung off the back end of the streetcars in summer, when the pull-down windows were all open. During swimming season, we took "free" rides up Fellsway West to the end of the line, near Wright's Pond. We all much preferred spending the five-cent fare on a Hershey or Mars candy bar to dropping it into the streetcar fare box.

Medford's old streetcars were discontinued on the Fellsway while I was still in grammar school, and we young free-riders watched in dismay as crews removed the tracks from the middle of the tree-lined parkway. Then the immediate

MEDFORD PUBLIC SCHOOLS

Report of _William Cummings_

Grade _I_   School _Curtis_

Sept. 9 to Nov. 16	*unable to mark William because of his short period of attendance.* Teacher *M. Veronica Dyer*	Days Absent / Times Tardy / Times Dismissed	0 / 0 / 0
Nov. 16 to Feb. 1	*Unsatisfactory. He is not up to standard but is doing well on his own level.* Teacher *M. Veronica Dyer*	Days Absent / Times Tardy / Times Dismissed	0 / 1 / 0
Feb. 1 to Apr. 12	*Satisfactory on his level — has a slim chance of promotion.* Promotion Prospect *Doubtful* Teacher *M. Veronica Dyer*	Days Absent / Times Tardy / Times Dismissed	½ / 0 / 0
Apr. to June	PROMOTED Teacher *G. Andrea Murphy*	Days Absent / Times Tardy / Times Dismissed	13 / 0 / 0

Bill's first-grade report card shows "PROMOTED," although his prospect of promotion in April was described as "doubtful"

rebuilding of the roadway that summer presented me with the ideal opportunity to develop my first business venture. With the construction underway practically in my backyard, I purchased bottles of cold Pepsi Cola, orangeade, and 7-Up for a nickel each, and then quickly sold as many bottles as I could carry on my red Radio Flyer wagon for a dime each. Joe Costa, the variety store owner who sold me the drinks at regular retail price, encouraged my nascent sales career by supplying me with a perfectly shaped laundry tub for my cart, and lots of chopped ice each day for several weeks. I had a great time with this early enterprise for the month or so while the construction was active nearby.

❧ *With unemployment in the United States at 25 percent, accompanied by a 50 percent drop in international trade, The Great Depression of the 1930s started in the United States, but became a worldwide economic catastrophe. Thereafter, it was most certainly an overriding lingering cloud over all of my formative years. Saving money, working hard, not wasting, and "making do" were ever present in my parental lessons.*

❧ *What we are is God's gift to us. What we become, and what we do with our lives is our gift to God.*

[2]

Well Grounded in Medford

IMMEDIATELY following the war, Dad returned to his former work as a house painter. Through a referral network of satisfied customers, he gradually built up a steady residential painting business, often with one or two helpers. During the summers, he mostly worked seven days a week, usually until nearly dark.

When he did arrive home, he was more than ready for our late supper. He typically then took a thirty-minute nap before relating much to anyone.

| *Dot Cummings at 23 Cherry Street, Medford*

After that, and for years, Dad and I would play checkers, chess, or Monopoly until it was my bedtime, while Mom read or enjoyed her favorite records. A compulsive reader, Mom loved biographies and best-selling fiction, and she was a regular patron at the Medford Public Library. The library's East Branch was a particularly convenient little storefront on Salem Street. Holiday gifts for Mom were always easy. If we bought her any kind of a novel or biography, or an Al Jolson record, it was sure to be a big hit. She would certainly have gone to college if she had been born a generation later, but college for young women was not common in her day, at least not for those with limited financial resources. She had an impressive vocabulary from voracious reading, and she always kept a dictionary handy, along with her current book.

In 1946, Dad and Mom achieved their dream of purchasing a two-family home, at 23 Cherry Street in Medford. We occupied the second-floor flat with two bedrooms. Paying off that mortgage became the great new family goal. Mom always felt pleased, and I think proud, when she could send in an extra six or seven dollars to Malden Savings Bank on the monthly due date. Her attitude was surely a strong precursor of what turned out to be a defining characteristic of my eventual mortgage-free business style with Cummings Properties. Like Dad, Mom had many lessons to teach, but the biggest one here was about how all those small additional payments would add up to major savings on interest.

By then, Marian had graduated from Medford High School and left home to join a Roman Catholic convent, though she later left the convent and became a registered nurse. With my sister having moved away, Mom decided, much to Dad's consternation, to rent out the front bedroom. Mom was the taskmaster on family finances, in part because she had worked several years as an accounting clerk and then as a secretary in the old Boston Safe Deposit and Trust Company, before she and Dad married.

Although Dad was always his own guy, he was also a loving husband who gave in whenever Mom took a strong stand on anything. Accordingly, for the first five years we lived on Cherry Street, Mom and Dad slept in what would normally have been the dining room, not unlike the way they had slept in the living room of the Salem Street apartment. A man named Mr. Williams rented the front bedroom, in a private corner of our flat, for five or six dollars a week— sort of like an early B&B without the breakfast.

DAD WAS AN EXTREMELY GOOD candlepin bowler, especially during the Depression, when he rarely had work. I later learned that in those days almost all of the family's funds for groceries and rent consisted of the cash he picked up hustling bets, either from bowling or at a billiards table. Mom was also an excellent bowler, and that and an occasional movie are the only things I remember them regularly doing together for entertainment. On couples nights at the former Hobbs Bowling Alleys in Davis Square, the prize was always a one- or two-pound box of scarce Fannie Farmer chocolates. Mom and Dad seemed to win almost every Saturday night, by having the highest average.

Dad particularly liked the bowling in Somerville because there was more liquor around Davis Square. Although he would never think of taking a drink himself when he was bowling, Dad knew that when his betting friends had been drinking, they became both more vulnerable and more liberal with their betting. He told me they were much more interested in "getting even" with him after they had enjoyed a few drinks. I knew when he told me— repeatedly—about the role other people's drinking played in his success that he was on a teaching mission to instill in me an early sense of the importance of liquor moderation.

Although he didn't really like to *gamble*, Dad said, he was pleased to earn money by betting on himself. To him, such betting wasn't gambling because he felt he was "working," and because he simply avoided bets that he was unlikely to win. He seemed to know immediately just how many pins he could spot the other men to entice them to bet with him.

Dad never glorified any of those "games of skill," and he did not want his son anywhere near them. Indeed, the only time Dad was really upset with me was during my junior high years, when he discovered me working as a pinsetter after school at the Medford Square Alleys on Salem Street. He was beside himself. It was as though I had broken his heart. He loved that I wanted to work, but he wanted me far away from what he believed was a seedy environment.

Setting pins—an essential job before machines were created to do that work—I quickly learned how to avoid being seriously injured, or worse. The danger was real, especially when bowlers were firing balls down my two lanes at the same time, as often happened. Eastern Massachusetts bowlers, particularly in those days, mostly used the slender, lighter-weight candlepins rather than tenpins, and the pins occasionally careened and ricocheted about violently, even between the alleys. Several of my classmates set pins there too, but that did not matter to Dad. He was extraordinarily smart about how things worked and how to get things done, and he was always conscious of wanting me to "make it," although he never did tell me what that meant to him.

Sunday afternoons were our family time. During the late 1940s, if Mom was not cooking her favorite pot roast or chicken Sunday dinner, we would frequently shunpike up the back roads to US Route 1 in Saugus and on to Chickland, which each day had 100 or more chickens roasting on spits on the other side of the large plate-glass windows. Dad made a point of explaining to me how smart the restaurant people were, blowing the enticing exhaust from the barbeque out into the parking lot. He also thought they were pretty clever for offering large portions from a limited menu at bargain prices. "The chicken dinners were about seventy cents," Dad would say, "but look at all the cocktails they're selling at fifty cents. That's where they make their real profit."

There were three Boston newspapers in those days, and the daily editions cost two or three cents each. Ice cream cones were five cents, or ten cents for a rare double dipper, while gasoline was about fifteen cents a gallon. When Dad would sometimes ask for "a buck's worth of regular, please," no one ever laughed at him. And any trips we took were in the family car, which was also

Dad's "company car," as he joked. We always had the smell of fresh paint with us, and maybe even a ladder or two on the roof if we were not traveling too far.

Weekly family time aside, from his earliest married days Dad's primary role was as family provider, with never much time for things like Little League or Pop Warner football, if they even existed then. Maybe that is why I never got involved much with organized sports or even pick-up games, though I loved shooting basketballs incessantly in my backyard after we moved to Cherry Street. Dad did turn out to be a lifetime role model in other ways, however, with his strong "can-do" attitude. So many times I heard, "You surely won't be able to do it"—whatever "it" might have been—"if you don't try."

Cub and then Boy Scouts became an important part of my Medford upbringing. My best Scouting experiences were overnight camping trips and two weeks each summer at Camp Fellsland, in Amesbury. One year, I won two extra free weeks at camp by selling the most tickets door to door of any kid in town for the annual Fellsland Council Jamboree.

MY MOTHER WAS mostly a stay-at-home mom, as were the mothers of all but one of my close friends. In her Irish tradition, and much to Dad's liking, dinner, except on Fridays, was invariably meat and some kind of potatoes, plus a fresh vegetable, and almost always a homemade baked pudding or other dessert. My parents must have thought my motor skills were greatly lacking, because until I was at least six years old, one of them always saw to it that my carrots were fully mashed on my plate when I got to the table. It was almost like a rite of passage the first time I prevailed and mashed my own.

In keeping with Catholic tradition in those days, Fridays meant baked fresh fish, canned salmon, or sometimes Gorton's canned fish cakes. We loved both cod and haddock, and Mom would decide at the fish store which one to serve after she saw the price. And in true Boston tradition, Saturdays were reserved for baked beans and frankfurters, with the beans always "from scratch," with molasses. Milk was another constant, and while growing up, I never once saw wine or any other alcohol on our table. Dad would occasionally pour a shot or two of Canadian Club whiskey before dinner, but only when we had company. Mom always took great pride in how our home looked on a daily basis, but there would be a special feeling in the air if "company was coming."

Mom was often recruited as the neighborhood collector for all sorts of community fundraising efforts. In those days, much fundraising was conducted through annual door-to-door appeals by the March of Dimes, Community Chest, Easter Seals, and several other groups of that ilk. Aside from wanting to help these causes, Mom enjoyed making the assigned rounds because she was such a good talker, and she always came back full of neighborhood news and chatter. She believed strongly that everyone on the block needed to help out, and her devotion to our neighborhood instilled a strong sense of community in her two children.

Her devotion to our neighborhood instilled a strong sense of community in her two children.

One night in 1950, Dad didn't come home. My mom became frantic until we received a call after midnight from Lawrence Memorial Hospital in Medford and learned that he had fallen off the roof of a home he was painting. Adding insult to injury, he arrived at the hospital awash in white paint. With multiple breaks in one leg and a serious back injury, he was out of work for six months, with no income.

Unfortunately, Dad did not realize that his customer's homeowner insurance policy should have been a source of assistance for him and his family. He also refused to apply for any kind of public assistance, and we never received any. In his view, the accident was "his fault" and no one else should have to pay for it. I remember Mom had purchased an early version of Blue Cross that paid twelve dollars a day to cover most of the hospital bill, but they had only a modest savings account, and the injury completely drained their resources. Dad's bowling days were over thereafter, but he did eventually return to the painting work he loved, and he continued to paint well into his seventies—long past the time when there was any need for him to continue working.

AS A YOUNG BOY, without ever thinking that I might like to be a builder someday, I always stopped longer and more often than other passersby to look in at construction sites, and I continue to do so to this day. Going back even to my third-grade days, I frequently let myself in to explore the construction site for the new bank building in Haines Square. Later, during junior high, in about 1950, I found great entertainment off and on for almost a year in exploring the "New Medford Square," consisting of fifteen or twenty stores under construction on Riverside Avenue. On several occasions, I recruited my friend Joe Hansen to be an accomplice as we wandered the ever-changing site, but never doing a bit of damage.

I was probably about fourteen and in high school when I committed my most memorable trespassing. That was inside the old, abandoned Charlestown State Prison, where Bunker Hill Community College stands today. Following a century and a half of dutiful service, this tired relic sat empty for many months after the new state prison opened in Walpole, and after riding past the crumbling penitentiary many times, including on the elevated subway trains, which rumbled down Rutherford Avenue past the prison walls, it was time for me to go inside. Intrigued, and seeing virtually no security or even a sign warding off trespassers, I rode there one day on my bicycle for an extensive private visit inside the prison walls. It was a full and exciting afternoon poking into all sorts of things that I would otherwise never have imagined, including about half of the old wooden electric chair.

WHILE A STUDENT AT ROBERTS Junior High School, I established a new venture that operated from May through August for three summers. I figured out how to arrange a study hall as my last class each day, and then cut out of that period during May and June. After purchasing a state peddler's license, I conducted a surprisingly profitable afternoon ice cream business from a large dry-ice-cooled box attached to the back of my bike, mostly at the former Ford Motors auto assembly plant in Somerville, where Assembly Row shopping mall is now.

That early business experience gave me lots of great training in talking myself into and out of all sorts of situations, many of them literally on the street. Some of those acquired "street smarts" have surely been invaluable throughout my adult life. I also discovered at an early age how easy it was and still is to earn cash, for anyone who was willing to devote the necessary time to an activity.

After three seasons, my own imagined peer pressure convinced me that fourteen years old was too old for me to be riding my bike, once it was time to enter high school. Instead I tried out several more-conventional after-school jobs for kids of that era. The first was at a store called Homier Music, on Boylston Street in Boston, where they had me doing all sorts of odd jobs for forty cents an hour. I learned to find my way around downtown Boston while making deliveries on foot. I also helped pack lots of orders of sheet music and books for postal delivery, and was everyone's first option to call for sweeping floors, straightening out display shelves, and running around the corner to pick up someone's sandwich.

I was happy to do whatever anyone wanted me to do to earn my keep, even if I often felt capable of doing a lot more. While working for others, I found it fun to do the best job possible, regardless of the task. Even then, my thought process was that I was being paid for my time, and I would accomplish as much as possible no matter my team. That was my mindset from my youngest years.

My next hourly job was after school each day for a few months at

Ruderman's, a small furniture store on High Street in Medford. I mostly polished tables, swept floors, and unpacked deliveries from the furniture factories. As it happened, there was a local Brigham's ice cream and candy shop directly across the street from Ruderman's. I often dropped in there to purchase an ice cream cone for my walk home, and came to know the manager. He didn't have a hard time convincing me how much nicer it would be working for Brigham's for sixty cents an hour rather than cleaning furniture for fifty cents an hour. The free ice cream was a bonus.

I stayed with Brigham's through high school, and then off and on through all four college years. The most enjoyable and worthwhile time for me at Brigham's was working full-time during all three college summers as a "vacation manager," moving from store to store, covering vacation weeks for store managers all over the forty-store system.

Brigham's was a terrific student work experience, especially when I was managing staff, almost all of whom were anywhere from a few to fifty or more years older than me. While there, I followed my dad's example as an hourly worker at the shipyard, routinely working as much overtime as possible, sometimes logging more than seventy hours a week. This was much to the (mostly

Bill, about 18 years old, and an unidentified Brigham's colleague

feigned) dismay of one of the senior supervisors, who fussed that because of all my overtime pay, my take-home pay was more one week than his was.

ANOTHER GOOD MONEYMAKER, and a valuable learning tool, was helping Dad buy and sell used boats from our backyard on Cherry Street. In those days, long before eBay and similar online auction sites, of course, people advertised items for sale in the newspaper. *Boston Sunday Globe* was especially prominent, often featuring a hundred pages of classified ads that usually included a couple of hundred used boats for sale. One of us would purchase an early copy of the *Sunday Globe* on Saturday afternoon, always without the news section because it had not yet been printed. We would then call everyone in our area who advertised a small boat for sale that looked like it might be a bargain. Showing up early on Saturday afternoon was not unlike showing up at a neighbor's 8:00 AM yard sale an hour or two earlier than the posted start time. It worked well for us.

We looked exclusively for small boats in the range of twelve to eighteen feet long. Oftentimes, people who were moving up to something larger would be selling a boat, an outboard motor, and, ideally, a trailer, as a package. Dad taught me about determining a boat's value and about how to bargain or negotiate with the seller on the price. We paid cash on the spot and then immediately towed our find-of-the-day home to resell it from our yard. Dad had the buying and selling talk down to an art form.

More often than not, we already had one of our own ads running in the same Sunday paper from which we made our purchases on Saturday. Occasionally, we would end up selling our Saturday afternoon purchase the same weekend, especially if it didn't need any cleaning or polishing. If a new acquisition needed to be scrubbed or painted, it paid well to do that work before offering the boat for resale. Looking back, the best part of our boat business was the one-on-one time I spent with Dad, and the opportunity he had to teach me about negotiating and finishing the sale. He was a terrific closer.

> *But he always wanted me to understand that the truest value of any item is "whatever you can get for it."*

Dad taught me few business lessons in any formal way, but he always wanted me to understand that the truest value of any item is "whatever you can get for it." A more formal definition of value is what a willing buyer will pay a willing seller, when neither party is under any compulsion to buy or to sell in a hurry, and when both parties are aware of any hidden defects or circumstances affecting the value.

The fact that he or we persuaded someone to sell us a boat at a bargain price, for instance, should have nothing whatsoever to do with how much we should ask a subsequent buyer to pay for it. At that early stage in his life, Dad also had strong feelings about the value of a neat, clear business signature—all the time. I was probably in second grade when he pointed out John Hancock's distinctive signature on a reproduction of the Declaration of Independence, and I recall reminding him then that I did not even know how to write in cursive. Dad also had a thing about wanting me to get into the purchase or the sale conversations, especially when we were trying to close the transaction because "someday you will be so glad for this practice," he assured me.

Even the simplest negotiating experience begins in the home and can be taught from childhood. Children who politely argue with their parents, cajoling for more freedom and privileges, are practicing negotiation. They are already honing their negotiation skills, which may foreshadow above-average ability, even in issues as simple as asking, "Why do I have to go to bed so early?"

For several years, Dad owned an older inboard motorboat, and he became a member at Cottage Park Yacht Club in Winthrop. He later joined a dozen or so other mostly blue-collar guys when they all became founders of Riverside Yacht Club off Ship Avenue in Medford. The boat club filled a void in Dad's life that opened as Davis Square gradually gentrified. His old haunts there gradually gave way to the boat club and the nearby Mystic River.

The club facilities consisted of an old twenty-foot-wide-by-fifty-foot-long wooden work barge. Dad and some of the other original members paid a few dollars to have a crane lift their new clubhouse onto some otherwise unused state-owned land at the river's edge, and they took it over. The members gradually also built a dock and a long string of floats in the center of the Mystic River for forty or fifty boats. No one seemed to care, and for decades they stayed there before they had anything more than squatters' rights.

It took less than an hour to travel down the river to Boston Harbor. Today, bluefish and striped bass are big attractions throughout Massachusetts Bay, but in the 1950s the available species were much different. There was excellent fishing in and around the harbor and the islands for cod, haddock, and flounder, and many summer nights we delighted Mom with freshly caught fish.

I WAS AN IMPATIENT student, and my three years at Medford High School were mostly just something to be completed. Sophomore English was my favorite high school class because we spent much time writing, and the teacher, Miss Bagley, gave us plenty of encouragement. She would have been so excited to know she played a meaningful part in my taking on this book-writing project so many decades later. Other high school details are more than a little sketchy now, sixty years later, probably because my high school years were simply not that interesting.

During my final summer vacation before college, I landed a fine work opportunity at what was then the upscale and iconic Blacksmith Shop Restaurant in Rockport, on Cape Ann. I had earlier worked a few weeks as a convention floor worker for the Massachusetts Restaurant Association during two of its annual restaurant shows in Boston, and the convention manager offered to help if I ever wanted a good summer restaurant job "on the Cape." I was thinking Cape Cod, which I knew would be great fun. But even though one of us had our "Capes" mixed up, I earned significantly more in tips on Cape Ann during that summer than ever anticipated, or than would have been possible at Brigham's.

Always one to broaden whatever experience I could get, I had a split shift at the Blacksmith Shop, with just enough time to drive a local taxi on weekday afternoons and meet the early commuter train at Rockport Depot. I had my driver's license for only a year, and at that age, the idea of getting paid to drive someone else's car was extra special. I never had a taxi driver's license or any training, but in 1954 that didn't bother anyone in Rockport.

Near the end of summer, a young woman I had never seen before hailed my cab just as I was crossing over the bumpy tracks and into the railroad station. She was disheveled and appeared to be in great distress from a visible pregnancy. She asked me to take her "to the hospital" and "right now." Unfortunately, neither of us knew where the hospital was (in the next town over, Gloucester). As she talked, I drove slowly back over the tracks, and her panic escalated.

She quickly became unable to communicate at all. It was, of course, decades before the advent of cell phones or GPS. Without asking, I turned immediately toward the Rockport Fire Station amid increasing clamor in the back. We made it to the station with my horn blaring, which seemed to quiet my passenger and brought an immediate response from the station, but the six- or seven-minute drive was quite an experience.

The firefighters gradually calmed her down and moved her into their ambulance. Meanwhile it became increasingly clear to me that they assumed I had a personal vested interest in the woman at least, if not also in the pregnancy. I became more and more anxious about extricating myself from this situation. When they told me I should follow the ambulance to the hospital, I did not ask about collecting my fare and quickly escaped in the opposite direction.

❀ *From an historical perspective, there never seemed to be any concern at all about gender discrimination until long after the urgency of the war effort began to bring millions of women into the workplace. Credit "Rosie the Riveter" for opening millions of new opportunities for women and for then starting the "Rosie" conversations about equal pay for equal work. I clearly remember learning that male teachers were paid more than female teachers because "the men had families to support."*

[3]

A Marvelous Pathway

WHEN I matriculated in 1954, Tufts University presented itself, as it does now, as a small Greater Boston school of special quality, squarely located within one of the greatest educational centers of the world. Founded in 1852 and located in Medford and Somerville, the university rises above much of Cambridge and Boston in the distance. Looking down as it does from the top of Walnut Hill, Tufts is clearly not in the shadow of Harvard University or Massachusetts Institute of Technology, although it is influenced in many ways by their proximity. It is also influenced by four dozen other degree-granting institutions, all clustered within a comfortable bicycle ride from one another in Eastern Massachusetts.

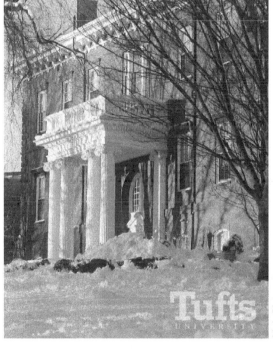

Tufts University

Tufts competes to some extent with its more prestigious Cambridge neighbors for students, teachers, and research money, and it tends to do so quite well, most of the time. It also understands what it is, as well as its place in the world. Tufts has been and continues to be comfortable with itself as an institution of excellent quality, fully capable of providing all the educational opportunities any student might need. I sent a well-prepared but late application to Tufts after I realized how many of my Medford High School friends were applying there.

During that winter of my senior high school year, Mr. Andy Lentine, my physical education teacher, who had earlier tried unsuccessfully to push me toward high school sports, convinced me to apply to Tufts. I also sent the application, at least in part, because there was no application fee. I could always drop out after my freshman year, Mr. Lentine suggested, and that notion was often in my mind.

Joe Hansen was my smartest pal since first grade. Joe knew I could get my mother's car on the Saturday morning he needed a ride to Tufts for his interview, and I was happy to drive him to the nearby campus. Joe was dressed appropriately, and I probably was not so well attired. But there was no reason for me to dress up for the visit, my having heard nothing on my application.

After waiting around outside the Admissions Office in stately Ballou Hall that early March day for Joe to finish, I chanced to meet Dean Grant Curtis as he escorted Joe to the door, following their fifteen- or twenty-minute meeting. Dean Curtis asked me who I was and where I hoped to

| *Bill Cummings and Joseph Hansen, 1966*

enroll. Without really thinking, I replied that Tufts was my first choice, but that things didn't look too promising, since I had not received an interview invitation, as was Tufts' practice at that time for local kids, or "townies."

Dean Curtis asked Joe if he would mind waiting while he met with me for a few minutes to talk about Tufts. After a casual half-hour chat, Dean Curtis excused himself to retrieve my application from a file somewhere. When he returned, it seemed that he had barely looked at the papers—that he just wanted to verify that he had them. Then we talked and even joked a little for another thirty minutes. To me, this felt more like a good audition than an interview about my qualifications, or lack thereof, to attend Tufts.

It probably helped greatly that my senior-year grades were much better than those of any previous year. I had a good bunch of A's among my fall grades. At that time, Tufts was much easier to get into than it has been any time since, but even so, I was lucky to get that impromptu interview.

Dean Curtis could not have been more cordial to me that day, and at the end he told me he thought I "might bring something special" if I came to Tufts. Within three weeks, Joe and I both received the proverbial "thick envelopes" with acceptance letters. Few candidates today would get a second look from Tufts with grades like mine, but there should always be a few places reserved for students whose abilities may be less obvious.

Mr. Lentine was the first person I told after receiving my Tufts acceptance letter. He said he was happy that he had finally figured out how to get through to me. But he was shocked to learn that I had not shared the news with my family. The problem was, I had not yet figured out the finances, though in due time I would. I did not know anything about scholarships, and no one told me about them.

Decades later, like shortly after my fiftieth birthday, I again crossed paths with Grant Curtis, who had retired by then. Although never much of a card player, I accepted an invitation to substitute for a few weeks in a local poker game in Winchester, where Grant turned out to be one of the regulars. This surprise opportunity to meet again as a peer with the man who let me talk my way into Tufts felt great, and I relished the opportunity to thank him personally so many years later.

JUST BEFORE MY FIRST COLLEGE YEAR—on August 31, 1954, to be exact—Hurricane Carol, one of the deadliest modern-day hurricanes ever to reach New England, hit Boston. There were sixty-five deaths reported in the six-state area.

Without knowing much about the danger of hurricanes, I drove to Memorial Drive in Cambridge to watch the effects of the vicious storm as it battered the Charles River basin, where Dad had kept our small powerboat the previous year. There, boats were breaking loose from their moorings, and one of the largest was splintering against the rugged stone wall. Several other people had come to the public boat club, apparently with the thought of somehow saving their boats, but the ferocious wind and waves prevented anyone from even trying. On the dock, one small cabin boat lay on its side, pushed right out of the water by a larger boat.

My attention focused on what I remembered as the fastest boat in the river, an old open-top Gar Wood speedboat, powered by a huge twelve-cylinder Scripps aircraft engine. Fortunately, because of the way the boat was dragging its mooring and was tangled with another boat, the waves were crashing into the Gar Wood sideways—enough to fill it quickly with water and prevent it from crashing against the rough-hewn granite wall. I watched it sink in about twelve feet of water. I not only knew just where it went down, but also that it went under softly and was likely not seriously damaged.

I reached the owner of the speedboat by phone that evening. He was thrilled to learn that his boat was salvageable, and we made a deal. He agreed to pay me $400 cash if I could save it, but otherwise nothing. Either way, he would be my helper, and he would pay to rent the small amount of equipment we would need to give it a try. I was back in the boat business again, just as my first classes at Tufts were about to begin. But this would take only a day, if all went well.

We picked up several large rubber flotation devices, plus a portable gasoline-powered air compressor to inflate the rugged rubber air bags, and some extra-long air hoses, all of which the owner rented from a friend of my dad who hauled boats for a living. How might this experience later benefit me?

Dad had a small aluminum boat in the garage and a block and tackle, which I used to hook the speedboat to the guardrail. By then, the boat was only about forty feet from the wall, although it was still not visible below the surface of the stirred-up river water. But because the upper part was only five or six feet below the surface, I was able to easily swim down, wearing a dive mask, and push the first uninflated flotation device under the bow deck.

Everything worked out perfectly, and the boat was floating by early afternoon, earning kudos from several onlookers. The Gar Wood's owner was excited and pleased to pay me, and $400 then was worth ten times more than it is today. And since the Charles River was mostly fresh water above the dam, the two mechanics the owner hired to work on the large engine were confident that the brief immersion would cause little long-term damage. This was the perfect example of finding a need and filling it.

KEEPING UP ACADEMICALLY at Tufts was never an issue. But shortly after I began my first year, an administrator decided that I really didn't know how to "read." As a result, in addition to attending the regular Saturday-morning classes and Saturday-noon chapel service that were mandatory for all first-year students, I found myself "learning to read" with several other classmates for six consecutive Saturday afternoons. I was thus almost eighteen years old before finally learning to read every line instead of every word.

For me, the single most worthwhile classroom learning experience at Tufts was the year with Professor Newlin Smith in his Business Law classes. Those courses and a basic two-semester General Accounting course fit nicely into my major of Business Administration. Another two-semester course in Industrial Psychology had some especially practical and worthwhile coursework that conditioned my thinking for decades to come, particularly in regard to logistical issues, time and motion studies, and things like that.

Freshman Writing, Composition 101 and 102, and two semesters of Journalism with Cecilia Van Auken in my second year were also invaluable. To this day, I often think how well they all served my lifetime needs. I remember using my hurricane-salvage story for one of my first Tufts writing assignments. The opportunity to retell the story here is special, too.

Notwithstanding my lackadaisical pathway to Tufts, everything there worked extremely well—not only because of the academic opportunities, but even more so because of the many extracurricular offerings. I never really bought into the allure of the party scene, which certainly had a presence, but I took great advantage of other social and organizational activities, often more actively than I did my studies.

I have spoken with many college graduates who strongly concur that the college years primarily serve to help many students grow out of their teenage awkwardness. I certainly know how much better prepared for life I was after four years of college. Students who are not planning a future in sciences, technology, or medicine will often learn more from their exposure to the other students and to the diversity of their college experience than they might ever learn in actual classrooms. For the most part, that was true in my case, because I always had many other activities going on. I might have been thinking even then about someday writing this book.

IN NOVEMBER 1953, after somehow knowing enough to take a Saturday-morning qualifying exam for appointment to the Naval Reserve Officers Training Corps. I was one of only three who qualified among the twenty-three Medford boys who applied. Then I learned that I did not have 20/20 vision, and that was the end of four years' free tuition somewhere and a possible Navy career.

Instead, I joined the Air Force ROTC during my first and second years at Tufts, participating on its excellent competitive drill team and on the rifle team. While the Navy program included full tuition, room, and board for four years, AFROTC provided no financial benefits for the first two years.

By the end of my first year, I had made myself conspicuous enough to receive a national award as Tufts University's 1955 Outstanding Air Force Cadet of the Year. It was the closest I ever came at Tufts to receiving an academic award, prior to receiving an honorary Tufts doctorate a half century later. The unit made a big deal about the Convair award, and I felt quite honored to receive it.

In my second year, I participated in several special Air Force flights out of nearby Hanscom Field, including one entirely unauthorized flight with a visiting fighter pilot—a young Tufts graduate and Air Force Reserves captain whom I had met at ROTC headquarters in Sweet Hall. He invited me to come to Hanscom Field in uniform and join him on his previously scheduled training flight early that following morning. It seemed he was behind on the number of training hours he was required to log, and he couldn't afford to miss this opportunity after his original partner dropped out.

The invitation to join my new friend was on the condition that I would "never say a word to anyone." But now, sixty years later, it should be okay.

We would meet outside the base, he said, to avoid my having to answer any questions at the base on my own. Before we drove through the security gate, I donned one of his flight jackets, thus effectively impersonating a military officer. We flew far out over the Atlantic, well beyond Halifax, Nova Scotia, and then back along the south coast. Although risky, this three- or four-hour joy ride provided me with my most exciting plane ride ever. I didn't have any idea what the rules might be about my flying as a passenger in his jet fighter, but this was clearly one of those times when it was better not to ask.

Don Knox

| Bill at Hanscom Field, February 1956

Back at Tufts, the rifle range was inside the old Cousens Gym, on an upper floor. Sometimes it would be active all day long. The housekeeping protocol required each user to sweep up the brass casings from the mostly .22 caliber shells as we left our positions, but no one had any concern about recycling then. I never thought much about the brass either, but I realized that the lead bullets themselves had been accumulating for many months at the far end of the range. Never one to pass up a good opportunity, I volunteered to clean up under the target area, several times shoveling hundreds of dollars' worth of spent lead into burlap bags for recycling, a half hour's drive away in Chelsea.

After two successful years in AFROTC, I made the exceedingly difficult decision not to go forward with the advanced program. I knew by then that my sight deficiency would have disqualified me from flight school, just as it had from Navy ROTC. I was also aware of a latent bias against non-flying officers.

Medford Daily Mercury

| *Bill (center) receives the Outstanding Air Force Cadet of the Year Award, May 1955*

Although I have never regretted that decision, I have often reflected on how different my life would have been had I managed to get into the Navy program or stayed with the Air Force all those years ago.

FORGETTING THE LESS-STELLAR aspects of my academic experience, I always knew I would become proficient in the art of business—in part because of some of my previous money-making experiences. I determined early on that grades were not going to be important to me, and though none of my friends regarded me as a saint, I was dead set against cheating to achieve a better grade. I would not and did not.

Knowing how focused my parents were on managing their financial affairs for their later years, I quickly convinced myself that I could pay all my own college expenses through four years. I managed to do that by working hard whenever I saw the opportunity to earn money. And with that approach, I learned so, so much.

After previously eschewing any interest in fraternities, I joined one of the two unaffiliated local fraternities at Tufts. The driving force in this decision was an upperclassman, Bruce E. Gordon, who was persistent in his endeavor to convince me to join what was then called Theta Delta Theta. Coincidentally, I later learned that it was Bruce who nominated me for the Outstanding Air Force Cadet award I received at the end of my freshman year. After his years at Tufts, Bruce went on to become a career fighter pilot in the U.S. Air Force, and we are still in occasional contact.

I surprised myself by becoming involved in administrative politics and leading our local fraternity's negotiations with two national fraternities, each of which was seeking to establish a chapter on the Tufts campus. Tau Kappa Epsilon, the first interested organization, was quietly rejected by a Tufts trustee and prominent Boston lawyer, who happened also to be the national president of Delta Tau Delta, another fraternity with a Tufts chapter. This trustee at first told me he much preferred the idea of Tufts retaining its local fraternities, and he urged our local fraternity to abandon the process of joining any national fraternity. Many national fraternities in the mid-1950s still openly practiced racial discrimination, but not Tau Kappa Epsilon which was our first choice.

I soon realized that this man was giving me all his good reasons, rather than his real reasons, for our remaining an unaffiliated local fraternity. After he eventually confirmed that he really "did not much care for" the *politics* of Tau Kappa Epsilon, I introduced the other national organization that had been equally interested. Shortly afterwards, our local fraternity was happily inducted, without any opposition, as Iota Tetarton Chapter of Phi Sigma Kappa, a national fraternity that also had no racial restrictions. I was delighted when David Jackson and Mark Anderson from my old neighborhood in Medford followed me to Tufts one and two years behind me, and then both became fraternity brothers too.

> *Skillful negotiation is the highest and most critical business art form.*

This experience was the first of many that taught me a valuable lesson: Few business skills are more important to an executive than the ability to negotiate. Day in and day out, formally or informally, the most critical parts of an executive's day are likely to be the time spent negotiating. Skillful negotiation is the highest and most critical business art form, and people who do it well must be carefully encouraged and nurtured. Good negotiators will often relish a back-and-forth "rehearsal" and will often appreciate hearing suggestions from colleagues before beginning any major session. Successful negotiations so much depend upon learning early on what is important to the other side and then figuring out what the other side can easily do in return for receiving something it wants or needs.

The best negotiators are competitive and quick-thinking. With an air of fairness and confidence and strength, good negotiators become careful listeners and even better observers who usually know exactly where the other side is coming from. Empathy and understanding are so important, as is the ability to read and play off another's ego. This is often particularly true when dealing with insecure people who are in positions of power or influence. Knowing where the other side is coming from can often be even more helpful when we don't let on that we understand the hidden objectives.

Since Phi Sigma Kappa now needed a fraternity house, I immediately went door to door through the neighborhood near Tufts, eventually locating a large and suitable house at 25 Whitfield Road, Somerville. The owner, the McManus family, seemed to love the idea of perhaps selling to Tufts, and I effectively acted as their *pro bono* broker. Their asking price of $25,000 was acceptable to the university, and we had our house almost immediately. Simple as that. This transaction fit so well into my later professional career.

There was some interesting jousting with my earlier nemesis trustee, but eventually he let me win him over, and he became a helpful ally when it came to buying the property and arranging the needed rebuilding and furnishing. Ironically, this was exactly the type of adaptive reuse real estate work I would later engage in professionally when I started Cummings Properties, albeit with much larger buildings. The fraternity house conversion work, with its high-level give-and-take between me and what I think was called the Student Life Committee of Tufts' board of trustees during the approval process, gave me some valuable student exposure. The university's administration and trustees proved to be extraordinarily supportive of my efforts.

STILL REMEMBERING my tiny but highly profitable ice cream business, I started my second seasonal business as a Tufts student, in December 1954, with Don Knox, a classmate and fraternity brother. During that first Christmas season, Don and I paid $500 to rent a vacant one-acre paved lot in Medford Square, where we sold more than 2,000 Christmas trees—well beyond our wildest expectations. Don's dad and mine both helped us take in the cash on the busiest weekends.

A former used car lot, the parcel directly abutted the original Carroll's Diner, a Medford institution opposite the Medford Police Station and, for decades, a major upscale night-out place for Tufts faculty and students. A small, twenty-square-foot building served as our office for overnight security, and we filled the surrounding lot with Christmas trees. Don and I took turns in sleeping bags to guard our investment. We both spent most days and every night there for three weeks, and took only strategic visits back to campus, especially for important tests and an occasional shower. My dad was a regular volunteer.

We bought our trees from among the many huge lumber trucks that lined up each day outside various produce distributors in Boston's old Faneuil Hall Market. The trucks from Maine and New Brunswick backed into their loading spots in the crowded site in the center of historic downtown Boston. Some days Don scouted out the trucks lined up in the morning, and then when we returned at day's end to make a purchase we had a better idea of which drivers might be the most anxious to make a deal. The drivers were always excited to sell their loads and drive back north, rather than spend another overnight curled up in the front seats of their logging rigs. Everything was, of course, sold for cash.

After doing so well that first year, we each sold trees for three more years, but as separate businesses with no need to split the profits—though we both hired several other fraternity brothers to assist us. During the subsequent years, in different towns, Don and I individually sold more trees, and we each made more money than we had made together in 1954. Notwithstanding the close and enduring friendship that developed during that first business partnership, neither of us ever entered another business partnership with anyone again. We both shared information about our tree businesses with the highly practical chairman of the Tufts Economics Department, Professor Lou Manley. We received his enthusiastic understanding, if not his full endorsement, of our seasonal absences. More giant doses of great entrepreneurial experience.

ONE ACTIVITY OTHER than fraternity and ROTC that maintained my special interest at Tufts was the Tufts Mountain Club, with which I learned to ski. I also occasionally participated in intramural sports, worked several months as a paid referee, and as a volunteer sold considerable advertising for the 1957 and 1958 *Jumbo* yearbooks.

I was also quite active in the Tufts chapter of the National Newman Club Federation, a loose association of campus clubs for Catholic students at mostly nonsectarian colleges and universities, as well as in the overarching National Newman Club Federation itself. Another good Tufts friend and classmate from Medford, Alfred Shiner, had served as president of the club in his sophomore year, and he nominated me for the position in my junior year. I was also encouraged by the then-new Catholic chaplain at Tufts, Father Walter Gouch, PhD, who became an influential person in my college years.

A member of the Paulist order, Father Gouch came to Tufts from Johns Hopkins University in 1956, I think, and was the first priest with whom I really related in a meaningful adult way. He strongly encouraged me to think beyond the Baltimore Catechism when making moral decisions in such an ever-changing world. Without his early teaching about the need for educated people to forsake a "one-size-fits-all" attitude toward the Church, I might have had much more difficulty considering myself an observant Catholic today.

Tufts was historically a Unitarian/Universalist school, but in the 1950s the undergraduate population seemed to include about 25 percent each of Catholic, Protestant, Jewish, and "other" students. The Newman Club was at the time the largest student organization on campus, and we offered well-attended programming on Tuesday afternoons. Speakers mostly focused on contemporary issues with student appeal. During my time in the office, we changed the club's name to Catholic Club of Tufts University, so people would more readily understand who we were. Then, in part to prove that we were not moving away from the umbrella organization, we hosted a convention of Newman clubs from throughout the Northeast, for which I was pleased to serve as chairman in 1957.

Holding the convention at Tufts required me to communicate extensively with the Archdiocese of Boston, particularly to secure a greeting from then Archbishop Richard Cushing, and to obtain his approval to arrange the first public Catholic Mass ever held on campus, in Cohen Auditorium. Everything went extremely well, and the whole process was another valuable learning opportunity.

I HAD ALWAYS wanted to own my own business and first started talking about it during my years at Roberts Junior High School. With likely no idea what the consequences of that ambition might be, I had a clear goal. Yet it would be several years later, at Tufts, before I first heard the word *entrepreneur*, during a sophomore French class, and I remember feeling empowered by it. The word fully defined my interests in business, and I knew I was already well on my way to satisfying the definition.

As my final semester of college wound down, it might have seemed inevitable that I would become an entrepreneur upon graduation—after all, I had played around with so many different self-directed business activities from grammar school on. But when the time came to go out into the real world of business, I did so determined to find out what was out there before deciding what I truly wanted to be "when I grew up."

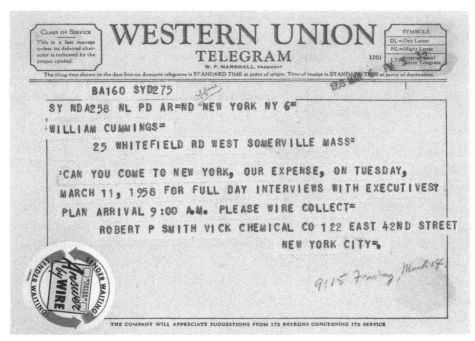

Telegram invitation to interview with Vick Chemical, 1958

During February and March of 1958, I interviewed with seven or eight firms that conducted in-depth visits at Tufts through the placement office. I remember how excited I was to receive invitations from five companies to visit their corporate offices, and I subsequently received formal job offers from four of them. This job-search process felt a little like the college-application process four years before, except that now the travel and expenses were all generously reimbursed by the respective firms.

The spring of 1958 was a highly opportune time to be a new college graduate. In those days, Vick Chemical Company interviewed at the same dozen or so college campuses each year, with a goal of hiring one new sales trainee from each school. Vick sent a hand-delivered paper telegram to invite me to my interview, a perfectly routine business practice at that time. A short time after the interview I was delighted to accept the offer from Vick, feeling as though I had won the job lottery. Then located in Greensboro, North Carolina, Vick Chemical was the maker of Vicks VapoRub and numerous other proprietary cold remedies. Vick offered one of the best business training programs anywhere.

Tufts' placement director, Viola Saltmarsh, urged me to sign up for the Vick interview, and I later learned that she was also instrumental in influencing the interviewer to offer the Tufts position to me, after three of us interviewed in New York. The starting rate was only $270 per month, as compared with other offers of up to about $500 a month for engineering graduates that year and maybe as much as $450 for liberal arts graduates like myself.

But I began the new job fully imbued with the Depression-era thinking of my parents. They had taught me from an early age to work a little harder than the next person and to always save whatever and whenever I could. This was the surest, if not the only, way for people of little means "to get ahead" in this world. They were great teachers, and I learned that lesson well. This mentality has followed me throughout my life.

COLLEGE TUITIONS had not really begun to skyrocket then, but Tufts' rate did seem like it was soaring when it increased from $600 per year in 1954 to more than $1,000 per year by graduation time. I was determined to pay all my tuition and my other college expenses myself, and was eventually able to do so. In what then seemed like fanciful exaggeration, Tufts trustees predicted in 1958 that by the time our kids attended college, tuition might be as much as $6,000 per year.

❉ *From retail to food service to internships, there are so many traditional ways for students to make money while gaining experience. Those who are entrepreneurs by nature, however, often find it more satisfying, exciting, and indeed, educational to launch their own ventures such as small one-time projects like salvaging a boat or harvesting spent lead, or longer-term repeatable undertakings like the annual Christmas tree sales.*

❉ *These types of early work experiences clearly demonstrate how creative thinking and extra effort can result in additional income. A student working for an hourly wage at a fast-food restaurant might earn raises over time, but would not typically be able to realize immediate returns on his or her investment of effort. He or she would always gain the commonsense background experience of learning what being an "employee" is all about.*

[4]

On the Road with Vicks

Bill is shown (eighth from the left) with the well-outfitted Vick Chemical 1958 recruiting class as they started a sales campaign in Detroit

MY WORK EXPERIENCE immediately after college showed me it is naïve to assume that a person will be good at conducting business simply because he or she has studied business successfully in any school. Instead, I have found that some people are happy to fill up their minds with facts and information to store, like a squirrel hoarding nuts, with little capacity for ideation. Oftentimes they can recite the information with scant ability to interpret it, or even fully understand it. Education is working when it teaches us to synthesize information into our minds and effectively apply it. Increasingly, it seems to me, students of business learn disproportionately more about theories and theorems, and about computer models for maximizing profits, than they hear about how to "do business." They may learn about real estate syndications, limited partnerships, tax strategies, and how to make the numbers work, but what do they learn about how to build or create? They may also learn all sorts of ways to convert other people's money into their own. How much do they ever learn about the wonderful side of business; managing production, motivating people, and creating jobs? Job creation, I think, is the single greatest factor in evaluating new businesses.

Certainly, undergraduate and advanced degrees can be highly valuable, but businesses make great mistakes when they persist in focusing so much on academic qualifications before considering what an applicant might really bring to the company. When making hiring decisions, examine a person's drive and determination. What about honesty, character, and personality? Steer your conversations with a job applicant to determine whether he or she has the ability to size up situations and opportunities and achieve positive results. Obviously, there is no science in this subject, but often a personal interview will reveal vastly more about character than will any résumé.

Even in an age when it is highly fashionable to be an entrepreneur, many people remain averse to risk-taking and innovation. Especially in large firms, which, perhaps only coincidentally, have more than their share of MBAs, there seems to be a great fear of doing something wrong. Many employees don't want, or care enough, to rock the boat. Similarly, many managers lack the confidence and maturity to encourage suggestions, or even involvement, from the employees they supervise; instead, they persist in treating them as underlings. Events, staff, and entire companies will often just drift along.

While it is true that I studied economics at Tufts University, my professional interests have always been more directed toward business, and I took enough practical business courses to receive my bachelor's degree in either economics or business administration. In the end, I selected the latter to the mild consternation of my department chairman, Professor Louis Manley, and was likely one of the last Tufts graduates to receive a Business Administration degree from Tufts' Department of Economics.

That Economics Department today is probably staffed entirely with academic economists, to the exclusion of any practical teachers of how to do business. They may not look down on the more plebeian side nearly as much as they did when I was a Tufts undergrad, but they are well aware that there is a difference. Ironically, however, my degree never once made an ounce of difference to me or to anyone else over the sixty-plus years since I graduated. A degree in philosophy would have been almost as useful, as long as I had picked up the few practical business courses that I was fortunate enough to find.

JACK KEROUAC READERS will surely remember his timeless classic *On the Road*. Kerouac included in that book many of his own memorable experiences while he completed the same Vick Chemical Company sales training job I was about to begin. Indeed, it was perhaps his only real job before he attained great fame as the "voice of the Beat Generation." Kerouac's mass appeal was surely one of the reasons for Vick's special employment allure in my age group in 1958, but I had not yet read the book, nor did I know then anything about him or his history with the firm.

By some accounts, Vick may have played an inadvertent role in the actual writing of *On the Road*, which Kerouac supposedly completed in just three weeks. Some historians have suggested that many writers of that day used stimulants made from wads of crushed up Vicks inhalers that contained the decongestant L-methamphetamine, the less potent component of the dangerous street drug known as "speed."

Although the Vick job paid less than any of the four other offers I received through the Tufts placement service, it held unique value and potential. A seven-day expense account covered 100 percent of my living expenses, with the exception of personal air travel and entertainment. I spent every night between early June 1958 and Christmas week in a hotel or motel, for instance, and was able to bank my entire paycheck every month. There was also a significant salary increase after the first nine months—just wait until March.

The Vick orientation team had a carefully arranged program and did a superb job of conditioning and exciting each year's new class of trainees. They emphasized the large number of candidates interviewed and how carefully we were selected. The majority, plus another dozen summer trainees who were hired for ten weeks only, were mostly from far more privileged backgrounds, and I found myself quietly learning from several whom I came to know fairly well. I particularly noticed their easy manner and smart attire, even though I was never the type to buy luxurious Hickey Freeman suits.

The formal training program began with several jam-packed days and nights at Vick's administrative headquarters in the Chanin Building, at 122 East 42nd Street in New York City, and at what was then the Commodore Hotel, directly across the street. A half century later, I learned from Roger Lowenstein's 1995 Warren Buffett biography that Buffett, whom I have long looked up to, was affiliated with the mutual fund Graham-Newman, and worked in the same Chanin Building shortly before I worked there.

Vick's program was well-known and respected in the proprietary drug industry, but after the first ten weeks, the wide range of sales and marketing challenges in which new staff participated was even better for building substantial general sales skills. The other trainees and more senior colleagues with whom I worked were an extremely talented and interesting group. Their drive, when aligned with their good training and high self-confidence, made them strong team members.

One of the first lessons business leaders must learn is the importance of identifying their own and their colleagues' strengths and weaknesses, and the Vick management team did that with great skill. For some managers, that may be difficult, especially if they equate evaluating other people's abilities with being "judgmental," but that task remains one of any manager's prime responsibilities. From an employer's

One of the first lessons business leaders must learn is the importance of identifying their own as well as their colleagues' strengths and weaknesses.

perspective, the end goal must be to keep staff engaged by having them do the things at which they excel, whenever practical.

Even though I did well on the graduate school aptitude tests, I never considered returning to school after being "deferred for two years" by Harvard Business School, which I fully interpreted as being rejected. Rather than using standardized management styles learned in business school, most good entrepreneurs will develop the management styles that are appropriate for their businesses. They generally have a strong bias toward acting ingeniously, discounting overwrought explanations, and discarding excuses. They make things happen.

For a not-so-poor-anymore Medford kid, always mindful of being from the less-affluent side of the tracks, my Vick training eventually served my needs better than any MBA degree might have. The Vick job, with a brand-new company car, expense account, and constant travel all over the country, was a dream job for almost any young single guy of my day, or at least it was for me.

Known around the world by its familiar blue glass jar, Vicks VapoRub was a mentholated chest-rub for relief from the symptoms of the common cold. It was widely promoted during the almost-worldwide influenza pandemic of 1918. John Barry, in his book *The Great Influenza*, chose, however, to liberally asperse Vick as an almost villainous predator of that day.

VICK MANDATED a rigid dress code of business suits with white or blue shirts and conservative ties. Probably every new hire in my twelve-member "class" also had to go shopping for his first straw hat before showing up "properly attired" on his first day. (There were most certainly no female colleagues in 1958.) We then needed to purchase our first felt hats immediately after Labor Day. Although business dress codes elsewhere were much less stringent by 1958, we always respected our program. We were much in the minority regarding our clothing, but most of us felt a quiet pride in our roles as "the Vicks guys."

Our clothing style may tell others a great deal about us, but clothing is only one small part of anyone's lifestyle. How do we act, talk, and think about things? How do we live, work, and treat others? What guidelines do we try to live by? Individually, where are we going? What are our objectives? What is our overall lifestyle? Where do all the pieces fit together? Do we have a separate business lifestyle, too? How do we meld the often-conflicting forces in our lives to achieve real fulfillment? What examples do we try to set?

> *How do we meld the often-conflicting forces in our lives to achieve real fulfillment?*

Each of us has dozens of opportunities every day to demonstrate the style we have programmed for ourselves. We may often flounder and waver in this regard as young adults, but with age we gradually develop consistency and responsibility. Vick mandated the image that it wanted us to project at all times as representatives of the company.

Eager and ready to soak in each new experience, I worked to be the best first-year recruit Vick ever had. And according to the weekly recap summaries Vick shared with me, I typically made more sales calls, had higher average sales per call, and had much higher sales of new products than my peers did, and I just had so much fun doing it. This was especially true during the company's big campaign every summer to promote oversized orders of Vicks cold remedies before the start of cold season. I made it a game to attain the best results I could. We never saw any kind of interim cash incentives, but my sales record paid off well in terms of salary after early 1959.

The setting of realistic life goals is one of the biggest decisions most of us will ever make, because we may spend the rest of a lifetime pursuing them. To many of us, the next question may inevitably be, "How hard am I willing to work to achieve my goals?" Some people achieve their goals because of extraordinarily good luck, just as others may be destroyed by really bad luck. Sometimes good luck is as simple as positioning ourselves and conducting our lives in such a way that good things can happen. Positioning ourselves often involves taking chances on colleagues, including our superiors, and making determinations about *their* character, presumed good intentions, and reliability.

One of the most important things to remember about good luck is that we must train ourselves and our colleagues to recognize it when it comes along. Although mudslingers love belittling people with whom they disagree as "opportunists," they are entirely missing the point. Indeed, taking advantage of opportunities is really the essence of how and why businesses exist. Businesses thrive by recognizing a need as an opportunity and then filling the need. My dad liked quoting Thomas Edison: "Most people miss opportunities because they look too much like work."

Knowing that I probably worked harder, completed more sales calls, and had better results than anyone else of my rank, I felt comfortable taking off most of one weekday to explore Imperial Coal Mine in Clymer, Pennsylvania. I had serendipitously met the mine's maintenance director at a nearby restaurant, and when he invited me to venture underground with him the following morning, I nearly leaped off my chair to accept. The only way in and out of the mine, however, was through a narrow tunnel, lying face down on a rubber conveyor belt. One mistake could surely have ended my days, but at least my last one would have been the most exciting. I also took time that summer to rendezvous with my parents along Lake Michigan where we all pulled up for a day at the beach. They were on their way home by car after visiting with friends in Chicago.

| Dorothy Cummings

| Bill Cummings

| Gus Cummings

AFTER LESS THAN A YEAR with Vick, my professional career was briefly interrupted when, in early 1959, I was called (not unexpectedly) to six months of active U.S. Army Reserve duty at Fort Dix, New Jersey. Many young men in that era elected to join military reserve units rather than perhaps being drafted for longer periods of active duty under the Selective Service process. I had assumed that my call to active duty would come eventually, and had alerted Vick of my status as a member of an Army field hospital reserve unit in Boston.

I reported to Fort Dix and after eight weeks of basic training was assigned as a recruit to Company D, Specialists Training Regiment, otherwise known as Cook School. Vick was liberal about almost all benefit issues, but I did have to give up my company car for the duration of my service and was without a vehicle for the first time in quite a while. Since hitchhiking was still common then, especially for men in uniform, there was never one bit of difficulty hitchhiking to Boston whenever there was enough time off to make the trip worthwhile. One time, I took a bus to New York City and had a fine time crashing the after-hours portion of a Vick sales meeting while still in uniform.

Ralph Nader

Bill (center) is shown above with U.S. Army Cook School classmates Barry Rich of New York and George Sexeny of Winchester, Massachusetts, in 1960 at Fort Dix, New Jersey

U.S. Army Cook School was an enjoyable two months, especially because I was selected as class leader for the twenty or so other privates who needed someone in charge. The job included a temporary promotion to acting sergeant, albeit with no change in pay status. The other interesting part of Cook School was working and living with the now illustrious Ralph Nader.

I first met Ralph earlier at the old Boston Army Base, now part of Boston's Innovation District, when we were both receiving our pre-active-duty physicals. Later, we also sat together during our Greyhound bus trip from Boston Army Base to Fort Dix, and by the time we again ended up together at Cook School, we knew each other fairly well.

Ralph, my *de facto* assistant class leader, had recently graduated from Harvard Law School following his undergraduate years at Princeton. He made my job as class leader much easier because he was such a steady, no-nonsense type of guy, and he always tried to assist me in making our class look as good as possible. Two classmates, however, were constant troublemakers.

Being the class leader gave me the luxury of a private bedroom on the second floor of the barracks, whereas Ralph was on the main deck below. I had few responsibilities beyond keeping track of the other recruits. One night, when I was sound asleep, however, Ralph rushed upstairs to wake me up. Even then a take-action kind of guy, Ralph already had my camera in his hand. "Come quick," he said as he hurried out of the room. "We can get the goods on them." Sure enough, our two troublemakers were excitedly conducting a craps game on the ground floor of the barracks. Ever the diplomat, at least in his Army days, Ralph decided that the photographic evidence of this "serious transgression" would be most useful in simply encouraging better behavior from the participants, and his logic did work, at least for our final two weeks together. My commitment to the U.S. Army included several years of service in the Reserves following six months of active duty between the years of the Korean conflict and Vietnam. At one point I was actually transferred to the U.S. Navy and the USS Loeser in Norfolk, Virginia, but then was honorably discharged after moving to California with Vicks.

Ralph quickly went on to much greater things, including publishing his 1965 blockbuster book *Unsafe at Any Speed*, much to the chagrin of General Motors and the rest of the American automobile industry, though probably in their long-term best interests. Ralph's national social activism led him to become a five-time candidate for the presidency of the United States, beginning as a write-in in the 1992 New Hampshire primary. It was no surprise to me that Ralph became so prominent. But where was he in November 2016?

It would be several decades until we reconnected, in early 1992, when Ralph called in advance of a trip to Boston. I was publishing just one weekly newspaper then, and it included Ralph's syndicated column. The two of us spent some enjoyable time catching up during that visit, and we have kept in touch ever since. In September 2015, Ralph opened this country's first tort law museum, the American Museum of Tort Law, in a former community bank building, in his life long home town of Winsted, Connecticut. Located less than two hours' driving time from Boston or New York, the museum fully justifies an educational stopover.

RETURNING TO VICK CHEMICAL in late 1959, for my final assignment with the company, I covered a terrific sales territory within Vick's West Coast Division. That meant working out of Long Beach, California, and managing the company's sales business in Arizona, Utah, Colorado, Nevada, and part of New Mexico. And for some reason, my only accounts in California were in San Diego County. What a fun region that was to work in at age twenty-four. Instead of my constant driving each week, there was an all new routine of flying off to a different region each Monday morning. Once there, I would be off in my rental car until Friday afternoon, unless I chose to remain on the road over weekend as was often the case.

By the start of that third year, Vick had me doing some interesting promotional work along with primarily calling on key accounts. This meant dealing with some of the largest accounts in the country, including a mammoth regional headquarters of Safeway Supermarkets, promoting wider displays and thus greater sales of Vicks on the shelves. There were also opportunities in representing the firm and its products at events such as the annual conventions of the American Dental Association and the American Medical Association.

One special project was helping to promote a major campaign in the fall of 1960 called the Vicks Care Crusade. The objective was to showcase numerous large display bins of assorted Vicks cold remedies on retailers' floors, with each display featuring advertising for the CARE organization, a prominent national charity that sent enormous numbers of food packages all over the world.

The campaign included a drawing for a grand prize: free passage on the first commercial flight into space. I have often wondered whatever happened to that grand prize. Was the prizewinner perhaps among those hundreds of high rollers who, in 2018, were reportedly on the wait list for the inaugural flight of Virgin Galactic?

In addition to doing guest interviews on a half-dozen regional radio stations, it was great fun doing live television interviews, promoting Vicks and the whole campaign, in Salt Lake City and Denver. The live TV interview in Denver was on a regional daytime show, where the host invited me to rehearse, on the evening before the actual show, just how he felt the presentation should go. He was passionate about doing well by the Vicks Care Crusade, and I was grateful to have the opportunity to practice.

This interview had a full crew in the studio for the dry run and included everything except the makeup routine. The next day, the host seemed quite excited with the net results of the extra effort, and I was certainly impressed with his work. I then learned this was the first time he had done a live interview.

KSL – Salt Lake City

Bill is pictured, in 1961, appearing on KSL TV, Salt Lake City. Bill did live interviews with two Rocky Mountains television stations (He was not discovered to be a television star)

I CONTINUED what turned out to be my final year at Vick, still feeling that as long as I was on Vick's payroll, it was up to me to do my best possible work in return. But weekends were still all mine, especially when stationed out West, with fun stays in several great ski resorts or national parks, depending on the season. There were more carefree weekends then than I would have for the next thirty years. Weekend lodging was always readily approved as part of the give-and-take that Vick managers encouraged. Resort lodging which frequently came with built-in opportunities for activities like snowshoeing, group horseback riding, and equestrian care, were especially enjoyable. My most adventurous weekend out West involved taking the famous mule ride down the trail that is cut into the south face of the Grand Canyon and is only three feet wide in some places. The mules were aging but apparently fully experienced.

Vick Chemical filled a critical role in my life and was an ideal first real job. I learned so much about what one version of corporate America was all about, and was able to do the job my superiors wanted done more than adequately. It was a magnificent learning opportunity, specifically because it frequently put me in meetings with other guys, just a few years older, almost all of whom could help me to learn. We greatly enjoyed the associations, and as a group they really helped me broaden my skill set. There was a real art form to learn about not taking "no" for an answer, and how to do it tactfully and gracefully. I learned to seek out colleagues who felt the same way and who would revel in finally closing a difficult account. When a prospect just would not say yes, we all wanted to at least change that to "not yet." Among people with whom I talked regularly, I found that little trick of the trade often led directly to breakthrough moments.

But there was also the restlessness factor, which has sometimes seemed so frequent in my current life at Cummings Properties. Sometimes, irrespective of anything a company does, excellent employees will simply get antsy because of factors that are entirely unrelated to their work. Employees may be ideally suited, well paid, respected, and secure, but when some almost insignificant thing pops up, they will chuck everything and go elsewhere, often resulting in a great waste of talent. On the other hand, quite frequently such valued employees will quietly pack up and move on because they have been working, frustrated, at the whim of underperforming or disgruntled supervisors. Careful exit interviews with departing employees can be extremely useful in uncovering situations that senior managers might easily modify or correct.

Today at Cummings Properties we sometimes hire young people for professional positions that will be their first jobs, but our longevity factor with that sector is always troublesome. We have a much higher retention rate among new recruits who have first worked for a couple years elsewhere. The average seniority among our entire Cummings staff is slightly shy of eleven years (as of January 2018), with many employees now at or approaching forty years.

❋ *A college education has become more and more important over the years, especially given the rapid advances in technology. Entrepreneurs, however, should never underestimate the value of on-the-job learning and should not blindly follow a path to an MBA simply for the prestige that might come with it. Whereas a higher degree may be beneficial for some business owners, others will gain so much more practical knowledge—like I did—by launching their careers and actually experiencing the world of business. Key colleagues at Cummings Properties have worked their way into top leadership positions with only bachelor's degrees. Among them are the firm's first four presidents.*

❋ *For me, job creation is the greatest single factor in evaluating new businesses.*

[5]

Still on the Road

I WAS NOT consciously thinking about leaving Vick, but in late 1960 Don Knox, of my Phi Sigma Kappa and Christmas tree selling days, unexpectedly called me. Don told me he was on a mission to recruit me to join Gorton's of Gloucester, Inc., in Gloucester, Massachusetts, where I soon accepted a great offer to manage the marketing of a new liquid fish fertilizer. At that time, Gorton's was pushing to help develop at least a regional local market for the sale of "fish solubles," a semi-viscous, nutrient-rich substance loaded with proteins and minerals that often produces extraordinary growth with many types of plants.

| *Bill in the early 1960s, during his time with Gorton's*

I was not in any way unhappy with Vick, but left for what seemed like a long-term career with Gorton's, a classic old Massachusetts firm. With Vick, I had worked in thirty-five states, after spending my first 180 consecutive nights in hotels and motels. Before eventually leaving Gorton's too, my assignments there brought me to all the remaining lower forty-eight states not previously worked in with Vick.

I was hired by Paul Jacobs, Gorton's late president, and by the late E. Robert (Bob) Kinney, its chairman. Bob later became chairman of General Mills, after it acquired Gorton's, following my years there. I once had the good fortune to have both of these men, whom I so greatly admired, quietly mentoring me at the same time, but independently of each other. I much appreciated and took advantage of their generous coaching at every opportunity.

A good mentor helps, but most people who do well in business ultimately do so because at some point in their lives they decide what they want, they set goals, and they make up their mind to sacrifice in order to reach them. Having brains and friends who are willing to help you is great, and those things can surely make life a lot easier, but nothing is as important as hard work, desire, persistence, and dedication.

I knew nothing about fertilizer products and not much more about things horticultural. And while it is not necessarily true that a good salesperson can sell anything, it was true for me when it came to non-technical products and services, which certainly include VapoRub, fertilizer, and fish. My new product was essentially the liquid byproduct that resulted from processing fish and fish oil. We chemically strengthened and stabilized the natural product, and added a coloring agent. And that was that.

First, Don and I dreamt up the name, Mer-made Fish Emulsion Plant Food. Then we created a family of both retail- and commercial-sized containers for marketing what we called "plant food" rather than "fertilizer," because market research showed that household users preferred the former term. We used translucent high-density plastic bottles and offered three retail sizes of this fine, natural product, starting with an eight-ounce flask. Each had a small plastic insert in the neck of the bottle, allowing users to neatly squeeze out just an ounce or so of liquid at a time. For use on houseplants, most people would mix an ounce of the highly concentrated product into a half-gallon of water and then either root-feed or foliar-feed.

The professional-sized containers came in one-gallon and five-gallon sizes, as well as fifty-five-gallon drums for use by commercial flower growers, several of whom I personally visited and sold to, including many in northeast Ohio. It was this specialized commercial market we most wanted to crack. This was particularly so because a competitive "Atlas" product, from the West Coast, was not a major factor there.

One of the first things Don and I did on the retail side was to take a booth at the annual Boston Spring Flower Show, where we could easily talk with hundreds of retail shoppers, many of whom were fascinated with our new local product. Don was in his element there, especially because of his considerable experience with landscape work and design in graduate school. Our key reason to present at the Flower Show was to have firsthand access to the opinions and attitudes expressed by home gardeners toward our new product as we assessed the retail market. We wondered if we should try talking about East Coast fish being better for plants than West Coast fish, but we never tried that pitch. If we were to do the same thing today, however, I can readily imagine playing the "buy local" card.

The most helpful thing we learned at the Flower Show was that a large percentage of people who purchased a bottle or two of Mer-made first unscrewed the cap and took a sniff. Many shoppers were mistakenly, but naturally, concerned that Mer-made might smell up their homes. Unlike two other West Coast fish emulsion brands, which were a sort of yucky brown, Mer-made had enough inexpensive coloring in it to give even the diluted product a pleasant green color. But the product was not formulated with enough deodorant, or reodorant, to completely mask the mild fish odor. That first evening, Don and I returned to Gloucester to investigate possible solutions, opting to forgo the night out so often associated with trade shows.

Someone suggested adding vanilla extract, but instead of adding anything to the contents of our bottles, we took about 500 of the small plastic inserts that we typically pushed into the top opening of each bottle to restrict the outflow and soaked those inserts overnight in the vanilla

> *We effectively marinated the plastic inserts in real vanilla extract.*

extract. We effectively marinated the plastic inserts in real vanilla. The next morning, before the Flower Show opened, Don and I opened the entire inventory we had there and substituted the newly sweet-scented plugs.

Customers that day may have wondered why we appeared so pleased when they continued to open the bottles. "Mer-made just smells so great," they told us over and over. Some of them, who were users of other fish emulsion products, even mentioned those products by name. We knew from a few growers, who by then were starting to use large quantities of the product in their indoor greenhouses, that neither Mer-made *nor* our competitors' products caused any odor problem at all when diluted and used, but we certainly provided a much better first sniff. Don and I gave ourselves merit badges for innovation.

BEFORE MUCH OF anything was really "done" with Mer-made, I was asked to transfer to the "real" Gorton's, but at its Blue Water Seafoods Division in Cleveland, Ohio. This assignment came as Gorton's and the Mer-made developer accepted an offer to sell the partially developed Mer-made line, although Gorton's local firm continued for some time to do the manufacturing. The Gorton's interest in the fish solubles really had much more to do with the company trying to help Gloucester's overall economy by building the market for this fishery byproduct than it did with actually making a market for itself.

When I moved to Cleveland, my sales area started in Toledo, in northwest Ohio, and extended all the way to Montana, Idaho, and beyond. I was tasked with creating a supply chain for our frozen seafood products in my "frontier" market, especially the vast area between Minneapolis and Idaho where we had almost no distribution. Ironically, my most substantial problem also yielded my greatest opportunity, and, in my mind anyway, the net result was as much a logistical masterpiece as it was an impressive sales success.

In an effort to make this new sales territory work, I needed to plan carefully when assembling and shipping orders and was able to organize my sales calls so that full truckloads of frozen product could be dropped off in logical sequence to the many new distributors I established. Our fresh frozen cod portions were cut with high-speed band saws from forty-pound blocks of cod fillets that were often processed at sea and were promoted as "fresher than fresh." These blocks were cut into four-ounce sandwich-sized pieces, lightly breaded, and then used primarily by fast-food restaurant chains for their hot fish sandwiches. "Fishwiche" was our trademarked name.

Blue Water had recently been designated as the exclusive national supplier of frozen breaded fish portions for all the McDonald's restaurants. There were not many McDonald's in New England in 1961, but the chain was strong in the West. In my territory, that contract was a huge tool whose power could be measured by much more than the amount of fish actually consumed in the McDonald's outlets there.

Each new distributor we signed up to serve the McDonald's outlets gave me many opportunities to sell other Blue Water brand products to these same new distributors, which would, of course, resell to their other customers, we hoped, as well as to McDonald's. The distributors benefited by reaching the minimum-size orders necessary for effective shipping costs.

If Gorton's brand was available, each McDonald's in the area was required by McDonald's national office to use our brand. That proved to be a marvelous selling tool. Whichever distributor was bringing in the frozen fish portions to its local McDonald's knew that it, too, would have an excellent opportunity to supply some of McDonald's other needs. I would then, of course, use the same logic with the distributors, motivating or enabling them to stock Gorton's or Blue Water branded shrimp, scallops, and lobster tails, as well as other sizes and shapes of frozen fish, in order to meet our shipping minimums. Everyone was delighted over my consideration for their needs. All of this ultimately made for a successful distribution and sales experience.

It always helps to show people that you are on their side before trying to get them on yours. Consider other people's points of view when plans and procedures change. Work on decisions until they are as fair as possible to all concerned to avoid building up sides and cliques. Respect the inevitable cultural or philosophical differences that will cause people to see some things differently from how you might see them. Always listen carefully to find things that might be thrown into a deal to sweeten it for the other side, at little or no cost to you.

Unlike most salespeople in the company, I left my home base of Cleveland to start out on my sales itinerary almost every Sunday afternoon, often flying then to the far end of my territory. I then worked my way back from places like Billings or Helena to Fargo and Cheyenne, and then perhaps to accounts around Milwaukee. Other times, I would jaunt up to the Twin Cities area, then to Omaha, down to Davenport, and maybe Milwaukee again. I was always working to instill excitement in the distributors and their sales staffs about our Blue Water products, and I often attended regional restaurant shows. I pretended (to myself, at least) that the whole company was mine.

Working for Gorton's, I, surprisingly, found myself once again happy to travel almost every week. Although it would hardly be newsworthy today, my picture appeared one day in a Cleveland daily newspaper with those of a half-dozen other inaugural members of what must have been a predecessor to United Airlines' frequent flyer club. In those days, United Airlines awarded membership in its 100,000 Mile Club for accumulated lifetime mileage: "In Appreciation for your Outstanding Contributions to Air Transport Progress." While it was easy for a businessman to accumulate air miles, they had zero value. They were not redeemable for anything then, other than access to priority reservations and a fancy walnut plaque, which I still have. Women

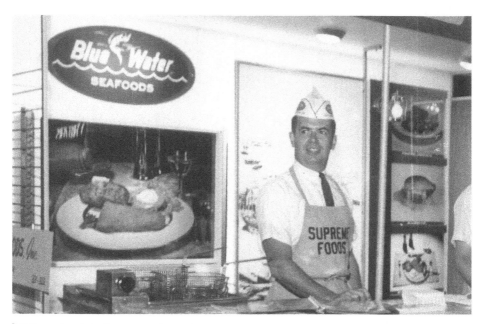

| *Bill at a booth for Blue Water Seafoods at the Minnesota Restaurant Association Show, 1963*

were rarely seen on weekday flights then, except for flights heading to vacation destinations, and flights were almost never full or even close to full. So, we can all now readily see what wonders women have done for the airline industry.

JUST AFTER NEW YEAR'S 1964, following my two years of frequently praised and highly productive work at Blue Water, the senior vice president there started my day by calling me aside. "I have some bad news for you," he said. "We've thought about this a great deal, but the appointment as the company's new assistant sales manager is not going to you." Instead, the attractive new job would go to a much more senior salesman who, I was told, had a family and really needed the new job and a raise. "You might have been the better choice for this job, Bill, but surely you are not going to let this get in your way now, after all you've accomplished here."

I suggested that they give me the new management position and give the money to the other guy, whom I certainly liked and who supposedly really needed the money. "Tell me in a year if I deserve a raise then," I argued, but I got nowhere. The SVP offered me a great raise and my choice of whatever territory I wanted as a consolation prize instead of the promotion, but I was not interested. I had been thinking for some time that any kind of a bump in the road with Gorton's would be my signal that it was time to go off on my own. So it did not take me long to decline the generous raise and give my notice.

Here, let's re-emphasize some of what I discussed earlier in this chapter. Managers must be constantly aware of opportunities to improve and enhance relationships with their key employees, lest they later be required to train replacements. It is generally far less expensive and less stressful to salvage existing employee relationships than it is to create new ones. Some of the most critical ingredients in employee satisfaction are consistency, opportunity, and fairness on the part of the company. Businesses that take the trouble to carefully think through and codify their employee policies provide a strong emotional bridge in times of individual employee stress. Access to easily understood information concerning company personnel policies seems to be of immense value in reducing employee frustration and turnover. If employees feel their employer is fair with them, they are far less likely to quit when some little thing goes wrong.

Job security, and the simple knowledge that staff members are truly appreciated for what they contribute, can never be overemphasized. When managers are overworked or rushed, it is easy for them to take people for granted. Every one of us needs to know that what we do is worthwhile, and when employees don't hear this from their superiors, the employees might prove how valuable they are by leaving.

There were bruise-colored clouds and a cold wind blowing in from the Cuyahoga River as I walked out of the office that day but my heart was really excited. I did not have any hint about how to start out on my own, except that I would take a few months' vacation first. Like my decision a few years earlier not to continue with advanced AFROTC, I have reflected many times on this pivotal decision to leave corporate America, but never have I one time regretted it.

I SOON BOARDED the RMS Queen Mary in New York with a low-cost windowless cabin akin to steerage class, and a first-class Eurail Pass good for three months of unlimited deluxe and first-class rail passage throughout most of Europe. On the Queen Mary, however, I managed to insinuate myself easily into the first-class routine of the ship with the help of a couple of older women as accomplices, whom I met the first night, and an underground booklet called *The Inside Route to First Class on Cunard*. These ladies changed their table assignment so there was always an empty seat for me at their table in the first-class dining room. I even coupled with one of my new best friends to win a three-day bridge tournament. The other essential tool I brought with me was an early edition of Arthur Frommer's *Europe on Five Dollars a Day*. The book took care of two-thirds of my hotel rooms in Europe, and the comfortable high-speed trains provided most of the rest of my lodgings.

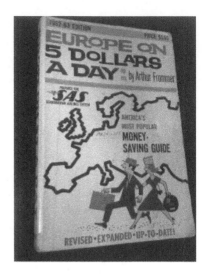

Though my passport was brand-new when I left the United States, I still needed to add extra accordion-style pages to accommodate what I anticipated would be dozens of back-and-forth border crossings, plus Russian and eastern Mediterranean visas. By entering Russia via Finland, I found it no problem to get there. I will never forget watching Swan Lake at the Bolshoi Theatre, or enjoying a live hockey game in Moscow, and hearing the Star-Spangled Banner played to start the game, even though the score ended up at about 11-1, the wrong way.

I probably visited every nation in North Africa and Europe by rail, boat, or plane, and enjoyed a fabulous winter. Later in my trip, when I traveled to Egypt, Syria, and Kuwait, the added pages in my passport allowed me to snip off evidence that I had earlier visited Israel—otherwise I would not have been allowed into those Middle Eastern countries. That would have been a great loss.

In Damascus, I once found myself surrounded by a dozen soldiers, all with drawn guns. I had rented a bike and was riding around and innocently taking pictures of the wrong things during a short revolution there, but after yanking the film from my camera, they let me go.

Later, in nearby Lebanon, I met up with a friend from Vermont whose brother had given her, and seemingly everyone else she knew, the use of his chalet on a mountain at Cedars of Lebanon for a week-long ski blast.

That ski trip turned out to be almost my only real "vacation" during my four months of constant travel—that and my one-night respite from all of the inexpensive fourth-floor walkup hotel rooms when I booked myself into Athens' King George Hotel to top off the splendor of that beautiful city. Clearly not an Arthur Frommer choice, the King George, in a single night, gave me all the super luxury I needed for the entire trip.

RETURNING FROM EUROPE in May 1964, I was excited to begin looking for my new start in life. Having just enjoyed a four-month "adventure of a lifetime"—or so I thought then—it was time to get to work.

For me, business is enjoyable for its own sake—even more than it is for the financial rewards it may bring. The money we earn will, to some extent, serve as a score card, but successful entrepreneurs may otherwise pay only the scantest attention to their financial bottom lines. I have never once tried to add up my net worth, at least not in the last forty years, anyway, and to the best of my knowledge no one else has either. Neither have we ever failed to pay a debt, or to pay it on time.

Starting my formal business career with Vick Chemical Company and then Gorton's of Gloucester was especially beneficial to me, because those firms gave me an essential close-up view of how solid, established businesses operate. Those five-plus years of traditional business experience in two smart, highly principled national companies would be so valuable to me even decades later.

———————————

❀ *Management experience at two fine national companies showed me firsthand the importance of seizing opportunities to enhance relationships with employees through thoughtful communication and expressions of genuine appreciation for work well done. Many employees, in fact, crave fulfillment more than money alone—at Gorton's, for example, I would have happily taken greater responsibility and no raise in preference to the inverse, and readily embarked on my own adventure when I felt the secure job no longer aligned with my goals.*

[6]

Fruit Punch and Lemonade

Joyce Cummings

| *Bill Cummings with a Starline refrigerated dispenser*

AS I SETTLED in following the grand trip, my Dad at first expressed no opinion about what business he thought I should get into. Little did I know—until later—that he was biding his time, and he waited just long enough before asking me to humor him by taking a look at the "funny old business" he had mentioned to me in passing months before. Funny indeed: It was a fruit-punch business. What would Dad know about which kind of business I should buy? I thought. But for that matter, what did I know?

The business was Wilmot H. Simonson Company, and its owner, Llewellyn H. Farnsworth, was a well-to-do West Medford resident who had begun spending the warmer months in Jonesport, Maine, where he grew blueberries. He was about seventy years old, tall and lean, and favored blue jeans and red plaid shirts. Except for the large gray cowboy hat he wore most every time I ever saw him, he was a pure Down East Yankee.

Mr. Farnsworth met me in his lovely West Medford home on a Friday afternoon in June 1964 after Dad took me to the business location, five blocks from Cherry Street, that morning. "My dad says I should buy your fruit-punch business," I said, "but I don't know why I would want to pay anything for a business that had almost no sales and no income."

Mr. Farnsworth immediately began telling me about the vast potential of the business and about what he considered its valuable secret formula. Wilmot Horatio Simonson had supposedly acquired this formula in 1890 from the makers of Old Medford Rum. Mr. Farnsworth suggested that the price to purchase the business should be "at least a six-figure number," but he would let it go for $40,000 because he knew I "would not be able to finance much." The total gross sales for the business the entire previous year had amounted to a scant $10,000 or $11,000.

We had a friendly conversation, but eventually he came to realize that the business itself was not worth anything at all if the maximum earnings to be made from it, based on its then-current volume, might be about twenty cents an hour—a small fraction of the minimum wage even at that time. Eventually I offered him 10 percent of his asking price, with full payment that day, but "not a dime more." When he finally agreed on my offer of $4,000, he did so based on the value of the sugar and other ingredients, and the gallon-sized glass jugs he had in inventory, but he still wanted $2,000 for "goodwill."

> *"The most important thing about being lucky," he said, "is recognizing good luck when it comes along, and then taking advantage of it."*

I told him again, "That was it." He could have my friendship and goodwill for free, but there wasn't any more money to give for his. He was not at all happy with the price, but we shook hands at $4,000 in 1950s dollars, say perhaps $40,000 today. At the end, he seemed satisfied and pleased, saying, "Old Medford will soon be out of my life."

Dad was visibly pleased with the Farnsworth purchase. He was excited that I had agreed with his assessment, and that we closed this deal at what he thought was such a bargain price. He seemed especially proud that he had just played a significant role in his son's career path. "Mr. Farnsworth just wanted to get rid of the business," Dad said. "You bought it for a song."

That evening, Dad gave me some advice that has remained extremely meaningful to me. "The most important thing about being lucky," he said, "is recognizing good luck when it comes along, and then taking advantage of it. Life is mostly what we make of the opportunities that come our way." Good genes or good luck may be the same thing, but wherever they lead us is highly dependent upon what we do with them.

Simonson Company, as it continued to be known during our first two years, was supposed to have been an aging descendant of the Old Medford Rum

Company, but Simonson made only one product—Old Medford fruit-punch concentrate. The company received an award from an advertising association in the 1920s for holding the oldest brand name in continuous use in North America. It sold its product mostly to catering firms and fancy restaurants in and around Boston and the North Shore. But the customer list for this delicious product also included two university accounts, Harvard Law School and Massachusetts Institute of Technology—both in nearby Cambridge. Over the next few years, we (which I use here as a pontifical "We") built the backbone of the company on what we soon did with these two tiny college accounts. Though their Old Medford orders initially were limited, these two prestigious schools became extremely important steppingstones for far greater business.

Wilmot H. Simonson Company at 54 Fulton Street with Whiting's Milk Company picking up Old Medford fruit-punch base, 1964

Another especially interesting new account my first summer was Whiting's Milk Company on Rutherford Avenue in Charlestown, directly next door to the area's milk giant, Hood Milk Company, and a few blocks from the old Charlestown State Prison. Coincidentally, Whiting's Milk was the company to which my grandfather, also named Augustus Cummings, sold his small milk-delivery company, including his three horses and their milk wagons, in 1936.

In late June, I telephoned Arnold Bullock, Whiting's president, hoping to convince him to have his drivers sell our Old Medford fruit-punch concentrate in retail-sized bottles for home use. As it turned out, he liked the product's taste so much that he decided to buy our concentrate just as it came, and we had our first real volume customer. Impracticable as it was, Whiting's chose to add water and sell a ready-to-drink fruit punch.

Someone at Whiting's could easily have concocted a comparable product from scratch. Alternatively, we could have delivered a far more concentrated product at a much lower cost, to which Whiting's could have added even twenty parts water instead of five parts water, and its own sugar. Instead, through early September Whiting's continued purchasing many truckloads of our completely standard fruit-punch concentrate. They added five parts water and then sold it as "Whiting's own original recipe" old-fashioned fruit punch.

The only thing we did differently for Whiting's was that we bottled our concentrate in Whiting's own gallon-sized reusable glass milk jugs and issued a credit for the savings on the cost of the jugs we would otherwise have used. We were surprised that it took someone at the milk company nearly the whole summer to realize that it did not need us for what it could do on its own for a dramatically lower cost.

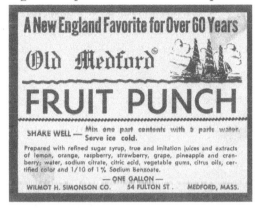

We operated out of Mr. Farnsworth's twenty-four-by-forty-eight-foot, two-story wood frame building at 54 Fulton Street, Medford, for more than a year. The facility was tucked behind two homes, but the regular visits of large delivery trucks began to pose a logistical challenge for our busy residential neighborhood. One memory from those early days was how much Mr. Farnsworth seemed to enjoy dropping by on the first or second of each month to see how we were doing, pick up the $50 rent check, and cheer us on. "It has been so long since I've made any money off this old place," he once told me.

THE MOST SUCCESSFUL entrepreneurs I have known almost always demonstrated great self-confidence, optimism, and often, personal magnetism, as well as a willingness to work prodigious hours to make things happen to their satisfaction. There is almost always a way to get the job done, and the true entrepreneur will persevere with some things to the point of obsession. Entrepreneurs hate to lose every bit as much as they love to win. Entrepreneurial mistakes, however, must be freely accepted because calculated risk is inherent to the concept of entrepreneurship. Oscar Wilde may have been the first person to write, "Experience is the name that we give to our mistakes."

Entrepreneurs must have an aggressive risk-taking nature, tempered by a reasonable understanding of how great any impending risk might be. Purchasing Simonson in one day, without any due diligence, was my risk-taking nature in command. I knew that this little business could be turned into a successful venture with a combination of creativity to improve the efficiency of production and hard work to dramatically cut costs and sell a better product. I have always had a wealth of intellectual curiosity, along with extra ability to innovate in the face of adversity. And innovate we did.

Sales and production steadily increased during our first year, as our original two-person sales team and I were out on the street peddling our concentrated fruit punch. We went from ordering 500 or 1,000 pounds of sugar at a time to 5,000 pounds per delivery, all in 100-pound bags. But one day, I personally unloaded and stacked 20,000 pounds (200 large bags) of sugar by myself to stock up before an upcoming price increase. We soon thereafter switched to liquid sugar syrup, delivered by tanker trucks, which was a far more appropriate form

| Student worker Jack Kerins in the bottling room, 1965

of sweetener. The liquid cane sugar was pumped directly from the delivery truck into a 2,000-gallon stainless-steel storage tank we had set up in an adjacent garage.

The meager bottling equipment from the original company was almost immediately inadequate to keep up with the production demands our sales results generated. We installed a pressurized water tank with a half-inch inlet, but with a two-inch-diameter discharge valve to accommodate the increased need for water in a hurry, and we configured the piping to allow the liquid sugar and water to pour into the mixing tank simultaneously. A new six-bottle siphon filler allowed one operator to fill six jugs much faster than two operators had previously filled two jugs. We also purchased a used electric conveyor belt to replace a rope-pulled dumbwaiter that brought the finished products from the basement up to the loading-dock level. Our one-gallon glass jugs soon gave way to less-fragile plastic jugs that worked far better for our needs, cost less than the glass jugs, and were lighter to ship. Every penny per gallon we could save on the cost side created a substantial difference in the profits, and we were always looking to save those pennies.

Penny-saving principles of cost control are frighteningly simple, and they come into play so often, but they are sometimes maddeningly ignored by smart people. Saving money through efficiency and eliminating wasted motions and unnecessary repeating costs is easy, once one starts to look out for it, though even well-meaning staff will sometimes surely mislabel cost control as miserliness.

WHEN WE FIRST took over the tiny wood-frame building on Fulton Street, it contained considerable ancient-looking equipment from the days prior to World War I, when the company also made Mrs. Simonson's Lemon Pie Filling Mix, which was packaged by hand in small retail-size boxes. Before we removed these large antique wooden mixing machines, I used them a little disingenuously to make the company sound busy when visitors were in the one-room front office. These loudly clunking machines had huge, old electric motors, and wide leather belts connected the machines to one another. The whole building seemed to rumble when we turned them on. It was impressive, even if, for decades, the antique equipment had done nothing more useful than make noise on command.

And judging by the buzz around the office on November 9, 1965, one might have thought that Simonson Company/Old Medford Foods was undertaking a massive office changeover of some sort. In reality, the "big occasion" was that we had transitioned that day from an ancient Underwood click clack typewriter to a new IBM "Selectric" model.

Before my mother joined us at Old Medford earlier that year, she had not worked outside her home for thirty years. She was always an excellent typist, however, and she loved her work at Old Medford. At the same time, she was completely spooked that she would now have to "learn to type all over again, after all these years." Mom wanted nothing to do with this "totally unnecessary" new contraption, but nevertheless we proudly made the momentous change to our new Selectric.

How ironic it was when that same afternoon brought the Great Northeast Blackout, supposedly the largest power outage in American history at the time, affecting more than 30 million people in the northeastern states. Mom, in her *post hoc* thinking about the monster outage, attributed this blackout, only half-jokingly, to her new electric typewriter. Late that afternoon, she was elated to put the old Underwood back into service one last time, to type out the final few bills of lading.

Dot Cummings at 54 Fulton Street, 1965

THE CHALLENGE OF developing new recipes that were efficient to manufacture and profitable to sell kept my mind churning while I worked. The first new formulas were for lemonade, Concord grape, and orange, because we were already utilizing all of the frozen juices for these flavors with the fruit punch. These three new varieties and the punch all had about the same ingredient cost. The last three new flavors we developed were lemon-lime, wild cherry, and black raspberry, none of which had any meaningful juice content at all. These were not as popular on their own, but most buyers who used any flavors other than fruit punch soon tended to rotate all seven flavors.

One important business question here was pricing. Should we vary the selling prices to reflect the 30-percent-lower contents cost for the three juiceless varieties? We quickly determined to price all seven flavors the same, and the subject of price differential never came up again. Old Medford fruit punch was the fastest seller, with Concord grape and lemonade a close second. The other four flavors all about tied for third place. The uniform pricing was certainly also to our advantage, as it kept everything simple. We determined that reducing the selling price of the less expensive flavors would not have helped us sell any more product and would have only reduced our profits. The single most important factor in determining how much something is worth is finding out how much customers will pay for it.

> *The single most important factor in determining how much something is worth is finding out how much customers will pay for it.*

The first important new growth for Old Medford started at Massachusetts Institute of Technology, one of the Company's thirty or so existing small customers (there were no large ones) when we purchased the firm. MIT had been loyally serving Old Medford fruit punch at conference sessions, parties, and other special events for decades, but while the purchases were steady, they had historically totaled about $1,000 per year. Perhaps we had that account because of an early "buy local" initiative at the school.

Although MIT's food service team loved Old Medford punch for its staff parties and special events, no one ever considered serving it to students—even though the person who ordered it for the administrative and faculty parties was the same person who supervised the school's broader food and beverage purchases and ran the Walker Memorial Dining Hall. But when we floated the idea, he immediately pointed out how impractical it would be to set up punch bowls in the cafeteria service lines.

This was an urgent challenge, and as soon as we could find an appropriate-sized "institutional punch bowl," I knew we would convince this highly supportive MIT manager to give it a try, and we would then be able to convert Walker Memorial into a prized account. Two days later, we purchased our first two oversized refrigerated dispensers from the former Dripcut Starline Corp. in Santa Barbara, California, each equipped with a fourteen-gallon clear Lexan tank. We immediately received MIT approval to set them up, filled with Old Medford fruit punch, next to the milk dispensers, and the students loved it. Then a day and a half after the Walker dining hall installation, we were asked to install dispensers in the dining rooms at MIT's Burton House and Baker House dormitories, and soon thereafter for all other student dining halls and cafeterias on campus. Those first two oversized refrigerated dispensers started a whole new business for us.

Moving forward, we eventually provided these refrigerated dispensers to hundreds of large institutional users to display and dispense Old Medford drinks, but almost exclusively in college dining halls and large hospitals. That was in 1965, shortly after most college cafeterias had started moving their classic Norris milk dispensers off the serving lines and into the dining rooms. Rather than be limited to one or two glasses of milk per meal, as was previously typical, students could now drink all the milk they wanted, and of course, all the Old Medford fruit punch, too. Students loved having the choice and were often vocal in their support of the change. If only we had had Twitter in 1965 to spread the news faster and farther.

Aside from selling the quality and appeal of our delicious product, the most important factor in marketing Old Medford fruit punch drinks was the "free" Starline dispensers we installed. Many customers often needed four or even six machines in a single large dining hall. Old Medford drink concentrates had a uniform list price of $10.60 per four-gallon case, including a $3-per-case premium until we recovered our cost of whatever equipment was provided. Thereafter, we automatically reduced the invoice price to $7.60 per case, but we still owned all the dispensing equipment and maintained the machines at our expense. If another supplier had come along trying to compete with us, there would have been little or no room for it to replace our dispensers and still make a profit on its juice sales. A strong point here, however: "Don't get greedy." Our customers were already benefiting from our substantial discounts for purchasing large volumes and paying promptly. Most of our college accounts used enough concentrate to fully pay off the surcharges for whatever equipment they needed during the first semester's use. And in some years we had absolutely no bad-debt expense.

Large accounts paid about two cents, again in 1965 dollars, per serving for our concentrated fruit drinks, compared to their approximately five-cents-per-serving cost of milk. Food-service directors tended to feel that their thirsty students would drink every bit as much as they could hold. With that in mind, the more Old Medford they consumed, the more money the school would save on milk. Sugar was not a bad word in those days, and even if it had been, we soon converted all the flavors to sugar-free products at an enormous savings to us in production cost.

With MIT using Old Medford at a marvelous pace, we quickly turned to the other school account we had inherited from the original business, Harvard Law School. Like MIT, Harvard also used Old Medford only for its special parties and for conferences. Along with hot beverages and a few trays of brownies or cookies, the school often served Old Medford during afternoon break periods for meetings and seminars.

Pauline Harkovitz was the highly regarded food-service director and an American Dietetic Association dietician

| *Old Medford delivery case, circa 1920*

for Harkness Commons at Harvard Law School. "Sure, we can try it," was her prompt response to my pitch for offering Old Medford in the Law School dining hall. Once again, Old Medford provided the extra-large capacity dispensers, and the account needed only to purchase the concentrated drinks. Before we knew it, America's top-ranked future lawyers were drinking Old Medford at a pace that I could never have imagined a year before.

Once we established ourselves with the Law School food service team, who were employed by Stouffer's, we thought we would, of course, soon be talking with the university's own dining staff who handled all the many remaining dining halls, but we made no such headway. After several months, however, Fred McCauley, one of Old Medford's first two sales associates, was attending a food service seminar at University of Massachusetts in Amherst when he noticed a key food service director from Harvard walking into a men's room.

It happened to be Charlie McCarthy, who for many years ran Kresge Hall at Harvard Business School, and Fred followed him into the UMass restroom. All of fifteen minutes later, they finally emerged from the restroom together, with Fred obviously happy. Fred recognized that opportunity when it came along, and Harvard Business School soon led all of the remaining dining halls into the Old Medford camp.

Tufts University was another early Old Medford client, for obvious reasons including the campus' location, which was just two miles from the Old Medford facility on Fulton Street. Despite being an alumnus, I was not known there at that time. Yet, to my surprise, Tufts' food-services director, Richard Ballou, remembered that I had worked for a short time as a kitchen helper and food monitor at the school's Carmichael Hall during my student days. Tufts students soon joined the ever-growing throng raving about our delicious fruit punch and six other tasty flavors.

At about $400 each, the Starline dispensers sometimes created a strain on cash flow, even as Old Medford sales grew rapidly (thanks to those exact machines). The results clearly justified the investment, but these high up-front costs did compel me, in mid-1966, to apply for a business loan at the local branch of what was then the Middlesex County National Bank. By that time, we had been doing all of our banking with Middlesex for a year. The bank didn't exactly say no. Instead, a snippy assistant branch manager told me, "Get your mother to co-sign it, or there will be no loan." I was sure he had never met my mother. Moreover, I was twenty-eight years old at the time (and looked my age) and stood more than six feet tall. As far as *he* knew, at that point, we were still friends.

How pleased I was when, just a few days later, an up-and-coming assistant manager from another bank came to our front door at 54 Fulton Street late one afternoon. Lawrence J. King from the old Malden Trust Company, in Malden, Massachusetts, came to make a sales pitch, after he had somehow found out about us. I told Larry all about our history and our current cash need and why we needed a loan. He quickly said, "Sure."

"Take this, and open the account for us," I said, handing him the week's receipts, "and let's get going." As he was leaving, instead of asking me to get my mother to co-sign, Larry said, "Are you sure you don't need board approval or something?" Larry's entrepreneurial attitude won him a new customer on his first surprise visit. If the old wooden mixing machines had still been there, I would have surely turned them on for effect.

Eventually, some twenty years later, I was delighted to introduce Larry to the owners of Saugus Bank and Trust Company, who we knew had a highly attractive opening at their bank. Fred England of the Saugus bank quickly liked Larry enough to hire him as the bank's president. We then for many years maintained a substantial relationship with that bank and later with Eastern Bank, which absorbed Saugus Bank in 1994. I had earlier become acquainted with Fred England, and his wife, Valerie, when we served for a number of years together on the board of his family's former Tanners National Bank in Woburn. Joyce and I enjoyed being around Fred and Val and came to know them quite well.

Saugus Bank grew dramatically under Larry's leadership, while Fred and his close colleague Don Lewis, whom I did not know then, were engineering the rise of Hastings-Tapley Insurance Agency. This was nevertheless the start of what is today still a significant relationship for Cummings Properties with Don, and with the firm that is now USI Insurance, in our building at 12 Gill Street, Woburn. USI has for many years handled insurance for all of Cummings Properties' commercial real estate and is also a key Cummings client.

Watching a business develop momentum and establish a sustained pattern of growth is so satisfying in itself to the entrepreneurial people who make that growth happen. Seeing the month-to-month and year-over-year improvements in sales and profits will stimulate competitive urges that drive business leaders and give them the resources to engage more and more qualified colleagues and eager clients at every level.

❀ *The successful entrepreneur embraces risks with informed optimism—with Old Medford, I took a chance in acquiring the company while knowing virtually nothing about it, but knowing that the (bargain) price I paid justified this with a huge potential upside.*

[7]

The Perfect Partner

| Bill and Joyce Cummings at 23 Cherry Street, Medford, 1965

DESPITE THE FINANCIAL SUCCESS of Old Medford Foods, the best thing by far about that business venture was meeting my future wife. I was making a call at Massachusetts Eye and Ear Infirmary, where Joyce Jutkins was the hospital dietician. She was not far removed from her days at the University of Alabama and her subsequent dietetic internship next door at Massachusetts General Hospital. I was smitten the first time we met.

I had noticed and talked with Joyce in mid-1965, the same day I met with her boss, Mass. Eye and Ear's food-service director, Herb Kirshnit, and driving away I could not get her out of my mind. After reaching my office I called Herb and when he told me that Joyce was not involved with anyone, I went back into Boston to ask her out that same evening, directly after work. She said, "yes."

I had never dated a southern woman before, and in those days, all of the Miss America winners seemed to come from Alabama and Mississippi. My days were so much sweeter after I got to know Joyce. And yes, the hospital did start ordering more Old Medford (although Joyce has vigorously denied any involvement).

Claiming that I "tricked her" into going out, Joyce still fusses at me occasionally for having taken her that night to a fancy grand-opening party at Boston's brand-new Prudential Center. It seems that her white uniform was not at all what she would have imagined wearing to such an event. Suffice it to say, Joyce did not take off her coat, and we did not stay long, but things went exceedingly well from then on. More than fifty years later, we still exchange Christmas cards with Herb and Charlotte Kirshnit.

When Joyce first asked me, "How come you're not married?" I was slow to answer. For her part, she was ready, but perhaps other guys were scared off by her notion that she had always wanted to have six children—"all boys, please." I was not necessarily opposed to the idea of a large family, but I had been focusing much more on remaining single than on family size. Early on, we talked with some specificity about work-life balance regarding my career, setting the tone for a lifetime of open and frank discussion.

Entrepreneurs thrive on challenges, problem solving, and new ideas, and they tend to love their jobs.

In time, we also had conversations exploring our respective attitudes about things like race and religion. The talks about race were in light of Joyce's strong southern background and all the racist turmoil right at that time in her hometown of Birmingham, Alabama. We tested each other's viewpoints on this issue a few times and found complete compatibility, and we always have since. Joyce's thoughts much more closely mirrored those of my Boston-area friends than those of some of her hometown acquaintances.

UNLIKE THE MAJORITY OF MEN I knew, my identity gradually became closely intertwined with my newly launched entrepreneurial career, even if I did not yet have any idea what that career would eventually be or where it might take us. Serious entrepreneurs seldom feel satisfied working "normal" hours, and I was convinced that drive, determination, and sheer willpower will overcome almost any obstacle. Entrepreneurs thrive on challenges, problem solving, and new ideas, and they tend to love their work.

As success blossoms, there is tonic-like satisfaction that helps justify all the extra efforts of entrepreneurship. While many others may find the pressure stressful, serial entrepreneurs I know thrive on it, sometimes wondering why they enjoy their work so much.

Before Joyce and I married, my Old Medford salary was $25 per week. Living with my parents on Cherry Street did not suggest much of a career perhaps, but I was putting everything possible into this tiny fruit punch factory and enjoying considerable great sales gain each month. I did not believe that this particular new business was my lifetime career, but it had plenty of potential to keep me plugging.

With no demonstrated career certainty, we married in 1966, when Joyce was twenty-five and I was twenty-nine. Before then, I had agonized for years over choosing the right partner, but now I knew she was the one. As I write this paragraph in August 2016, we have just returned from celebrating our fiftieth anniversary in Venice, Italy; and on the Dalmatian Coast of Croatia; and in Montenegro.

I have always recognized how important it is to have a partner's "buy-in" well before marriage.

It is so important to have a partner's "buy-in" well before marriage. Choosing the right person to share both the highs and lows of a family business has to be one of life's greatest challenges for people with that career path. Joyce has been that supportive partner for me. New and thinly financed companies will rarely be successful without extraordinary personal commitment, and Joyce understood that I would put much more energy than most people into my work, while also being fully committed to her.

Still, I was extremely lucky that she was so tolerant of her busy husband and that she readily took primary responsibility for the daily activities of raising our four (not six) children—two boys, two girls. The allegiance of our marriage grew stronger still through our mutual interest in community service and involvement, which would truly blossom much later.

Joyce had been a food and nutrition major at the University of Alabama, Tuscaloosa, during some of that school's early sports glory in the Bear Bryant and Joe Namath era. In college, she was active with Phi Mu, a national women's sorority, and she excelled academically. She was also heavily involved in Girl Scouts and served as head swimming instructor and waterfront director at an Alabama Girl Scout summer camp. In her senior year at University of Alabama, Joyce completed a student internship at Walter Reed Army Hospital in Washington, D.C., and, after graduating from Alabama in 1962, went on to her American Dietetic Association internship at MGH in Boston.

Joyce eventually gave up her daily train commute to Boston in order to raise our family, and we soon had three of our four children. Daniel, Kevin, and Marilyn were born in 1967, 1968, and 1969, all at Winchester Hospital. Looking back, she still regards the "three under three" stage with considerable disdain. Nevertheless, Joyce showed uncommon patience with our children and my work life, despite the full house.

We have not had a storybook marriage every single week throughout the last half-century, nor should anyone expect that. By constantly learning and understanding more about each other, however, we have developed our own deep, enduring romance built on ever-growing love and respect. We have somehow survived all the pressures I probably still bring to our life together, and we have every hope for a couple of even better decades yet to come. But just in case, we rarely go to bed or wake up in the morning without telling each other, "I love you."

After noting how important Joyce has been to me and how critical her ongoing attitude toward the company and Cummings Foundation is, I would be greatly remiss to not recognize how important every management spouse can be to the ultimate success of any organization.

AFTER WE SOLIDIFIED the Harvard account, the team's most common sales pitches usually sounded something like: "We would not begin to suggest that you should like our program just because someone else is using it, Mr. Jones. At the same time, I can tell you that this is exactly the same product and the same dispensing system now installed in every dining room at Harvard, MIT, and Tufts." The implied endorsement resonated well with other colleges, and we used it to great advantage, especially because so many of the local-area school food-service managers shared ideas with one another. Mentioning our highly successful programs in three such prestigious local universities was extremely influential with prospective clients.

Leapfrogging personal referrals from existing accounts to other prospects was Old Medford's principal means of growth. We never purchased any media advertising, relying instead solely on personal contact and word of mouth. After we received an unsolicited endorsement from the home office of Saga Food Service of Menlo Park, California, then one of the top college and university food-service management firms in the country, we were really off and running.

FOR DECADES, we have regularly delegated many of the most difficult decisions to trusted colleagues. If we have carefully considered the reasons to resolve an issue one way or the other and have not seen a compelling reason to decide either way, I will almost always invite a colleague to make the final call. If the colleague is going to bear responsibility for carrying out such a decision, then let it be his or hers from the start. The key thought is that decisions can often be called in either direction with no net difference. In those situations, delaying or waffling about a decision will often be the worst thing.

Most companies have clear personalities, just as people do, but the personalities of true entrepreneurial companies are often indistinguishable from the personalities and styles of the individuals who founded them. Several things have characterized the essence of my business style from well before the start of Old Medford Foods: precise writing, strong negotiating, and ever-present frugality. None of these are specific to any one firm or industry, but they should be thought of as indispensable for any entrepreneurial business.

The personality, motivation, and reputation of the founder or founders are crucial to the success of a business. Their personal skills and dedication will often outweigh all else. It is also essential that an entrepreneur have a broad understanding of all the key positions in the firm, so that incompetence masking as sound professional advice is easily spotted.

I am more than a little bothered when information offered by a staff lawyer or accountant contains errors so obvious that they jump out even at me. Thereafter, I may pay particular attention to that person's work and find myself often more than a little disappointed if the shoddy thinking or careless work reappears. Usually then there will be serious consequences for that person's future with the firm. Résumé credentials can never be assumed to mean what we might like to think they should mean. Always hire the person, not the résumé.

I have repeatedly learned how important it is to recognize that few business owners know all the answers and that fewer still can run their businesses alone. At the same time, the business owner must know and understand the needs of the business enough to fully recognize which key staff members are competent enough at their respective roles to be implicitly relied upon. I have often thought of my business interests as being like a baseball team's. I must be able to accurately assess the ability of every position player on the team, and be able to either personally jump into, or at least fully understand, every position.

AS A RESULT of Old Medford's exponential sales growth within the first two years or so, the company soon needed larger manufacturing space and more office quarters, even if we had to give up paying our $50-per-month rent for 54 Fulton Street. Additionally, the "funny little business" located behind two old houses that had been there since well before many of its neighbors were even born was increasingly perceived as a neighborhood nuisance. Our rapidly growing truck traffic on Fulton Street was also problematic.

In February 1966, we began searching for a new home for Old Medford. Ironically, considering my profession today, it never occurred to me to explore leasing rather than buying. We eventually purchased a beat-up 6,000-square-foot concrete-block building on one acre of land at 10 Henshaw Street in Woburn, for which we paid $60,000. Five miles north of Fulton Street, the new location was also just off Interstate Route 93 but still inside Route 128, metropolitan Boston's well-known circumferential highway.

Old Medford's new concrete home was only forty years old. After clearing everything out, we engaged Telfer Construction Company of Salem Street, Medford, to expand and remake it to suit our needs. The price for the needed construction was about $80,000. Many years earlier, Elmer Telfer had been one of my regular Salem Street window-washing customers, and his daughter Nancy was a classmate at Medford High School. Not by coincidence, from the earliest beginnings of my career as an entrepreneur I have always tried to patronize businesses owned and run by qualified people we know and with whom we have had other interactions. I have a strong sense of give-and-take, and mutual loyalty has been a significant factor in my success.

After substantial planning and a little waiting for the right time, Doug Stephens, another Phi Sigma Kappa fraternity brother, joined Old Medford as treasurer, in August 1966, just before we moved the business to Woburn. Also, a retired U.S. Navy chief petty officer joined us as a full-time warehouse shipper. As he learned the production side of the business, this shipper soon transitioned and completely took over the day-to-day product manufacturing as volume steadily grew. By then, Steve Collins, Fred McCauley, and Don MacEachern were the sales force, and all three of them, plus Doug, remained for as long as I owned the firm. Fred and Doug later worked with me at Cummings Properties for many years, as well.

Few things are more vital in business than employee satisfaction and continuity. Well-trained, experienced employees don't appear anywhere on the balance sheet, but their value in a properly run organization is often far greater than managers realize. Not everyone will be a superstar or future leader, but the core strength of a firm is the high-quality workers who get the job done, day in and day out, year after year. Failure to properly recognize the value of the firm's staff at all levels can be extremely damaging.

Jobs that can be tailor-made for certain workers often pay big dividends. Businesses are far more productive when they can find and feature people's strengths. It is the job of managers to carefully observe new workers and form opinions about where they will best function. Assigning work to people who enjoy doing

Fred McCauley, the company's first sales associate, sampling Old Medford at a Restaurant Association event

it well will exponentially improve the quality of the work. If managers keep employees busy enough working with their strengths, many weaknesses can be overlooked. This is one more area where flexibility and accommodation in the workplace can be to everyone's advantage.

An important corollary to knowing others' strengths is for managers to know their own strengths and weaknesses, and then capitalize on their strong points. For example, my mind works quite nimbly. I am extremely comfortable bouncing among multiple issues simultaneously. I also tend to assess the issues and make generally good decisions quickly. I am equally as fast to change direction when new information is introduced. On the down side, Joyce hates it when she catches me tinkering with our family plans or other social plans as they progress. She tends to be extremely thorough and beautifully organized and never appreciates my last-minute "interfering."

In addition to the stainless steel liquid-sugar storage tank we moved from Fulton Street, we now had a new 5,000-gallon heated tank to store much more viscous high-fructose corn syrup. We mixed this sweetener at a 50–50 ratio with liquid cane sugar from Domino, a recommended blend to achieve our best drink taste and "mouth feel," while still yielding significant cost savings.

With the new plant open and two liquid-sweetener systems up and running, Old Medford's production capacity immediately quintupled over our former 40,000-cases-per-year capacity at Fulton Street. The new facility could comfortably yield about 210,000 cases per year. Though the new plant was by no means a modern marvel, it was no longer a quaint backyard cottage industry, either. Without serious changes, we could easily have increased our volume to about $5 million in today's dollars, or $15 million with automated equipment, if there had been that much demand.

With ongoing changes, we achieved great savings with no detectable difference in product flavor or mouth feel, according to our unsophisticated taste testers. There was nothing scientific or democratic about the way I handled product development, but it worked at Old Medford. We carefully adjusted all our ingredient labels to reflect any product changes and prepared staff members on how to best handle anticipated questions about revised recipes and processes. We heard so few comments and no complaints or concerns whatsoever from customers.

New accounts soon started coming in unsolicited, and our sales group was both delighted and excited. Much of this business resulted from colleges served by one of our several large food-services management companies referring us to other colleges within the same management group or geographic area. It was highly satisfying to challenge the production team to keep up, especially with all the fast-paced process changes being pushed through as we learned more and more about the business. We fell into the college food-service field at a propitious time and rode beautifully with the trend.

ONE DILEMMA WE faced at Old Medford, with our growing geographic spread, was how to accommodate the fast-rising shipping costs. We considered increasing our price for the more distant clients, or making the product more concentrated, perhaps, say a ten-to-one rather five-to-one concentration.

Instead, within a year of relocating to Woburn, we developed a completely new sugar-free product, which we first used exclusively for all of our new clients outside New England. We followed all required labeling requirements, of course, including the mandatory message that the product was "sugar-free" and contained non-nutritive artificial sweeteners. We did not, however, otherwise differentiate between the two versions. Our profit margin was noteworthy before, but with the entirely sugar-free product, the cost savings were extraordinary. The contents cost with all

> *The contents cost with all non-nutritive artificial sweeteners was less than half the contents cost when made with sugar, but there was simply no reason to reduce the price.*

non-nutritive artificial sweeteners was less than half the contents cost when made with sugar, but once again there was simply no reason to reduce the price. Any possible competitors continued to use all sugar.

We, however, soon converted all of our production to the sugar-free variety, and because of its significantly reduced product cost it was now practical to travel even farther for business—even to the Caribbean. Although we necessarily had less direct contact with our three large Puerto Rican colleges, it took no arm-twisting to convince Fred and Don to make occasional winter visits there. Joyce and I even managed to work in a long weekend around some customer calls there in 1970, for some rare vacation days alone. It did seem counterintuitive, however, for us to be shipping fruit punch to tropical Puerto Rico, though we were delighted with Old Medford's expanding reach.

We liberally referenced our "delicious sugar-free fruit beverage bases," but never spoke of the recipes as being "new and improved" or anything like that. We didn't hide anything, but neither did we call attention to what we had changed. We also referenced the "empty calories" of other fruit drinks and were as matter-of-fact as possible. As with the situation a year or so earlier when we blended the cane and high-fructose corn syrups, we never heard any complaints. This move proved successful beyond our wildest dreams, and the sugar-free version was soon well received across all accounts. Our later good friend, famed Harvard nutritionist Jean Mayer, who eventually became the tenth president of Tufts University, was unknowingly helpful to us at that time as one of the early and most vocal advocates for reducing consumption of sugar-sweetened beverages. Today there seems to be near-unanimous condemnation of sugar-sweetened colas and other carbonated drinks, but non-carbonated drinks like the sugar-sweetened Old Medford would deserve almost as much bad press. Artificially sweetened carbonated drinks are nearly universally common in college dining halls, but now they, too, are receiving great criticism.

When I sold the business in 1970 to Green Textile Associates, Inc., it signed a five-year market-rate lease for the building at 10 Henshaw Street to go along with the sale. The firm that Llewellyn Farnsworth handed over to me in 1964 for $4,000 yielded more than $2 million in today's dollars, and that was at a time when having cash to bankroll a real estate business really meant something. These sale proceeds from Old Medford made an enormous difference as I started in the next—and quite different—chapter of my early business career.

While it was not always customary for business owners to personally guarantee any debts, I always did so and still would, although no one asks anymore. That is just the way I have always managed our finances. I always wanted every creditor or lender to be comfortable giving us the lowest selling price or interest rate because of the certainty of payment. For any business owner or prospective owner, having a personal relationship with a bank and its manager can be highly valuable, and any relationship based on personal trust must be treated as different from all others.

Good business people will be innovators, but even more important, they should be opportunists. First, they will see the opportunity to make something better or to make it less expensively, and then they will innovate the best way to accomplish this goal. They will continue to always think about what something costs before they make decisions to buy. They will think about how to get large potential purchases at a better price and will hate getting "taken."

I soon arranged our first bank mortgage on the then fully leased Old Medford plant at 10-14 Henshaw Street. The mortgage proceeds, plus the payout from Old Medford, provided us with extremely valuable working capital at a time when market interest rates were going sky high. That increased capital-in-hand enabled us to always avoid the hassle and time-consuming process of finding financing for our typically all-speculative construction. Doug Stephens initially stayed with Old Medford, but eventually, he returned to work closely with me for another quarter century.

> *Any relationship based on personal trust must be treated as different from all others.*

After we next completed an entirely new 30,000-square-foot rental structure next door at 8 Henshaw Street we had more than enough cash to pay for it all, and again avoided the endless verification and documentation that any kind of construction loan would have entailed. The management time alone that we thereafter saved on each building was dramatic, not to mention the far more detailed and sophisticated building plans we did not need, and the whole process construction lenders seek, and the cost of it all.

When I first began building things, most decisions were made by the seat of my pants. Many still are. For the first two buildings on Henshaw Street, I kept a handwritten spreadsheet for all construction costs as I made each deal, but even then, there was absolutely no budget in advance. After the rudimentary plans for each of the earliest buildings left our dining room table, I purchased each component and kept a running total showing me how much I had already committed, and the paid invoices became our "budgets." There was so much margin between what it cost me to build these single-floor buildings and their value after they were leased that I simply never needed to know their precise actual cost. As a building was completed and leased, I was able to easily borrow enough on that new asset to pay for the next property.

———————————

❁ *Through all of this, an essential resource was dedication. I loved what I was doing— opportunistically creating value and jobs—more than any financial return. Would- be entrepreneurs who, instead, launch into something merely for the money may inevitably struggle to muster the requisite commitment.*

❁ *The continued buy-in of clients is equally important, frequently yielding referrals (or, at a minimum, the implied endorsement that can be drawn from an ongoing business relationship). This word-of-mouth advertising is bolstered when a business "speaks for itself" through the quality of its offering. At Cummings Properties today, this thinking is evident in our account managers, who are responsible for both servicing existing accounts and securing lease renewals. By doing the former consistently, the latter should be a cinch because clients are already bought in.*

❁ *Outside of the workplace, buy-in from family "stakeholders" is also essential, and only achieved through open communication and mutual willingness to give and take. This support can make all the difference in buttressing an entrepreneur during the critical early stages of a venture.*

❁ *The collective company borrowed extensively during the early years, but we always borrowed against the equity in our occupied buildings, so there were never any so-called construction loans. I also routinely personally guaranteed virtually every mortgage loan to achieve the lowest available interest rate. The biggest advantage from avoiding construction loans was avoidance of having to document construction methods and expenses and all of the time and energy such documentation always entails.*

❁ *Empathy and patience are two of the most important but most overlooked aspects of deal making.*

❁ *A huge advantage to small private companies without outside investors is the ability to avoid a focus on short-term profitability in favor of long-term equity.*

❁ *Success is much more a journey than it is a destination.*

[8]

Cummings Properties Emerges

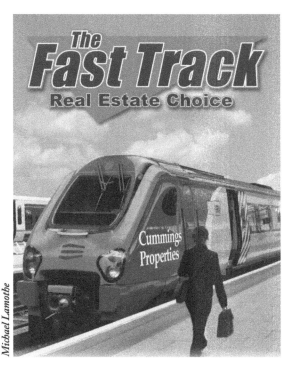

THE REAL FOUNDING date of what, in time, became Cummings Properties is 1969. The first property I built then for rental purposes was the well-located concrete-block structure directly north of Old Medford on the same one-acre lot. We engaged Albert Finethy Company, a Woburn general contractor, to build this two-story addition at 12–14 Henshaw Street. At the time, I thought of it simply as an opportunity to invest in a one-off building to lease to others, and it never occurred to me that I was laying plans for a new career that would quickly supplant our fruit-juice syrup business. Our first leasing client, Eastern Tool Warehouse, Inc., leased the lower 7,500-square-foot warehouse at a lease rate of a $1.90 per square foot/per year. We leased the unfinished upper floor to Wakefield Engineering with no office space for $1.50 per square foot/per year.

We already owned the needed land for this additional 15,000 square feet, for which there would likely never have been any use in connection with Old Medford. Additionally, the existing utilities were either readily available or already of sufficient size. The necessary site work also had been almost all completed in connection with the original cleanup of the property. The economics of this kind of investment, then, were extraordinarily good. We were taking advantage of what for the next fifty years I would continue to call free extra "buildability" that came with the deed. Identifying such additional construction potential from newly acquired properties became a regular occurrence in the new commercial real estate business that was about to take shape.

After promptly and profitably leasing this newly constructed addition, we purchased an adjacent two-and-a-half-acre vacant parcel on the south side of the Old Medford building for $90,000 in cash. If this vacant field next to Old Medford had not become available when it did, my foray into property development would likely have started and ended with that single addition at 12–14 Henshaw Street. Instead, we built out 2–8 Henshaw Street, in three phases, as our first from-the-ground-up building.

Opportunistic in every sense of the word, top businesses, like athletic teams, must be aggressive and active enough to make things happen. Only then are they capable of converting opportunities into success. Overall awareness and the ability to react quickly to opportunities are often characteristics of the best teams in business as well as in sports. Disappointingly, many athletes in their later working years appear to have no idea how to carry over the same competitive principles to a business setting.

Sometimes good business people will try to take advantage of opportunities that are not at all in their best interest, as I did in late 1969 by purchasing the Gift Boutique card shop, now a Starbucks, at 542 Main Street in Winchester. That was the first real business mistake that I recall making. We bought and sold it all within three months, but the purchase price was low enough that we escaped without any damage. There was a large lesson there, however, about business owners not diluting their attention with extraneous enterprises, like a gift shop. There is a lot to be said for "minding one's own knitting."

After deciding that we wanted no part of retailing, and that we really enjoyed building and leasing commercial real estate, I then purchased twenty prime acres on Washington Street in Woburn, and we started building what is now Cummings Park. During those first years, each of the buildings was laid out and designed on Joyce's dining room table at 23 Ash

| *Joyce with Patricia, Daniel, Kevin, and Marilyn, 1976*

Hill Road, Reading, where our growing family lived from mid-1967 through November 1970. Drawn with not much more than a $10 drawing board, a couple of plastic triangles, and a yardstick, my designs were simple but functional enough to get by. The Cummings Park land cost was $26,000 per acre.

At about this same time, notwithstanding Joyce's reluctance to leave Reading, we made an offer on a house we both really liked at 2 Mayflower Road, Winchester, but it was a low, low offer. It was low enough that the seller's broker, who later became a good friend, was more than a little annoyed. The home had everything we wanted, plus a sizable swimming pool that we had yet to appreciate. On the other hand, the lot was unkempt and overgrown, the pool water was a murky brown, and the shrubbery looked as though it had suffered for many years. It became a standoff with the seller for several months, and Joyce would not let me raise the offer. When the broker eventually called to tell Joyce, "You have won," she cried for having to leave Reading.

We already had a few roots in Winchester, including three Winchester Hospital births by then, and several friends in town, and Joyce soon accepted that Winchester could be nice. One of Winchester's major community events there is the En Ka Street Fair, operated by a women's service organization called the En Ka Society, founded in 1902. We had taken our kids to this fair twice before we moved to town, and we all already liked

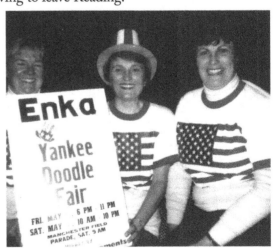

Sandy Thompson, Joyce Cummings, and Joyce's Co-chair of the Fair, Dennis Clarke's mother, Nancy Clarke

it. *Aha*, I thought, Joyce might become involved in the En Ka Society, because she is such a well-organized, type-A person. While she never really became active in my business, this venerable service organization could be a great way for her to meet interesting people. Joyce initially laughed at me for what she clearly took as an almost outrageous suggestion.

By the time our children were at Winchester High School, however, Joyce was co-chair of the En Ka Fair. And after serving in many other roles with En Ka, she was elected president of the several-hundred-member organization in 1990 and later served for six years as the society's historian. Joyce's En Ka work turned out to be one of her most cherished activities, and she has so many excellent memories from her almost forty years of service. We have had and continue to have a marvelous life together in Winchester and are still heavily involved, both singly and together, in many aspects of the community.

IN THOSE EARLY days of what grew to become Cummings Properties, the company avoided any construction that required municipal zoning variances or special permits. That was true of the Henshaw Street buildings and also of our two much larger Cummings Park developments on either side of Washington Street. There, we purchased the twenty-acre commercial lot from Kenneth Anderson in April 1971 at what even then was a remarkably low price of a half-million dollars. By way of comparison, a twelve-acre parcel on South Boston's undeveloped waterfront reportedly sold in late 2015 for $300 million, or about $25 *million* per acre, versus our $26,000 per acre for Cummings Park.

Aerial view of Cummings Properties' first significant development, Cummings Park, a 340,000-square-foot mixed-use development in Woburn at the junction of Interstates 93 and 95

With its great highway location and proper zoning for our needs, our large and mostly level Cummings Park lot could not have been much better or easier to develop. And over the next two years, we improved that parcel with three highly similar single-story, multiple-occupancy buildings designed for office, research and development (R&D), and distribution space.

It is really remarkable how Cummings Properties emerged as a significant factor in the north suburban Boston real estate market. Although I never specifically planned it that way, the business fed upon itself. We routinely took almost no cash out of the business, preferring to reinvest all that we could. My equity was always 100 percent, and I could always borrow easily against a recently completed building as needed, with minimal red tape at local banks.

Most important of all, there was never a time when we ever even once talked with anyone about construction lending. Such borrowing is probably the most common method by which local construction projects are funded, but I would not even know how to go about it. Financial independence has always been central to all Cummings construction. By never having a need for any kind of private financing, we saved huge amounts of time, as well as cash, on every building we built. We have the added benefit of not having to prepare the *ad nauseam* cost documentation normally required to satisfy lenders. Never having to deal with things such as lenders' inspections and architects' documentation in order to obtain funds to pay our bills allowed us to focus solely on building. With no outside investors or unwarranted city interference, we were able to move and change plans and strategies with barely a nod to anyone, as long as whatever we did met all codes.

We also process tasks on an accelerated basis from a design perspective. Our colleagues, working together, need to be free to make frequent changes as we go along with any project. Avoiding redundant layers of regulatory oversight from financial partners is a true blessing in any building or construction activity. We have also been exceedingly fortunate in that city inspectors came to know we would never take shortcuts with building code issues. In most towns, they have always been relaxed and helpful in expediting our plans. In Woburn, they also have been acutely aware of our strong local hiring policy, and that we have generated huge increases in the city's tax base.

While we obviously know the cost of all the components as we carefully negotiate them, we never estimate the total cost of a prospective new building for decision-making needs. Partly, this is because our buildings have never involved anyone else's fractional ownership. But also, it is my philosophy that the right answer will never be determined by the project cost. Clearly, we are in a much different position than if we were doing construction work for a third-party payer, who

We almost never estimate in advance the expected cost of any of our own new construction.

would certainly need to have a clear understanding of what the exact project cost would be before making any commitments.

Instead, we will typically review any newly proposed project, thinking about what needs it will fill and how efficiently we can build it—if indeed we do want to build it. We carefully track all capital and maintenance expenses for tax purposes, but the construction costs are never featured or discussed, even among the company's senior management team. There is simply no need for us to know in advance how much new structures will cost to build or remodel, because we know we can always secure competitive pricing for components and labor, and the buildings are always profitable. Today, the only number we think about is how much after-tax income we can provide to Cummings Foundation.

FROM THE BEGINNING, ours has been an extremely vertical business model. Relying, for instance, on the extraordinary talent of our in-house engineering, design, and purchasing professionals, and a marvelous team of supporting contractors of all sorts, we will carefully shop every phase of the development to obtain the best prices as we go along, and then we just do it. We have our own large staff of building tradespeople, along with our business professionals. With 360 or so full-time, year-round staff members at Cummings Properties, we have a fascinating array of mechanics and technicians, including, for instance, dozens each of electricians, plumbers, carpenters, and maintenance technicians, plus painters and roofers and at least sixty grounds workers. Our in-house legal team includes four attorneys, while about a dozen other lawyers fill other professional positions. For the company's first twenty years, and especially for active construction projects, I was personally at every building site almost every day. When there was site-work going on with excavators, trucks, and bulldozers, I was usually there—all day, every day, and always with my boots on.

I was not one bit distressed when a *Boston Globe* reporter once described Cummings Park as "plain vanilla" buildings that were "very neat and very full." They were neat, and they *were* full, and so "plain vanilla" was okay with me. All those early structures were built in a solid but economical manner, at a cost averaging under $18 or $19 per square foot, at a time when space was leasing at a gross rate of $2 or so per square foot. The three single-story flex buildings at Cummings Park totaled 340,000 square feet.

While fast project turnaround speed results in part from the use of a somewhat standard palette of materials, we also have the ability to fully customize build-outs to meet almost any client requirement. Cummings has designed and built dozens of specialized facilities, including Tempest rooms, clean rooms, TV studios, biotech labs, hospital operating rooms, and complete medical centers, as well as many thousands of office, retail, warehouse, and R&D spaces. Over more than forty-five years, we have accommodated multiple clients that have leased more than 100,000 square feet, as well as hundreds of office spaces as small as a few hundred square feet. Residential uses have never been a major factor, but altogether we presently operate some 600 residential units.

By October 1973, all three Cummings Park buildings, plus the first of six major buildings in what later became West Cummings Park, were completed—a total of a half-million square feet of space. By the end of the year, all of it was leased.

TWO YEARS AFTER we completed Cummings Park and 200 West Cummings Park, it was time to get going again in what continued to be a wonderful market for our eminently flexible multiple-occupancy buildings. During 1977 and 1978, we teamed up with the Woburn Redevelopment Authority and purchased many separate newly developed North Woburn lots on which we busily constructed another half-million square feet of floor space. Doug Stephens ran all our financial affairs, allowing me to spend the large majority of my time on the construction sites. Dennis McClay was our first field manager as we did more and more such work in-house, and Steven Frohn was leasing manager. All of this talent really solidified our comprehensive vertical integration.

| *Rick Freeman*

In June 1977, our first official designer, Fred Wilbur, began working full-time, and he effectively ran both the design and purchasing functions. Other than having taken part-time courses at Boston Architectural College at that point, Fred had little in the way of professional credentials. Even so, he brought a practical approach and did a wonderful job in all of his work. His plans represented a huge improvement over any plans I cobbled together in those early days.

While Fred did most of our design work, a local structural engineering firm sold us all of our structural steel and created the necessary stamped plans to get building permits for the earliest buildings. George (Butch) Olson and, later, Rick Freeman, both longtime Woburnites, otherwise capably handled the field engineering work on all the earlier Cummings buildings. Rick worked full-time for seventeen years and was a uniquely valued and trusted colleague.

During the early 1970s, between getting buildings built and then filled with happy clients, I gradually adapted a Standard Commercial Lease form from the Greater Boston Real Estate Board to create our much shorter Cummings Commercial Lease. We proudly printed this up as four pages in small font on a single 8.5-inch-by-22-inch sheet, and we used it effectively for more than forty years each time we prepared a lease for a prospective new client. It wasn't until April 2017 that we finally abandoned that process in favor of computer-generated leases. In all of our thousands upon thousands of lease transactions, except for leases with the federal government and the commonwealth of Massachusetts, every lease is prepared on our standard form, with whatever negotiated changes might be necessary. Our evolving standard form lease as such, however, was reprinted at least fifty times over forty years—a thousand or two at a time.

Back in 1974, we were the first firm we knew of to include a cost-of-living escalation as a standard clause in virtually all of our leases, to keep lease rates in current dollars. Later, we also became adept at including an automatic extension provision in the large majority of all leases. Both practices produced extraordinarily good results. Many long-term clients have operated for decades under their original lease agreements.

Cummings Properties has always offered only full-service leases with gross rental terms, generally including the cost of real estate taxes, snow removal, landscaping, structural and interior maintenance, and building insurance. Especially because all our leased properties are relatively close together geographically, it became practical to keep an ever-growing maintenance and construction staff. The members of that team tend to become really exceptional at doing whatever needs to be done. Communication among our field crews, the design department, property managers, and client firms happens smoothly, because they all see one another so frequently and their interest in solving the client need is so strong.

Despite building only speculatively during our early years, we somehow managed to lease every building we constructed almost as soon as each building was ready for occupancy. Relations with the city of Woburn remained exceedingly strong under Woburn's enormously respected Mayor Thomas Higgins and its equally esteemed late building commissioner John Brophy, especially regarding permitting. And because many city functions in Woburn were so much more customer-friendly than they seemed to be in other communities, the ease of permitting helped us to create a large portfolio of taxable property in a short time. Indeed, the continuum of real estate taxes paid and the thousands of excellent new jobs provided in Woburn, decade after decade, has had an enormous impact. By calendar year 2016, we were paying $7 million annually in real estate taxes to Woburn alone.

THE COMPANY GRADUALLY learned how to build better, more efficient, and steadily lower-cost buildings. We had our own niche, which often included buying underutilized land with grossly neglected buildings. Most of the existing structures were highly adaptable commercial buildings, and the lots often included future buildability for substantial additional space. The early properties we acquired and built were virtually all multiple-occupancy speculative properties; none was ever pre-leased. As soon as one building was completed and in the process of being leased, we would find a place to build the next one.

Working southward from 200 West Cummings Park, we purchased a row of eight mostly single-story Washington Street houses. A former longtime Woburn teacher and real estate broker, Joe Crowley, worked comfortably with us for two years as a member of the leasing department. "They just gave me a bag full of money to buy up the whole row of small homes in the light industrial zone," he said. "That's where they built the rest of West Cummings Park, on Washington Street."

Those homes received a unique and extremely favorable federal tax treatment. Rather than tear down the homes we purchased, we moved seven of the eight homes to new lots a half-mile south, on a street off Washington Street that we created just for these homes (and named Marilyn Court, after our first daughter). By moving and upgrading the houses, we were able to allocate 60 percent of the sales price as a credit against their original purchase price, thus almost fully eliminating the non-depreciable basis for the West Cummings Park land.

The land from those house lots and the former city-owned Golden Elementary School *alone* has since generated more than $20 million in municipal real estate taxes for the city of Woburn. If we had demolished those eight homes instead of salvaging them, the entire purchase price would (by law) have been imputed to the cost of the land and would never have been one bit depreciable. It was a major coup.

All early buildings until then were one or two stories high, but then we learned how to build our first mid-rise structure, a six-story office building we called Tower Office Park. At the time, it did seem like a tower to us. We subsequently built four more six-story structures in quick succession, directly

The first management group of Cummings Properties: (shown left to right) Fred Wilbur, Doug Stephens, Dennis McClay, Dot Cummings, Bill Cummings, and bookkeeper Margaret Connor

across Washington Street at West Cummings Park where the row of homes had been. All four new buildings were almost identical to one another, and each contained about 180,000 square feet.

In every business I have owned, my employment goal was always to first seek capable colleagues from among people we knew or knew of. We were careful not to poach from other companies or to solicit people who already had jobs, but when I knew a friend or acquaintance was looking for a job, I was happy to match him or her to an open position at Old Medford or Cummings Properties or, later, at our *Woburn Advocate* newspaper. Surrounding myself with trusted people has always allowed me to coach them and hone their skills to use over and over again. That approach so often greatly improved their confidence and initiative, and their value to the firm. Today we have truly extraordinary corporate longevity. Our treasurer, Doug Stephens, who had been with me since starting at Simonson Company in August 1966, and Steve Frohn, who joined us in the late 1970s, allowed me to focus completely on land acquisition and construction, particularly the site work, which I have always enjoyed so much.

Real estate management combines elements of both art and science, and Cummings Properties excels at both. As an art form, property management is a people business, one of listening closely and responding definitively and promptly to client needs. Cummings Properties' real estate professionals at all levels use their experience and resources to fully address both elements. And no one is too important—or too junior—to be involved in any issue that may arise. All phones are still routinely answered with a live, personal presence, and I have a real fetish requiring that no one's phone calls, including mine, ever be screened.

The amenities offered at a major development are also extremely important. Good highway access and public transportation are vital, as are nearby food services, day care, fitness and exercise facilities, and well-kept, nicely managed open areas. Our experienced maintenance and construction staff are able to deliver highly efficient and prompt building services in part because of proximity—the relative closeness of our properties helps us greatly in delivering excellent client services. That is another way Cummings Properties differs from many of the huge national and international real estate giants, business cartels, and real estate investment trusts that dominate most big-city markets.

MOST START-UP FIRMS will commonly need an owner or owners to work seventy- or eighty-hour weeks, or even more; this certainly applied in my new venture into real estate, but at least it was mostly me putting in those hours. When partnerships are involved in start-ups, it is the uneven contributions and work commitments of the partners, more than anything else, that has the greatest potential to introduce serious discord. Other than working with Don Knox for our first college December in the Christmas tree business, I have never had a formal business partnership with anyone. Perhaps that is why I have always felt so close to so many of our extraordinarily loyal and supportive senior team members.

At Cummings Properties, one of our major early goals is to find out what good employees do best and then keep them busy doing it. Our once most-senior carpenter, Richard Irwin, liked to teach new carpenters the tricks of the trade. With his agreement, as he aged and grew less agile, we successfully made him a full-time mentor and job coach, and he continued working as our most highly paid carpenter well into his seventies.

Find out what good employees do best and then keep them busy doing it.

By the mid-1970s, I was becoming involved in the Woburn community. Because of my long-term interest in the city, I was delighted to become a director of what was then still the Woburn Boys Club, where I served for forty years (and still serve as an honorary director). As it turned out, my early Boys Club involvement paid huge dividends in an unexpected way with employee referrals from the club's executive director. He thought I was doing him favors, but it was the other way around.

In November 1976, Charles Gardner introduced me to George Holland in the first of what would be three such referrals. Before George became our first heavy-equipment operator, he had been one of the club's earliest "Boys of the Year." At the time Charlie made the introduction, George was a newly minted Marine Corps veteran. I hired him on the spot.

With forty-one years now of continuous service, as of 2017, George is today the dean of Cummings Properties' entire 360-person employee roster. At his thirty year milestone, George received a ceremonial captain's chair and told me he was looking to start a new tradition by receiving a company *rocking* chair upon reaching his fortieth anniversary—as he recently did. Now, he said, he is eager to see what the company will do for him when he reaches his fifty-year mark.

The thirty-year captain's chair award is named the Stephens Chair, in honor of Doug Stephens, the first colleague to earn one. The rocking chair will hereafter be named the Holland Chair in George Holland's honor. On the actual anniversary of his fortieth year with the firm, however, George seemed stunned to receive not only a suitably engraved rocking chair, but also the keys to the company's first-ever brand-new backhoe, which had his name painted prominently on the door.

George married Sue Ellen Martin, who, in November 1982, opened Little Folks School in West Cummings Park, our first children's preschool. After thirty-five years, Little Folks is still an important client firm, as are a dozen other privately operated daycare centers that now lease space in various

| *George Holland with a super snowblower*

Cummings buildings. All three of the Holland daughters worked during school vacations in the Cummings Properties home office, and George's now-grown daughter Emily recently opened a personal-training studio at our TradeCenter 128. The Hollands' involvement with Cummings Properties is now truly a family affair.

Charlie Gardner made a second employment referral in 1979. This time he recommended James "Jamie" McKeown, a Woburn native and a more recent Boy of the Year from the Boys Club. He was a 1977 graduate of Salem State University who had also just earned a master's degree in school administration at the University of Vermont. But fortunately, for me anyway, he had started looking for a full-time public school teaching position in one of those "off" years, when there just weren't many teaching jobs available. So, instead, Jamie joined us in what turned out to be the only post-college job he ever held.

In 1983, Charlie introduced us to a third long-tenured colleague. This time it was Charlie's own son, Kevin Gardner, who in 2017 had more than thirty-four years of service at Cummings Properties. Kevin takes great pride in ably assisting the administrative support team in the company's main office. Company records show an extraordinary history of employees with long tenures at the company. This is partially owing to our early practice of offering paid vacations, paid health coverage, 401K plans, and many other benefits at a time when this was an unusual practice for a small construction-related firm.

❋ *As we built up the nascent Cummings Properties, familiar themes of constructive opportunism and attentive risk-taking remained prevalent in business decisions as well as hiring. Quickly bringing on people we knew (or knew of) to support the company's growth embodied both themes. Taking a risk on capable employment referrals is often justifiable (they are effectively "known quantities" that a trusted individual is willing to speak for), and the unique opportunity such hires present for all parties can translate into unusually strong professional relationships.*

❋ *And, as with Old Medford, we continuously reinvested Cummings Properties' earnings with the goal of sustained growth. Entrepreneurs who opt for more proximate payouts (perhaps to announce "I've made it!" with expensive cars or houses) will often fetter their venture's long-term potential. We have also always made a point of investing in colleagues through mentorship. In addition to enhancing an employee's immediate abilities, this fosters trust, which, in turn, invites further mentorship, creating a highly positive feedback loop.*

❋ *Whereas many companies find financial efficiencies by "farming out" various functions, our dedicated in-house staff and hands-on approach has driven our success. This vertically integrated structure underpins our responsiveness and control over the final product. It also affords us exceptional flexibility in decision-making, which has won us many leases in situations where our competitors simply did not have the ability to respond promptly to the prospective client's requirements.*

❋ *Cummings has designed every one of its major buildings in-house, and always served as its own general contractor, with great success. Collectively, the combined organization owns and operates 11 million square feet of commercial space, all of it 100 percent debt-free today.*

[9]

Teaching and Family Years

| *Patricia, Marilyn, Daniel, Kevin, and Bill skiing at Zermatt, Switzerland, August 1981*

Joyce Cummings

ALTHOUGH JOYCE AND I had previously managed to take several international trips with our children, accompanied by one of our especially reliable high school babysitters, we took our first three-week, family-only trip to Europe in August 1981, when the kids were thirteen, twelve, ten, and six. We started out in Paris and then traveled to eastern France, Germany, Austria, and Switzerland. In Switzerland, we skied through the spectacular scenery in the Matterhorn area, where the greatest dangers were falling into open crevasses and getting a sunburn. Before the kids started off on their own, we managed a half-dozen big family trips abroad.

While sports in general have never been a significant part of my life, golf did become important to me after we moved to Winchester and joined the town's country club. Neither Joyce nor I had played golf before, other than when I played a little on Tufts University's former six-hole on-campus golf course at Powder House Circle, in Somerville. We had come to know Winchester Country Club mostly for its great dining room. Later, however, what we cherished most was its intense sense of community and camaraderie, especially as golf became an important, if limited, part of our summers.

Golf, I think, offers an interesting comparison to business. Golfers, like business people, will always need to make corrective shots, gradually closing the distance to the hole. How often in any business do we experience slightly or grossly wayward decisions in altogether the wrong direction? In business, our own errors will often obstruct our best-laid plans, or obstacles may come in the form of someone else's errors or bad luck, or from circumstances over which no one has any control. These trying moments represent the crucial time in any business when managers must address the problem and hit that next shot correctly, no matter how far off track the first shot may have gone.

Our business interests were still highly centered in Woburn, and we had little reason, it seemed, to change this. We worked closely with city officials and were often consulted, at least under Mayor Thomas Higgins and much later under Mayor Scott Galvin. City officials would routinely request advice on construction issues with which we had helpful engineering or building experience. This was also a period when I served on several local boards, including those of the Woburn Boys Club, Tanners National Bank, and, briefly, Choate Hospital in Woburn, including one period when I was simultaneously also on the board of Winchester Hospital. I also served several years as an elected member and then chairman of the Winchester Planning Board, and ten years as a charter trustee of Tufts University.

One of the greatest challenges any business owner eventually faces is that of learning to let go. But gradually, as more and more qualified people become involved, tasks must be moved from the founder's purview. Business leaders should look carefully at their own firms and determine who solves the problems. Who always seems to say the right things at just the right time? Who always listens carefully and *then* comes up with the right negotiated solutions? Who makes things happen?

WHEN JAMIE MCKEOWN started at Cummings, he was twenty-four years old and still quite unsure of himself about business issues. "Just a kid," I thought, "but extremely street-smart." And he was the kind of person everyone immediately liked, because he had such a genuinely congenial and unaffected manner. This was one reason he was so successful at Cummings, and in life.

Jamie grew up in a solid middle-class Woburn neighborhood within easy earshot of Interstate 95, then called Route 128. He once told me his proudest day ever as a kid was when he graduated from the "Goldfish" program at the Woburn Boys Club and got to swim in the deep end of the pool, "like the big kids."

One of Woburn's late chiefs of police, Leo McElhinney, was a founder of the Woburn Boys Club. When I hired Jamie, Leo told me he had first come to know a seven-year-old Jamie in 1964, and had watched him grow up as a club member. "Jamie always did his own thing, but he absolutely got along with everyone; even the cutups in the Club liked him, though he never joined with them," said Leo. "I remember watching one day when Jamie, as a teenage lifeguard, cajoled three of the tough kids into the swimming pool, and he somehow made them learn to swim, right then and there. It was just remarkable. Two of the three were even older than Jamie was."

Initially, into the summer of 1979, Jamie worked at Cummings under Stephen Frohn, the company's first leasing manager. Steve, who passed away in July 2018, was an especially talented salesperson, but he quit the firm to do general real estate brokerage, leaving an unexpected vacuum, which Jamie soon filled.

When I moved from manufacturing fruit-drink concentrates to constructing and managing real estate, I quickly became concerned about the importance of preparing and training others to genuinely understand the entire business, and to effectively keep all the parts functioning harmoniously. I foresaw one of these people emerging as a "right arm" in the short term, and, hopefully, a well-prepared successor in the long run.

Rapidly coming into his own, Jamie soon began figuring into that long-term planning. Owing to his extraordinary people skills, his strong work ethic, and his determination to learn everything he possibly could about business, the two of us gradually developed a close mentoring relationship. Within a year, it was clear that he would be the successor I had been looking for almost since I had started the firm a decade earlier. He would become the perfect first person to succeed me as president, before one of my own four children might, I then hoped, someday step in to succeed him.

Jamie's office was next to mine, and when routine business calls still used to come quite regularly to me, Jamie could pick up his phone and quietly click into any of my calls, learning from everything he was hearing. He also received copies of every letter I wrote, to learn from those as well. Soon, he was writing those letters and handling the most challenging calls.

As a business prospers, entrepreneurs must disengage more and more from the "do it myself" mentality or risk strangulation of the business. Once any company reaches a sufficient size, in-house specialists will be needed to handle many of the diverse responsibilities. With my office located directly adjacent to the main leasing conference room, I am today still often tempted to walk in and help out, but I rarely succumb. It is best when all the vital functions of a business can be capably handled by those whose responsibility it is to complete them.

Once they have proven everything they need to prove about themselves, successful entrepreneurs should be even more thrilled with their colleagues' successes than with their own. A business has reached a truly strategic plateau when the management team is deep enough and committed enough to ensure the continuing viability of the business even in the event of the unplanned loss or disability of the founder. Creating that type of corporate security was always a major concern for me.

In short, no one should even think of starting a business without believing he or she will love every hard-working minute of it. Additionally, I never started any new business without soon surrounding myself with competent people whom I respected for their values, their dedication, and their integrity as much as for their intellect.

WHEN I HAVE opportunities to coach people about the joys and perils of entrepreneurship, the concept of needing to be a resourceful problem-solver is near the top of my list. It is also totally foolish, it seems to me, for anyone to own or operate a business if the work itself and the sense of accomplishment are not always a major part of the reward.

It is also totally foolish, it seems to me, for anyone to own or operate a business if the work itself and the sense of accomplishment are not always a major part of the reward.

Most people who think they want to open a business will start out with little or no concept of how much is involved in the mechanics of doing so. The whole process of withholding and paying taxes, providing insurance, obtaining licenses, writing policies, performing government reporting, and conforming to a vast array of applicable regulations can easily become overwhelming. The intricacies of hiring, evaluating, and compensating workers can frighten many aspiring business owners, too, especially when it comes to meeting payrolls. Owners need to train employees, retrain them, and certainly replace them, sometimes much more frequently than they would like.

PURCHASING, TOO, IS AN extraordinarily vital part of any business, and buyers must know how to purchase what they need without spending money foolishly. Too often I have heard people describe their purchasing policy by saying, "We just get three bids for everything we purchase," or some other simplistic nonsense. There is so much more to it than that. Equally dumb is thinking one should never go with the low bidder, "because that bidder perhaps didn't bid enough." Buyers must recognize that a supplier's bid will often have much less to do with costs than it does with what the bidder thinks he or she can get. And sometimes if a low bidder honestly bids too little, it may even be reasonable to help that supplier to be successful.

Especially when it comes to purchasing things such as building or construction components, or whole buildings for that matter, there is a real art to buying at the right price. And just as anyone selling a product or service has a right to achieve as high a selling price as possible, so also does the buyer have the right to purchase the product or service at the lowest price. But the buyer has no right whatsoever to expect that any seller will easily give up his or her best price. Rather, the purchaser will usually need to coax out that best price.

Getting back to the one-dimensional concept of simultaneously "seeking three quotes," when one is not dealing with a sealed-bid situation, there is nothing wrong with anyone using information in the first bid to help the next bidder get to a lower number. Once we have a quote in hand, say for $120,000 to install a new roof, our buyer might well advise bidder number two to not even type out any bid if he cannot beat, say, $108,000. It is amazing how rapidly and how far bids will drop when they are managed or even just allowed to "ripen." When there are significant value purchases to be made, buyers can use the bidding process to effectively set up an auction for the work, and there is absolutely nothing unethical about the process.

When making substantial purchases, we routinely use the concept of ripening the bids. If there are a half-dozen good prospective bidders for a job we need done, a piece of equipment we need to purchase, or an order of construction supplies, we routinely seek quotes from the first one or two and wait for those bids before we call two more bidders and seek lower quotes from them. Only after the third and fourth quotes are received will we then go to the last bidders on our list, knowing much more about the market by then.

Cost control is something we think about a great deal—there may be no greater direct influence on the profitability (or even the viability) of any enterprise. This especially applies to any kind of a production business, such as Old Medford, where reducing *the cost* of any product sold will have a far greater benefit than increasing its selling price. Assuming product quality is maintained, all of the cost reduction goes directly to the company's bottom line. Simply raising the selling price of a product is not nearly as beneficial, as a significant part of that increase will typically be shared with distributors and/or retailers. Additionally, inflating the price will usually also negatively affect how many consumers ultimately place the product in their shopping carts.

One thing that greatly helps Cummings Properties achieve consistently low quotes is that we have been buying so many of the same products and services for decades, and all the regional suppliers know that we go out of our way to never quibble and always pay everyone promptly. It is in our best interest to make sure sellers are convinced of these things *before* they start working with us, lest they add to their quote to offset the risk of incurring collection expenses, or worse, of perhaps not getting paid at all. It is uncanny how often subcontractors who have worked extensively with us have then taken on work elsewhere and been badly burned, especially by not getting promptly paid. Too many unscrupulous developer types get away with cheating subcontractors or suppliers that way all too often. How sickening it was during the 2016 presidential election to hear one candidate brag on national TV about how skillfully he gets away with cheating suppliers and investors.

I worked to save money on every purchase, but then we also developed a reputation for unusually prompt payment and abundantly fair treatment of suppliers. We also sought to treat *all* customers and clients with the utmost courtesy and respect. I have worked with thousands of suppliers and subcontractors over the last fifty years, and no business we have ever owned or controlled has ever been sued for non-payment of any debt or non-performance, nor has any business we have ever owned. Never!

MANAGERS MUST DEAL with the exceptions. They must minimize losses when plans go awry. It is also crucial that executives analyze what caused failures so they can avoid making similar mistakes in the future. Managers who treat problems as challenges can thrive in dealing with them. They will teach others about what went wrong and help their colleagues see the lessons in the challenges. It will always be the next shot—and that extra effort—that makes the difference.

Business owners must be abundantly careful about establishing and enforcing company policies governing all aspects of their business. This is a hugely important aspect of entrepreneurship, and one that is frequently overlooked when new businesses are launched. One of Cummings Properties' important early policies was that, when dealing with large firms, or even small branches of national or sometimes worldwide firms, we would expect diligent compliance with all lease terms. For small businesses, on the other hand, we routinely try to take a far softer approach, especially regarding collection efforts in the event of a business default, at least when a defaulting client is being straightforward in his or her dealings with our staff.

Those same executives who enjoy dealing with challenges will instinctively look to identify and solve small problems before they grow into larger issues. A competent manager always must be concerned with not leaving problems to fester. When things are going well, a manager's job is, of course, much easier, but good leaders will really shine in adversity. Yes, managers handle the exceptions, and they need to spend far more time spotting and resolving problems than they do gloating over the latest successes.

With institutions, as in business, incalculable money, time, and effort are thrown away by relying on inaccurate or misrepresented "facts." Top management in any organization must have the intuitive sense to know when it is presented with puffed-up or misinterpreted information as fact. Management must instead be sure that the information it utilizes is absolutely reliable, and that solid data, not some third party's suppositions, form the basis for decisions. Add up the real facts and then intuit from there.

Many people are given credit for the phrase "management by walking around." Among them is Abraham Lincoln, who was said to have used it to describe his staying in touch with and more fully understanding what his troops in the field were thinking. It can be extremely effective as a consistent business practice to keep senior officials in contact with the people in the organization's front-line operations.

> *Another great concept is that of "catching people doing something right."*

The essence of managing in most businesses is contact. Many good executives greatly increase their effectiveness either by personally circulating throughout the physical work space or by being available at all times for brief comments or consultations to focus others or give them direction. Brief, unplanned interludes give a good manager the opportunity to react to work in progress so that shifts and adjustments can be made before effort is expended to complete a project or a product that must then be changed.

Another great concept is that of "catching people doing something right." Most good managers take note and likely say something when staff are behaving badly or performing inefficiently. But how much more valuable is it for managers to also send out an "attaboy" whenever they notice unusually good or caring workmanship or performance? Those certainly are the times to speak out publicly. I remember first reading this notion many years ago in Tom Peters and Robert Waterman's *In Search of Excellence*.

I urge colleagues to remember what we call our 80 Percent Rule. Different from the well-known 80/20 Rule (or Pareto principle), our version suggests that one person's answer to any problem will likely represent, at most, 80 percent of the best solution. It is only by collaborating with, or bouncing the idea off of, one or more other colleagues that we can collectively bring the solution to 90, 95, or even 100 percent of its potential. When time allows, it is especially important for managers to encourage their teams to improve on any solutions they (or others) may offer, and to be open to hearing suggestions of refinements. Some colleagues may instinctively react negatively at first if they think they are being second-guessed, but cooperatively improving upon other people's initial thinking is exactly what teamwork is all about. We adopted and often mention this 80 Percent Rule to strongly suggest that added collective input in most problem-solving situations will almost always result in either marginally or significantly better results.

Finally, at Cummings Properties we constantly preach to staff at all levels the need to go out of their way to smile and be friendly to clients, visitors, and passersby whom they encounter while working anywhere in or around any Cummings building. It is so much more enjoyable working in a place that is friendly and upbeat and where people will get into the habit of speaking and acknowledging others as their paths cross. This practice builds upon and perpetuates itself in giving Cummings Properties its reputation for friendly service. Doesn't this concept work with almost any business?

CUMMINGS PROPERTIES was becoming well established in commercial real estate immediately north of Boston, without ever doing any business in Boston itself. We were quite content in the near suburbs, along the northern portion of Route 128/Interstate 95, and along Interstate 93, from Andover down into Medford and Somerville—all solidly centered in Woburn. Growing rapidly, we were enjoying our role as the proverbial "big fish in a little pond."

Meanwhile, strangers routinely assumed in those days that I could not be old enough to have built Cummings Park. "Is your father still active in the business?" asked many well-meaning folks. Or, "How long has your family been in the real estate [or construction] business?" Yes, it was old fashioned, and people did think of it as a mom-and-pop firm, but there was no "pop" in sight, and the business was beginning to accumulate great unrealized capital.

As a cohesive property-management team, we were becoming ever more adept at accumulating properties. We focused then on purchasing slightly distressed properties at bargain prices, and we always paid in cash, sometimes early on using mortgage proceeds borrowed against other recently completed properties. In all cases, we either built or purchased rental properties and then continued to hold them. As I write this, we have never once sold any of our major commercial buildings, nor have we ever partnered with other parties or participated in any of the syndications that seem so common.

Speculative builders sometimes invest their own money in projects, with serious risks, but they somehow "know" those risks will ultimately pay off if they work hard enough. Syndicators, on the other hand, often leave legacies of unfinished or even unneeded structures to be picked over by vultures. The syndicators suck so much profit out of a project that there is often little or nothing left to be divided among the "limited partners," other than the sometimes-questionable tax benefits. They often play the game fully prepared to leave their debt with some bankrupt shell at the end.

If you need square feet we're just your size.

As the Cummings family business prospered, so did my own family. During the late 1970s we owned a family powerboat—a Chris Craft Sea Skiff. This fast twin-engine lapstrake boat frequently took us all to Provincetown or through the Cape Cod Canal into Narragansett Bay. We also traveled as far down east as Bar Harbor, Maine, and to so many picturesque spots along the way. Joyce and I enjoyed lots of day trips, often fishing with our kids, plus the occasional overnight trips alone, always sleeping onboard. For six years we lived our summer weekends on this boat, the Old Medford.

We were still living happily at 2 Mayflower Road in Winchester, but by the late 1970s Joyce and I had quietly started looking for "the house." As it happened, Joyce heard about an upcoming bank auction of a Winchester house lot at 4 Fernway, a large, heavily wooded, secluded lot overlooking Mystic Lakes and downtown Boston, nine miles away. The site was the former home of Reverend Howard Chidley, a long-ago and legendary pastor of Winchester's First Congregational Church, but successive fires had destroyed the home two years earlier.

We acquired the mostly empty two-acre lot at auction, in October 1978, and soon began hearing stories from several of the area's older residents about the day President William Howard Taft visited Reverend Chidley at his Fernway home. The President supposedly traveled from the Taft Summer White House in Beverly in his private railway car, via Boston, arriving at Winchester's Wedgemere train station. There he boarded an open-topped carriage with a team of matched black horses. Our new, quite-a-bit-older next-door neighbor, Martha Speers, delighted in telling me the story about how she chased along Everett Avenue as a young girl to watch the carriage cross Cambridge Street and bound up Fernway to the Chidleys' home.

Our main living accommodations have certainly been more substantial sometimes than they needed to be, but they have never been too extravagant. I built our second Winchester home, at Fernway, using a classic iron-spot red brick exterior. This new contemporary home had six bedrooms and commanding views of Boston, especially from its upper floors. Though the house was larger than we needed for daily living, we were happy to have the extra space for the many times we hosted large charitable and personal events. Joyce and I greatly enjoyed this home for twenty-five years before downsizing to a much smaller third home in town in 2003.

It was also during this period that I spent many, many evenings as a volunteer in much different surroundings, working alongside my sister, Marian. She served as a part-time registered nurse at Pine Street Inn, a major Boston homeless shelter. She was on a remarkable team of volunteers who treated the many minor medical needs of destitute overnight residents of the shelter, while I and others stayed nearby to intervene if situations got out of hand, which they sometimes did. That early personal experience benefits me, even today, in remembering the extraordinary good that so many magnificent not-for-profit institutions provide to untold throngs of highly disadvantaged citizens.

BY 1981, JOYCE AND I, along with Doug Stephens and his wife, Carrol, frequently socialized with Jamie McKeown at company functions and elsewhere. Jamie would occasionally bring an eligible date-of-the-season, until Denise Arndt first appeared that year. According to Denise, Jamie's friends all thought he was a confirmed bachelor, because marriage would have interfered with his skiing. The common joke, after Denise continued showing up on Jamie's arm, was that "Rent-a-Date must have run out of girls for him because they kept sending the same one."

"Jamie was twenty-five years old when we met," recalls Denise, "when he was leasing manager for Cummings. He was a laid back, easygoing guy who was always smiling. I thought at first it was just because I didn't know him that well, and eventually the smile would stop, and eventually I would see him lose his temper. I waited and waited, but it never happened. Sounds weird, I know. I thought, *Is this guy for real?*" I never once knew him to lose it either.

Their relationship blossomed quickly, especially after Denise moved from Chelmsford, Massachusetts, into a nearby apartment in Woburn, but then it seemed to stall for a couple of years. This was the most serious relationship Jamie had as an adult, but he was clearly in no rush to get married. Eventually, Joyce and I started nudging him not to let Denise get away. We may have been as happy as they were when they came to our home to celebrate the night of their engagement.

If I ever had any misgivings about the appropriateness of our bugging Jamie about getting married—in other words, about interfering in a colleague's personal life— Jamie later set me straight. Three nights before their May 1984 wedding, Joyce and I joined Jamie and Denise for dinner at Winchester Country Club. Just outside the clubhouse entrance, Jamie purposefully pulled me aside as Joyce and Denise went ahead. "You guys have both been so great. I want you to know that

| *Denise and Jamie McKeown at Sunday River, Maine*

my marrying Denise will be the best thing that has ever happened to me." Unrelated men did not hug each other much in those days, but that was how Jamie made his point that night. "There is nothing I won't do for the rest of my life but to try to make Denise happy," he told me. I had no more second thoughts about perhaps having become too personal.

Jamie was avidly athletic, but never seemed to have time for team sports or spectator sports. At a little over six feet tall and perhaps 170 pounds, he was always fitness conscious. He ran or swam almost every morning, and occasionally we did some great bike rides together, including one to Beverly where we had to work to find our way. He wanted to stay in shape for local triathlons, which he particularly enjoyed. We both logged in notable events of the business day on simple steno pads, year after year. But virtually every single day, Jamie's first entry would be his start and stop times for whatever early morning workout he had done, only occasionally writing "off."

Knowing that Jamie's greatest enduring sports love was downhill skiing, I was relieved when he got married: Maybe now we could stop worrying about his someday taking off to live in the Rocky Mountains as he had sometimes fantasized about. After running and skiing, tennis was Jamie's next individual sport of choice. He was skilled at it, too, especially for someone who rarely played the game more than an hour or two a week. In time, however, as he steadily built his business and life skills, he also began to find great satisfaction in the pursuit of business, especially in putting together complicated leasing deals and property acquisitions.

In all my years working closely with Jamie, we never once had an argument or even a disagreeable conversation about anything. He never disappointed me, and he once told me that feeling was mutual. I was beyond happy when Jamie added, "I trust you more than any other person I have ever known." Then he thoughtfully added, "Except for Denise, of course."

WELL BEFORE THE phrase "bucket list" came into common usage, Joyce and I checked off one of our longstanding dreams: a piloted hot-air balloon ride. One lovely morning in May 1985, we gently floated over central Connecticut, up to about a thousand feet above the ground. Once we eavesdropped on a conversation on the ground as we silently floated low over farmland and other areas where there was no traffic. We startled two people who were deep in a private conversation by yelling out "Hello" as we drifted close overhead. Going wherever the breeze blew us, we felt almost no sense of movement through the nearly still air.

Then, about fifty minutes into our first and only balloon trip, the balloon's gas burner began sputtering and failed, and we quickly lost altitude. The aeronaut could not really control the balloon's direction, but he had us frantically leaning over the left side of the basket, using our weight to guide us away from a house below us on our right that we were rapidly approaching. We missed the brick chimney by inches and then thumped down in the yard, with only a gash in the side of the balloon's big wicker basket. The family whose home we missed happily shared the champagne we had brought to celebrate our excursion while we waited for the chase car and trailer to figure out where we were and return us to our own car, twenty miles away.

About a year later, Joyce and I checked another adventure off our list with a pair of great glider flights near Truro, on Cape Cod. This time, Denise and Jamie accompanied us. Each glider was designed to carry a pilot and one or two passengers. We were dragged several thousand feet up in the air by small tow planes and then released to glide like hawks, using the air currents to sometimes soar high up over the ground. Remembering the angst we had experienced the previous year with the mild crash landing of our balloon ride, we did a brief wife swap, just in case, before we packed into the single seat directly behind each of the two pilots. It was a bit like riding on a motorcycle with two passengers lined up behind the driver.

Swooping along in a glider was more exhilarating than floating in the hot-air balloon, as we skimmed through the air with nothing propelling us, but both were terrific new experiences. Though we never thought about it this way at the time, the hot-air balloon and glider rides were the start of many exciting exploits all over the world with Joyce.

❋ *It is highly important for business and institutional leaders in any community to take active roles in their respective home or business communities. For me the most meaningful roles were serving as an elected member and chairman of my town Planning Board, especially because, by that time, I was routinely appearing on the other side of the table in Woburn and elsewhere. Membership on the board of Woburn Boys Club also paid enormous dividends for many decades.*

❋ *Although I managed to make time to serve on many hospital and bank boards and other similar groups, I never personally served in industry trade associations. I have been delighted, however, to watch Dennis Clarke serving in top spots with the Boston Chapter of NAIOP, while our treasurer and CFO, Bill Grant, has been similarly active in AIM, the Associated Industries of Massachusetts. All such roles are appropriate when organizations find they can make the time and there are suitable groups nearby.*

❋ *Managers must be constantly ready to recognize and react to whatever each day brings, and there is no possible way for managers to imagine ahead of time what new conundrums may arise.*

❋ *Many people, maybe most, don't want a career… they just want a paycheck, and then they meander through life to a different drummer.*

[10]

Branching Out,
But Still in Woburn

The 147-unit Place Lane Condominium in Woburn, Massachusetts, with the original Woburn Boys Club swimming pool and gym shown next door in the lower right corner

WOBURN RESIDENTS Douglas and June Brown contacted me through the Woburn Boys Club in 1983 to say that they had decided to sell an undeveloped nine-acre parcel they owned adjacent to the west side of the club, at the end of Place Lane. Mr. Brown told me that some attorney "had checked the zoning map and told him [erroneously] that his land was undevelopable for anything significant, because it had only a single access point and just forty feet of frontage at the butt end of Place Lane," a few hundred feet off Main Street.

We immediately doubted the attorney's advice, however, and could readily see that the Place Lane acreage was properly zoned to allow office or research uses as a "matter of right," or residential condominiums with a special permit from Woburn City Council if it had more frontage on the street. The needed frontage should have been easily achievable by utilizing a small portion of land to create a cul-de-sac at the end of the street. With the latter in mind, we purchased the land in December 1983, and, as an increasingly skilled middle manager by then, Jamie took on the political challenge of acquiring the necessary permitting to enable solid use of this highly buildable and centrally located vacant parcel. The Browns' legal advice fell hugely short.

Aside from zoning or legal issues, though, there was an overriding neighborhood issue. "Greedy Mr. Brown," so the story went, was selling this previously undeveloped privately owned land to "the insatiable developer" from Winchester. "Why doesn't he build his condominiums in Winchester, instead?" was a frequently repeated refrain as Woburn's *Daily Times Chronicle* appeared to be working to get everyone agitated over the possibility of a residential development there. Unfortunately, this mood set up a long and acrimonious back-and-forth, and discussions quickly turned antagonistic, especially with the recently installed Planning Board. At the same time, I certainly knew how planning boards worked from my experience as a member of the Winchester board. We were totally confident that we could make the land much more usable than Mr. Brown thought it was.

It was, however, critical that we prevail, because in return for a modest purchase price of only $250,000 for the supposedly not-usable lot, we had taken title with no contingency for our ability to secure a building permit. Eventually, we submitted a Definitive Subdivision Plan to the Planning Board to simply extend the length of Place Lane into the property to gain the necessary legal frontage for whatever the Woburn Zoning Ordinance would allow us to construct there. The timely submission also froze the zoning provisions for the next seven years and prevented any unreasonable rezoning attempt by the Planning Board, which we felt was a strong possibility, given its members' outwardly hostile attitudes during that era.

A break finally came when the Planning Board dithered around so long that it lost track of its own legal calendar.

This solution to the hypothetical major problem with lot frontage should have made the land developable, but our combative Planning Board at that time still did everything it could to challenge and delay approval of our fully compliant cul-de-sac plan. A break finally came when the former Planning Board dithered around so long that it lost track of its own legal calendar. Rather than simply approving or rejecting our Definitive Subdivision Plans, and delaying our efforts, the board inexplicably took no action at all within the allotted ninety days from the date of our submission. We knew it, but the board members seemed totally oblivious that Massachusetts laws provided a perfect legal remedy for such arbitrary behavior.

On the morning of the ninety-first day after our well-documented submission date, Woburn's city clerk, Attorney Jack Ryan, certified that the subdivision had become constructively approved by reason of the Planning Board's failure to act within ninety days. It was akin to recovering the other team's fumble in its own end zone to score in the final seconds of a tied football game.

Much of the lot consisted of a partially open grassy hill, known as Bucky's Hill, which had been used for decades for snow sledding and many other neighborhood activities. In retrospect, with all the flak thrown up to stop our development of the site, I was surprised no one tried to assert an adverse possession claim on the land. Once we created sufficient legal frontage and started building on the new cul-de-sac, there was little else anyone could do to stop our development of the property, and not surprisingly, there was no public disclosure at all about the board's glaring gaffe.

By that time, we had determined that residential condominiums were really the highest and best use for the lot, but since we had plans in a drawer for a small office building that fit easily on the lot, we requested and quickly received a building permit to construct the office structure. Immediately thereafter, Jamie went into his role as the designated Woburn native and submitted an alternative plan to build 150 high-end condominiums.

I personally made it my job to cobble together the complete set of condominium documents, using samples from other communities and making up new clauses as the need arose. This was a perfect example of entrepreneurs sometimes needing to play every position on the team in dealing with many unexpected situations. There are so many scenarios in any kind of business when work commonly performed by so-called experts can be readily accomplished by laypeople.

Jamie and I then both came under repeated fire for supposedly "holding a gun to the city's head" to get the condos approved, but we soon earned the necessary city approval and built the condos. We really had a last laugh over the issue when the condo market reached a fever pitch in the fall of 1986, and the highly successful construction year perfectly meshed with a great sales effort just before the epic market collapse in 1987. We could hardly have asked for a better storybook ending.

We self-managed the unit sales at Place Lane and then managed the complex itself for ten years after the resident owners took over the board of trustees, though the more common practice was for condo owners to throw out the developers at the first opportunity. This often occurred in the 1980s shortly after a majority of the condominium units were sold and when the owners had enough membership votes to elect their own slate of trustees, but such action was never even considered by the Place Lane board. In fact, it was Cummings Properties that eventually informed the trustees, much to their disappointment, of our decision to give up our property-management role.

Eventually we realized that one trustee seemed to enjoy questioning virtually every detail of many actions we took as the association's manager. Effectively, we were putting inordinate effort into satisfying her need to demonstrate just how demanding she could be. But, after a full decade, the constant need to act so defensively caused us to back away from the assignment in favor of a management firm better accustomed to dealing with such situations, and we were then out of the condo business for a long time.

WHILE GROWING THE firm steadily in terms of both staff and square feet, we also became an early and vocal supporter of the campaign to eliminate smoking in the workplace. This was decades before it became a popular concern.

From the mid-1980s, the firm paid annual cash bonuses of $500 per year to every employee who agreed not to smoke anywhere on company property or in any company vehicle, and we also all but stopped hiring smokers. Jamie

Jamie and a reporter during a television interview about the Great American Smokeout

was interviewed about this by a reporter from WBZ-TV who did a piece at Cummings Park in connection with the Great American Smokeout, arranged by Cummings and the American Cancer Society.

The TV report focused heavily on a former Cummings employee who filed what we, of course, felt was a frivolous lawsuit against the firm for "discriminating" against him because he was a smoker. Jamie had a good time pontificating about the great health risks of smoking at a time when many people still did not want to believe smoking was that harmful. The legal matter was thrown out after Jamie agreed that the employee had been discriminated against, but there was nothing wrong or illegal about this.

This anti-smoking campaign, coupled with the company's longstanding policy of overtly preferring non-smokers in its hiring practices, had a practical application as part of a whole collection of programs over the years to promote wellness among our staff. Certainly, it is not lost on corporate managers that healthy employees will generally perform better and will need less medical attention than those who do not make wise health decisions. Good employee health also means better lifestyles and lower health insurance premiums for both company and staff. The enemy in all cases has been tobacco—the most prominent legally manufactured product proven to cause disease and death when used as directed.

Illegal drugs and marijuana have been the other major targets in the workplace. The company and its corporate affiliates have conducted drug testing as part of the routine hiring process for all full-time employees at all levels for more than forty years, even though Massachusetts state law requires ongoing drug testing only for truck drivers and several other classes of employees. Random drug testing, plus targeted drug testing for cause, as well as the use of tobacco on the job, has always resulted in summary terminations if there is evidence of such usage. This zero-tolerance policy is still clearly laid out in all employment solicitations and the employee policies handbook. We learned from our earliest days that the best disincentive for drug usage is simply to keep users out of our workforce. Notwithstanding that Massachusetts recently legalized the use of marijuana, we do not currently anticipate any changes in the way things will be handled in future years, and certainly not for truck drivers and other workers in field positions.

For thirty years, we also have effectively used one-page business letters as editing exercises for all candidates for management or office-centered jobs. Many such applicants will be college graduates, but even then, it is truly remarkable how many prospective staff struggle with this test. The exercise consists of editing a single-page business letter that includes three dozen grammatical, spelling, or usage errors. A person whose job includes writing letters but who cannot compose a simple error-free business letter can be a huge liability. This comes at a time when most managers no longer have the luxury of a "secretary" at their disposal to make them look good. We also use the exercise to discover new hires who have particularly good writing and editing skills, which we can always use.

Skillful writers are also often especially good negotiators, even though they may agonize with draft after draft, as I often do, when they structure proposals or agreements. Strunk and White, in their classic book *The Elements of Style*, compare extra words in a sentence to extra parts in a lawn mower: Neither runs efficiently with extra pieces. The writer in any business communication must study all the words and know their meanings and their exact effects.

For a half-century, I have preached at Cummings Properties about the need for all managers to express themselves well in writing. While that goal was not always fully realized, we have gradually pulled together more than our share of excellent writers. When it comes to achieving personal goals in business, being able to write down and share our good ideas with others is a crucial step. Another key consideration in hiring decisions at Cummings is that we are always much more interested in the potential, and the character, and the innate abilities of the applicant than we are in trying to hire the perfect résumé.

Fixing written words must be done carefully, especially anytime we run into communications that could become a factor in confrontations or legal issues. All staff are expected to seek peer review or legal review before transmitting any written communications. Somewhat counterintuitively, staff at all levels must be even more careful to do this when sending off a "quick email." It is vital in business to recognize how damaging quick, casual responses can be when they subsequently resurface, sometimes years later, as discovery evidence in a legal matter.

When members of the management team must occasionally respond to captious correspondence, as inevitably comes our way from time to time, we find it is far better for us to be extremely temperate, careful, prompt, and accurate with any response. Since there are often many varied thoughts that might (or should) be incorporated, our response may involve three or more writers working together to clearly lay out the fact pattern.

FROM ITS EARLIEST days, the company established a firm policy of allocating 10 percent of all net earnings every year to support various community activities and charities, especially in Woburn and Winchester. Joyce and I were both personally active in a wide variety of volunteer roles and always found these activities highly rewarding. This spirit of giving ultimately inspired us to create Cummings Foundation in 1986.

We were both raised to do more than necessary and to "do good" for more than just ourselves. We realized early that there is a point at which it doesn't make a difference to earn more money. Rather, we were much more interested in helping the community, and we have found it highly satisfying to be able to do good things with what we have. It would be difficult to overstate how important our early upbringings were in our philanthropy today.

Cummings Foundation was created with a mission to invest in organizations that work to improve our society, and to mostly do it locally. The foundation emerged as a place to set aside meaningful philanthropy money for a later date, when we could better decide how to put it to work. Despite years of distributing funds to many different causes, we were still working on finalizing our ultimate long-term strategy, a process I will address in a later chapter.

Once the foundation was established, Cummings Properties and its affiliate companies all made annual financial contributions to it—as well as directly to many local organizations. Over time, however, we also gradually came to donate as many properties to the foundation as we found was legally allowed, providing a stable source of funding. The foundation now disburses funds derived from these properties primarily to community-based programs geared toward improving area residents' quality of life, particularly programs benefiting senior citizens and youth. Supporting such programs is a reinvestment in the same communities that are central to Cummings Properties and its affiliate companies and employees.

One of our earliest major gifts, in 1986, was a grant of $100,000 to the Boys Club of Woburn. That donation was specifically earmarked for the formation of the Charles H. Gardner Endowment Fund in honor of the years that Charlie had served the club as executive director. He had done so much to assist our work in Woburn, and we were thrilled to help support his legacy. Twenty-eight years later, Cummings Foundation gave the club $1 million in cash for a major rebuilding project, along with an additional $2 million challenge grant to be

| *Bill, Charles Gardner, and Jamie, 1989*

paid when the club reached 80 percent of its $8.5 million goal to rebuild and enlarge its home directly adjacent to Place Lane Condominium.

Joyce and I are so pleased to have played quiet but meaningful roles during many of the Boys Club's first fifty years, through some of its early struggles into periods of growth and great successes. Elsewhere, the foundation donated $1 million to build the Douglas Stephens YMCA Teen Center in Beverly, and it created a major high school scholarship program. Cummings Foundation has demonstrated a strong propensity toward gifts and grants to organizations with unusually strong volunteer support.

IN 1989, WE OFFERED to purchase a home on several acres on Arlington Street in Winchester, directly across from Winchester Country Club and directly abutting our own home, for Hospice Care, Inc., now VNA Hospice Care. Joyce had been particularly involved with the organization for some years, including two years as a hospice home volunteer. After Hospice Care managers decided they were not yet prepared to operate a hospice home, we also considered creating a large assisted-living community on the property, in what was formerly a motherhouse of the Medical Missionaries of Mary.

This period included the years when our four kids were getting up to college age, and I was increasingly active at Tufts and had additional community responsibilities as a bank director and a hospital trustee. I was also guiding a rapidly growing staff at Cummings Properties. There was not a lot of time or availability to actually do much with the foundation for several years.

But then we learned, in late October 1989, that Woburn's recently bankrupt Choate Memorial Hospital on Warren Avenue was closing, almost immediately, and that it would be auctioned off to the highest bidder. We were also told that any sale would be "consistent with the best interests of the city of Woburn." Our interests seemed to fit perfectly, and after several hearings, Judge Harold Lavian of the federal bankruptcy court awarded us the hospital for $3.1 million in January 1990, notwithstanding a competing higher bid of $3.21 million. When we decided to buy the hospital, Joyce was visiting her ill parents in Alabama and was more than a little shocked to hear we had purchased the community's hospital. We immediately began rebuilding the property as a 100-resident not-for-profit retirement community, creating our first major philanthropic presence, in the city where Cummings Properties had its beginning and its earliest successes.

There seemed to be no end to the number of medical records we found everywhere we looked. Symmes Arlington Hospital, a former corporate affiliate of Choate, had evacuated most of the remaining Choate patients. Its staff told us they had taken along all the medical files they needed, so we brought in a shredding company to process literally tons of multi-colored patient folders with highly confidential contents.

But much more sensitive, we thought, than the past patients' medical records were some of their remaining body parts. There were several shelves full of preserved internal and external human specimens in what looked like large two-gallon pickle jars. There was also a refrigerator with many other "fresh" body parts in a secure area near the morgue. Symmes Hospital eventually retrieved those specimens, as it had agreed to do, but only after much finger-pointing and cajoling.

Having become a licensed auctioneer specifically so Cummings Properties could hold its own auctions after purchasing just such a property, I particularly enjoyed personally arranging and conducting a major public auction sale of all the hospital's furnishings and equipment, netting well over $400,000 in a mammoth one-day sale. Before people arrived for the auction, we updated the signs for the restrooms on the operating-room floor. Signs limiting usage to "Doctors Only" in one restroom and "Nurses Only" in the other told something of the hospital's mindset as the time of its bankruptcy.

| *New Horizons at Choate, 1990*

On February 6, 1990, a remarkably short time following the bankruptcy award, the Woburn City Council granted the special permit we needed to convert the hospital. Two council members who had been highly outspoken opponents of our Place Lane development unsurprisingly cast negative votes, but their behind-the-scenes efforts to delay this project had little effect. We rebuilt the entire hospital within seven months of the City Council vote.

Fortunately, there was no need for anything resembling a gut-out of the old building. Instead, we incorporated a careful, adaptive reuse of what existed to create an extraordinarily comfortable and cozy community. Carrol Stephens, Doug's wife, volunteered her artistic decorating skills to the effort. Among many other things, she cleverly utilized the extra space in the building's original nine-foot-wide hallways, which were much wider than our plans required. It was Carrol's idea to expand closets into the hallways from the adjacent new apartments created by combining the former patient rooms. The hallways became a perfect width, and the apartments became that much more functional. Nothing was wasted. All the while, our in-house designers were working with our soon-to-be first executive director, Mary Ann Outwater, RN, and with Carrol on the final details of a furniture and decorating plan.

New Horizons at Choate welcomed its first residents in August 1990, and soon the entire complex was filled. We quickly paid off all of its loans by using the fully refundable entrance deposits paid by each arriving resident. Our first resident, Bill Young, unexpectedly arrived at the building one day early.

Not wanting to start on an unhappy note, Mary Ann, after what I imagine were a few hard gulps, invited Bill to move right in. She told me she was so concerned about her first resident being all alone in her big new building that she spent that whole first night in the empty hallway near Mr. Young's door reading a good book, just to be sure he would be okay. Bill Young went on to live *We quickly paid off all of its loans by using the fully refundable entrance deposits paid by each arriving resident.* at New Horizons for nineteen years, until just shy of his 100th birthday. He was always an outstanding booster and community supporter.

WITH THE PASSING now of many years, it has been so gratifying to Joyce and me to see how many of our older personal and business acquaintances and their close relatives have opted to spend their final years at New Horizons at Choate. In addition, many early buyers from Place Lane Condominium have established a delightful pattern of following their friends or family members from Place Lane to New Horizons as their own living needs change.

There is no question that New Horizons is a truly marvelous place, but it is also an economical place. One of its most surprising features is that no resident in the last twenty years has ever been asked to pay any type of an increase in his or her monthly rent or meals expense after moving in.

There has never been a need for any increase for services expense, either, because the foundation has done so much to keep operating costs low without compromising on quality. Residency fees are adjusted only as new residents move in. Charges billed by Winchester Hospital's home-services division for personal healthcare, when applicable, are separately billed by the hospital at its current rates.

Choate Medical Center, which directly abuts New Horizons, houses medical practices and other health services on the ground floor of the former hospital. It is an eminently convenient provider of on-site medical care for many New Horizons residents. It enables residents to receive high-quality medical care without having to leave their building. The medical providers also serve others from all over the greater Woburn community. Residents can handily arrange visits with any of the many on-site physicians and other healthcare practices, which include a twenty-bed dialysis center. The substantial rental income derived from these medical and physical therapy facilities defrays almost all of New Horizons' food-service costs.

Recognizing how little extra it costs New Horizons in both Woburn and

Marlborough to accommodate a second resident in most apartments, we made it highly attractive for couples to move in. Our additional charge for providing housing and three meals per day for a second person is extremely low. Partly for that reason, and because we offer special programs and activities for men, our gender ratio is typically about 30 percent male and 70 percent female, giving New Horizons a far higher ratio of men than most of the other top area communities.

The need for assisted and independent living units for Americans age eighty-five and beyond is expected to triple from 5.8 million today to 19 million by 2057. Most often, when couples consider moving to New Horizons, or any other similar group home, they do so because one of the two is in failing health. The more frail spouse is often keen to see his or her life partner settled into a new home before the ailing partner succumbs. Only rarely—indeed, almost never—does the surviving partner choose to leave New Horizons after the death of his or her spouse. Most importantly, the last months these couples have together are dramatically more comfortable and meaningful when they can be together in a highly supportive environment. We so frequently hear from residents, "We should have moved here sooner. Why did we wait so long?"

We are proud that there hasn't been a single time in more than fifteen years when the Woburn community was not 100 percent occupied as of the first of each month.

By this time Doug and I had begun getting considerable experience working with David Leland as the foundation's principal financial advisor. David was particularly attentive to any financial or investment issues at our not-for-profit assisted living communities and later with Cummings family issues, for which I was so grateful. David was another key connection involving members of Winchester Country Club, as Joyce and I actually knew David's parents before we knew him. Decades later, David in turn met Darin Byrne, who became one of his standout younger team members, through Darin's parents at the club.

❈ *"Getting to yes" pithily summarizes the creative and committed problem-solving approach that led to our successes at Place Lane, New Horizons at Choate, and elsewhere. This requires strong analytical and negotiating skills, as well as scrupulous attention to key details to avoid unforced errors. Those businesses most able to "get to yes" are in a position to reinvest in the communities to which they often owe so much—a goal to which every business should aspire.*

[11]

Jamie Takes the Helm

STARTING IN the mid-1970s, I became increasingly active at Tufts under President Jean Mayer, whom I particularly admired. In addition to minor roles and committee work, I served on the Tufts Medical School board of overseers before accepting a ten-year appointment in 1986 as a charter trustee of the university.

As my extracurricular activities grew, and as Jamie—by then executive vice president of Cummings Properties— became an ever more esteemed colleague, it was my special pleasure to nominate him to take my place on the board of directors of the Woburn Boys Club. That was particularly meaningful to Jamie, as he heavily attributed his success to his lifelong involvement with the Boys Club. He thus became the club's first former student member to serve on its board of directors. Before long, Jamie also became the first former student member to be elected president of the club, and he felt so honored to continue his long association with the place he cherished so much.

"Without exaggeration," Jamie's mother, Connie McKeown, recently told

Joyce and me, "from elementary school through his mid-teen years, Jamie spent almost all of his out-of-school waking hours at the club. He truly loved it. He was never home." When he was named Boy of the Year in 1974, it appeared as though he had reached the pinnacle of his Boys Club experience, but of course that honor turned out to be but a steppingstone. As the club's new president, Jamie—by then the father of two young daughters—quickly led the move to formally change the club from the Woburn Boys Club to the Woburn Boys & Girls Club.

Nineteen-ninety was a pivotal year for Jamie, beginning with his appointment as treasurer of the Woburn Industrial Development Finance Authority by Mayor Thomas Higgins. Then, in June, I named him president of Cummings Properties, twenty years after its founding and eleven years after he joined the company. Our company newsletter by that time bragged in its banner: "Serving 1,000 Firms in More Than 3 Million Square Feet."

I had no plans yet to go anywhere, but I was eager to see the company's next-generation leadership firmly in place. Still hoping that my children might have long-term interest in the firm, I felt it was important at that point for Jamie to be in position to someday help guide whichever of them might later qualify for the job. With Jamie so firmly set in his new position as president, I could not possibly have felt any better about the reality and wisdom of my succession planning.

By then, Jamie was universally respected, and his appointment as president was extremely well received. People were drawn in by his natural charm. At thirty-four years old, he was surely young, but his maturity and commendable personal commitment safeguarded him from negative feelings. He also had more time with the firm than anyone else who might have seen himself or herself taking over.

Thinking back, I know that the decision to have Jamie succeed me at his young age was informed by my own earlier experience that caused me to abruptly leave Gorton's in 1964, when someone else was selected for an available post over me because of *my* age at the time. I was several years younger than Jamie was when his time came, and I had less seniority with my employer then than Jamie did, but still I was the right person to assume the new management position in the Cleveland subsidiary of Gorton's. At Cummings, Jamie never once pushed me for a new title, but I felt that he had in effect "trusted me" long enough, and he always appreciated my strong public display of confidence in him. Jamie truly cherished the respect he had earned from his peers, especially in his hometown of Woburn. This major management change came just as the final push was underway to open New Horizons at Choate. That effort consumed much of my time for a while, giving Jamie plenty of extra room to become established in his new role.

In the fall of 1991, Jamie was also elected as an early president of the Woburn Business Association, which was morphing into a highly effective voice for business interests in the community. Woburn businesses formerly had the North Suburban Chamber of Commerce, but many Woburn business people at the time believed that the so-called regional chamber was disproportionately interested in fighting off further reductions in the dwindling Air Force presence at Hanscom Field in nearby Bedford. Thus, the WBA came into being as a Woburn-centric business group, and it has enjoyed donated Cummings office space for decades.

| *Bill and Jamie in West Cummings Park, 1991*

AS IT TURNED out, three of our four children, Daniel, Kevin, and Patricia, all occupied significant roles in the family business for a few years each, but each later chose a different career path. There never was a time, however, when anyone in the management team at Cummings had to compete with family members for career opportunities.

Our eldest son, Daniel, did well at Colby College, and he later worked closely with me for several years in various capacities at Cummings Properties. He always demonstrated exceptionally good business intuition, but he eventually chose to opt out while recovering from several major back surgeries following first a skiing accident and then a work-related accident in Florida.

Kevin received a bachelor's degree from the now closed New England Institute of Art and worked for several years at our much larger New Horizons retirement community in Marlborough, Massachusetts, which we opened shortly after New Horizons at Choate. Later, he started his own photography business.

Patricia graduated from Tufts University in 1997 and became a clinical psychologist in San Francisco, after first working for several years as associate director at our New Horizons at Marlborough. Although Patty, now a psychologist, had no Jewish connections, she later also served for several years as the assistant dean at San Francisco Orthodox Hebrew Academy.

Marilyn, the only one of our children to work only part-time in the family business, was a 1992 Phi Beta Kappa graduate of Dartmouth College. After then graduating from Tufts Medical School, she became an intensive care pediatrician at Children's Hospital of Philadelphia. She is currently medical director of the Clinical Trials Division of Columbia University Medical Center in New York and serves as chair of an institutional review board there.

Naturally, Joyce and I were proud of our children's successes in their chosen vocations, but I was still at least a little disheartened when none of them chose a career with the company. Their decisions forced me to continue making extremely careful selections of key managers who would eventually take over the business—but clearly, that process was coming together beautifully under Jamie.

BEYOND OUR TALENTED field staff, Cummings has other extraordinary in-house capabilities. For example, we manage all purchasing ourselves and always serve as our own general contractor. In fact, the company has been its own general contractor in every newly constructed building and in every major rehabilitation since its first building. That work includes almost all of the 11 million square feet we gradually developed and acquired over the last five decades. Among the hundred or so buildings we have built or purchased, the only buildings purchased that never required total makeovers were two small office buildings totaling about 80,000 square feet between them, plus a recent direct acquisition of about 100,000 square feet in Andover,

Massachusetts, from Boston Properties.

For most of the firm's early days, designer Fred Wilbur managed purchasing. As the construction intensified, architect Mike Pascavage took over Fred's design role in 1990, while in 1991 Susan Brand began as general counsel and as a member of our Executive Committee, as Jim Gillette started helping with purchasing. Fred left the company during that period but returned several times, always doing outstanding work as a construction manager during his later stints. His work included most of our more complicated and difficult projects. Fred

| *Jim Gillette*

even returned from his retirement in Florida for four months in 2016 to serve as a senior consultant for the building of our Elliott Landing condominiums in Beverly. Dennis McClay, who had been with us since May 1971, served as general superintendent until well into 1996.

Jim Gillette has been rock solid as our purchasing director. Jim has thoughtfully established an extensive purchasing protocol for the firm, which highly values its longstanding subcontractor relationships. His six-person department is one of the few groups we have that maintain offices in both Woburn and Beverly. Jim himself is among our most senior 20 percent of colleagues. Members of this group average twenty-five years' seniority.

The Jim Gillette era brought with it a much more organized set of written policies for dealing with suppliers of all sorts. Beyond simply paying vendors and contractors promptly, it is imperative for any company to work with vendors to help them reduce their cost of doing business with your firm. With suppliers of goods especially, reduce the frequency of small orders, teach your team to get deliveries offloaded promptly, and avoid quibbling over trivial details. Be careful to always check the accuracy and condition of incoming orders, ideally as they are coming off the truck rather than making more time-consuming claims later, which may appear suspicious and will be difficult to verify. While occasional favors can appear harmless, be exceedingly firm about employees not accepting gratuities or special treatment from customers, clients, or vendors, and make the policy well-known to those who might offer gratuities.

CUMMINGS PROPERTIES' longtime designer, now chief design officer, Jim Trudeau, has a full-time in-house architectural group that rivals most small architectural firms. As a 1984 graduate of the prestigious Rhode Island

School of Design, Jim originally worked directly under Jamie and then under Mike Pascavage. Jim now directs our three full-time registered architects, Mike Aveni, David Harriss, and Jennifer Davidson, and also our registered engineers and a dozen other professional designers. Jim himself has had more than thirty-four years of unfailingly solid contributions with Cummings, while his next four most senior design colleagues have another *ninety* years among them, as of 2018. Never in our corporate history have we ever subbed out any architectural assignment.

| *James "Jim" Trudeau*

Our design department handles building design, estimating, permitting, engineering, and project management, as well as graphics and web design. It constantly deals with multiple demands for its services from many different departments, including leasing, operations, facilities, construction, marketing, and communications. Jim commented on the company's unique style:

> *Team members handle the incoming work orders and then work directly with the in-house client or 'pass the ball,' asking their fellow designers for help, delegating tasks or turning to senior designers for review. This flexible arrangement finds tasks passed back and forth across a wide range of junior and more senior staff. This distributed system reduces bottlenecks, cross-trains employees, flexes with varying demands, and ultimately speeds task completion—always a Cummings goal. Whereas other firms might organize the work of a department like our design group more like a football team, with every play starting out from the quarterback, our staff likes its organization to be much more like a soccer team's.*

> **J.G.T.**

Substantially bucking the system used in many real estate and development firms, Cummings Properties has always been concerned about avoiding overused job titles. We have conspicuously few aggrandized titles. Typically, we have only two or three vice presidents, and only three times over forty-five years have we had an executive vice president. In addition to the four attorneys who staff our busy legal department, we have been delighted with lawyers who fill numerous other "non-legal" management roles in our sales, leasing and operations departments. There may be more, but for no particular reason, I know of only one colleague who holds an MBA.

PRIOR TO THE SUMMER of 1991, no one at our company had ever considered starting a newspaper to compete with Woburn's mostly excellent longtime newspaper, the *Daily Times Chronicle*. At that time, though, the "DTC," as we routinely called it, seemed to be publishing an increasing number of unflattering and sometimes anti-Cummings stories. They told me they could sell more newspapers by "stirring up" their readers but that had the decided effect of feeding a vocal anti-business attitude in the community.

In September 1991, the long-time senior editor, Jim Haggerty, was pretty blunt with me. He said the paper's approach was "nothing personal," but "if you can't stand the heat, you'll have to get out of the kitchen." It was not clear how I was supposed to handle the remark, but within a week of that meeting in the DTC office, we began working to start a new Woburn newspaper. Joyce described this new endeavor as the perfect opportunity "to invent my own midlife crisis."

> *We had no plans to tell anyone what to think, but we were intent on helping influence what they thought about.*

Prior to our paper's actual launch, however, Jim and I met one more time, again in the DTC office, to discuss whether his newspaper might possibly alter its dynamic. We were so much hoping it might move away from what we viewed as pandering to what was then a small but highly vocal group of naysayers. Unfortunately, the DTC was not open to any sort of accommodation. Jim even made a crack, warning me that Woburn readers would not like "rich people from Winchester coming in and trying to tell them what to think." My response was that this "rich person from Winchester" had worked for every penny I had, and most certainly grew up with many fewer economic advantages than he had. Still, he made it clear that he saw no reason to change the DTC's highly populist posture.

The DTC team did not seem to believe we would move forward with a real newspaper of our own or that it would be any good, but we did, and it was. I made the final decision to start the *Woburn Advocate* during that second visit to the DTC office. Now we had to figure out how to build the first edition. No member of our original staff had ever worked a single day for a newspaper, and we had a great deal to learn.

We had no plans to tell anyone what to think, but we were intent on helping influence what our readers thought *about*. Rather than writing reports of who said what at each City Council or School Committee meeting, we wanted our reporters to discuss the issues with the many public officials who made sense and ignore the several who did not. They should concentrate on the back story when there was one, about what was really going on, and write about the many highly successful businesses in Woburn and about the people behind them. Particularly, I requested in-depth interviews and feature stories about the people who helped define the fabric of the town. I wanted us covering some of those who seemed as though they had been here forever but were never before visible.

I happily justified creating the *Woburn Advocate* as a way to keep myself busy so that Jamie would not see too much of me as he grew into his new role as Cummings Properties' president and then CEO. At the beginning, a *monthly* paper seemed like the right idea, but then a late friend who once published the nearby *Winchester Star*, C. Peter Jorgenson, convinced me we would be foolish to build anything but a weekly paper from the start. He further told me we should deliver it free on Thursdays, for no better reason, he said, than "Thursday is the day everyone publishes a weekly when they can."

Conveniently, Boston's now-noted author Neil Swidey was looking for his first real job when he responded to our line ad in *The Boston Globe* classified section. I immediately liked Neil, even though his only prior real-world experience was some part-time work at the *Providence Journal*, in addition to working on the *Tufts Observer* while in college. But he had indeed been the editor-in-chief at the *Observer*, and he performed brilliantly on our simple editing exercise. If I remember correctly, Neil started working the next day.

Once we settled on the paper's name, our senior Cummings Properties designer, Jim Trudeau, produced a front-page banner design, which everyone liked. The paper was set for free delivery by U.S. mail to some 18,000 households in Woburn. For my part as publisher, I learned most of what I knew, including the U.S. Postal Service rules, from reading a small "how-to" book called something not too profound, like *Starting Your Own Newspaper*. That book

Bill Cummings

Editor Neil Swidey, Fred Phinney, Josh Resnek, and Joyce Cummings are shown in the Harte-Hanks pressroom with the first edition of the **Woburn Advocate**, *1991*

showed me how easy and surprisingly inexpensive it was to acquire items like crossword puzzles, cartoons, and syndicated columns from writers whose views we respected. The first columnist we added was an old friend, Ralph Nader. With some extensive extra tutoring from a helpful postmaster in Woburn, we were fully operational on October 24, 1991, and never missed an on-time delivery.

We found many local people who were good writers, including several who had been regular or occasional DTC writers. Eventually, we also recruited several with experience in regional newspapers. Collectively, they did a superb job of showcasing city leaders and helping to break down some of the class stereotypes so liberally proffered by Woburn's anti-business activists. They also helped get us into less of a crisis mode at each week's deadline.

We never set out to overtly challenge or in any way embarrass the DTC. Stories about our own firm were extremely rare, and for reasons I just don't remember, I do not think we ever once used the paper to advertise our own rental properties. I think it is accurate to say that there was never a story about me, either. Getting out each new edition was our weekly miracle.

Starting the newspaper would help to greatly lessen my real estate involvement, even though everything was under one roof. Jamie rarely had time to think much about the newspaper, and I relied instead on Doug Stephens and Jim Trudeau as our editorial sounding board, at least until the new newspaper staff became acclimated. Jamie did, however, occasionally use his knowledge as a Woburn native to catch potential gaffes in stories about Woburn or Woburn people.

Neil was always "the professor" and the perfectionist of the group. If Josh Resnek—another new hire for the *Advocate*—was the bold activist I was trying to control, Neil was the idealist I wanted to both impress and teach. Rick Friedman was our philosopher, and he wrote many warm, thoughtful stories, often involving Woburn's delightful Horn Pond. His stories had great depth and genuine emotion, to the surprise of some readers. Gail Carson, a former opera singer, contributed numerous stories about the arts. She occasionally delighted everyone on our floor when she would let her powerful voice fill the entire space as she strolled in with a good story that she hoped would excite the editor as much as it did herself.

David Harvey, another Woburn native in his first real job, turned out to be a naturally gifted sports writer, even though he was hired as an advertising sales representative. One of the most engaging young Woburnites around, David made friends for the paper all over town. Several knowledgeable readers went out of their way to enthusiastically praise David's often-endearing sports stories. He was the only original staff member to stay with the paper as long as I did. In many respects, he emulated the sincerity and sensitivity shown by Josh and Rick. After we sold the paper, David became a property manager for several years before eventually leaving to become a stay-at-home dad. David much later returned to the firm in 2018.

Josh, for his part, was also the romantic on the *Advocate* team, and he taught us all the mystique of the newspaper business, making it more entertaining—although not always without some peril from the occasional slight exaggeration. Nevertheless, Josh was a terrific storyteller, and he added so much to the team and to the paper. I still talk with Josh every couple of years. Last time we spoke, he was running a highly successful chain of suburban community newspapers, where he is likely sharing his insight with great flair, mild irreverence, and sharp wit.

In 1991, we were still at the earliest stages of using computers to create our small newspaper. PageMaker software was the new thing, and seemingly fast computers were quickly outmoded by still faster ones. The first edition of the *Woburn Advocate* featured a front-page color photograph of Woburn's much beloved late multi-term mayor Thomas Higgins. Starting with that image, the *Woburn Advocate* became the first Woburn paper to regularly use full-color news photographs. Well before the arrival of digital printing, photographic color separations were not inexpensive, but they gave us something special—a small edge, until the *Daily Times Chronicle* soon adopted color photos as well.

DENNIS CLARKE joined the *Advocate* in June 1992 as an advertising-sales representative and made a strong impression on me from the start.

Dennis is the son of Dick and Nancy Clarke, our longtime friends who are now Woburn residents. Dennis grew up in Winchester, however, and graduated from Winchester High School, where he

| *Jamie McKeown, Dennis Clarke, and Bill, 1992*

was prominently recognized as a *Boston Globe* scholar/athlete prior to attending Harvard. At six-foot-two with a strong build, Dennis also went on to be a Golden Gloves boxing champ. He gives great credit to his extra-long arms for his boxing success, but he would be the last person to ever throw his weight around, or to ever even mention his boxing days. Dennis is another of many colleagues sourced in one way or another through Winchester Country Club, which is where I first got to know his parents.

With only a year or so of corporate business experience when he joined us, Dennis was still pretty green in the art of business. During college, he sold a boatload of fancy kitchen knives door-to-door in Winchester, and before that, he had cut grass, raked leaves, and shoveled driveways throughout his high school years, in addition to playing varsity football and basketball. But he rapidly came to know more about the newspaper business than I did, and I was delighted to appoint him as general manager of the entire newspaper operation by the end of his first year.

The DTC clearly did not appreciate us, but we consciously treated it with the complete respect we felt it deserved after so many decades of operation. Its publisher, Paul Haggerty, who was Jim's uncle and not too active in the family's publishing business by then, was one of Woburn's finest, most polished, and most distinguished citizens.

When the DTC occasionally maligned us, we reacted quickly, but that was rare. Jim Haggerty Jr. once spelled out the situation quite succinctly with his "two straws in the punch bowl" analogy. The bottom line was always about not wanting to share the available advertising dollars—and certainly not with any unworthy newcomers.

During my three years publishing the *Advocate*, it was not at all unusual for me to write stories with no byline, and I do not think my picture ever appeared in any issue, nor did the words of any talk I ever gave. Thanks to strong encouragement from Josh, however, I did write one story with attribution as an editorial. "From the Publisher" was a tribute to my dad, who lived in Woburn during his later years and died here in January 1992. Dad defined his

> *I wrote many stories with no byline, and I do not think my picture ever appeared in any issue.*

life with his love of family and with his work: "Nowhere have I ever known anyone who ever worked harder at his job than Dad did, or with as great a sense of pride and accomplishment in trying always to do the right thing."

MEANWHILE, back at Cummings Properties, Jamie was as busy as ever. Between late 1992 and early 1993, we acquired eleven buildings during another

Executive Committee, circa 1993: Dennis McClay, Bill Cummings, President Jamie McKeown, Treasurer Doug Stephens; seated: Vice President Michael Pascavage and General Counsel Susan Brand

huge slump in the Boston-area real estate market, adding more than a million more square feet of mostly vacant property. Including properties in Wilmington, Medford, Somerville, Stoneham, and Sudbury, our total square footage now reached 4 million square feet.

Despite the extraordinarily low purchase price of these buildings—just under $10 per square foot on average—there seemed to be no one else with any appetite for purchasing such distressed properties. The most significant reason we acquired so many sites at practically giveaway prices was our ability to act immediately and to pay cash. We have many times assumed the risk of possible failure but have never thereafter failed to make something really good of any deal.

In April 1993, we created still another new buildable lot, this one at 17 Warren Avenue, Woburn, with some of New Horizons at Choate's unused land. This parcel was then donated to Supportive Living for the construction of a home for survivors of traumatic brain injuries. Supportive Living's fifteen-resident Warren House would be completed in 1997. The organization was formed by Doug and Carrol Stephens after their son, Scott, suffered a disabling brain injury in an auto accident when he was a teenager. Warren House became the first of four free-standing Supportive Living residences. The other residences are in Lexington, North Reading, and Rockport, Massachusetts. These not-for-profit homes offer long-term, semi-independent accommodations for their residents.

By mid-1993, Cummings Properties had reached a level of systemic success with all it had going on. Certainly, there were bumps—not the least of which was the wild economic upheaval of the early 1990s in the commercial real estate market. As buyers of mildly neglected commercial real estate, however, we were in a comfortable position, having made the best of the economic downturn. I had achieved a long-cherished goal of maintaining debt-free status by then, and

| *New Horizons at 400 Hemenway Street, Marlborough*

it was comforting never to worry about economic survival, while so many competitors seemed to be engulfed in old debt.

New Horizons at Marlborough, formerly the thirty-two-acre home of Madonna Hall School for Girls, opened on October 1, 1994, three years after the Woburn New Horizons community. We purchased the defunct boarding school for $1.15 million from the Sisters of the Good Shepherd, a Roman Catholic religious order that operated the school there for thirty years. After investing approximately $12 million to renovate and rebuild the well-constructed Madonna Hall property, Joyce and I donated it, debt-free, including the entire highly successful assisted-living business, to Cummings Foundation, as we also gradually did with most of our commercial buildings.

Supported by about ninety mostly local employees, nonsectarian New Horizons at Marlborough currently houses more than 460 seniors on its beautiful forty-acre campus a dozen miles west of Interstate 95, just off US Route 20. In addition to the independent- and assisted-living suites, the campus includes a forty-five-resident Hearthstone Alzheimer Care group, a collocated but separately run twenty-two-resident geri-psych wing, and a newly constructed convent for a dozen Sisters of the Good Shepherd, who have lived on campus rent-free since October 1994 as provided in the original purchase agreement. As of August 2017 we were able to accommodate an additional new group of Catholic women—twenty-six Sisters of St. Anne. This new group is now occupying twenty-six new apartments in the original convent.

WHILE THE PROPERTY side of the company was firing on all cylinders, the newspaper side was also expanding. Soon after we started publishing the *Woburn Advocate*, we added two more new papers: the *Winchester Town Crier* and the *Stoneham Sun*. Like the *Advocate*, the two new papers avoided devoting much space to topics such as accidents at Fourth and Main, or who said what at public hearings. We sometimes covered such events, but only when they occurred on Tuesdays and we could appear somewhat current in reporting them on Thursday. We mainly focused on positive developments in the business, educational, and not-for-profit spheres in each community. We wrote many in-depth feature stories about the people who were doing the talking and saying positive things at various events. We also concentrated on developing new advertising clients and were highly successful in this endeavor. Initially printing twenty-four pages a week, we were soon hitting a routine fifty-two to sixty-four ad-filled pages.

A most interesting and highly profitable Cummings Properties side-story came up during our newspaper adventure soon after we realized that none of the local Woburn residential real estate agencies would advertise with us. Realtor Joe Crowley, a good friend for many years, clued me in: "If one office starts using the *Woburn Advocate*, then they would all have to follow," which would increase their total spending for advertising. There was supposedly a clear understanding that none of the Woburn real estate offices wanted to be the first. I did not blame any of them for not wanting to take a chance with us, but the situation still presented as a major challenge.

Having greatly enhanced its success with the then-current condominium boom, Carlson Real Estate Company was at the time an impressive eastern Middlesex and Essex County chain of residential real estate offices, but with no Woburn office. So, I asked owner Dick Carlson to consider opening a Woburn office. He immediately told me Woburn might be a great location for him, but he had found that buying out an existing office was almost always a better pathway for him than building a new one. When I asked what his largest expense would be, he said that rental cost for an office was usually the greatest concern. He also said he was concerned that he might be stuck with a long-term lease if the office was not successful. I told him we had just the answer, and we had a deal within five minutes.

It just so happened that Cummings Properties had one especially appropriate ground-floor space at 800 West Cummings Park all built-out, and since we also still needed more advertising for the *Woburn Advocate*, we put those needs together. I offered Dick *free* office space for a year, and he in return quickly agreed to become a regular full-page advertiser in the *Advocate* every week for a year. Bingo, the lease was signed, and as expected, other Woburn real estate offices soon found the *Woburn Advocate* to be an attractive advertising vehicle.

The rent-free first year went by in no time, but the Carlson office remained at 800 West Cummings Park long thereafter. It became a regular rent-paying client, and soon it expanded this new Woburn office,

I offered Dick free office space for a year, and he quickly agreed to become a regular full-page advertiser in the Advocate *every week for a year.*

which Dick told me was the single most successful all-new location he had ever opened. Not only did he expand in 800 West Cummings Park, but he also later moved his entire corporate headquarters to our newly constructed office building at 18 Commerce Way in Woburn.

As it turned out, that one tiny "free-rent" deal, in addition to gaining us a much-needed advertiser, produced substantially more net *rental* income for Cummings Properties than the million dollars we later received from the sale of the three newspapers. And then, instead of moving the newspapers out of 300 West Cummings Park when its initial lease with us ended, the *Advocate* purchaser brought others of its papers in and it, too, leased a much larger space for five more years. The synergies were magnificent.

We enjoyed our foray into the newspaper business, but when the end came, we were more than ready for it. We were waiting for it. It began in September 1994, when William "Bill" Elfers, representing a Fidelity Investments affiliate called Community Newspaper Company, knocked on our door and announced that his firm wanted to purchase our three local papers. This was exactly what we had been quietly desiring. It was perfect timing: During the bad economic period, Cummings Properties had acquired an increasing number of distressed buildings at low bargain prices, so the decision to lighten our management load by selling our three newspapers to CNC came easily. After publishing the papers for three years in the red, we sold them quietly and quickly, at the end of 1994.

CNC already owned about ninety mostly weekly Boston-area newspapers at that time. Many of them were much like ours, because we had unabashedly modeled our three papers on some of theirs. And not at all by accident, our three towns of Woburn, Winchester, and Stoneham filled a significant gap in their coverage. Although we never made even the slightest direct overture to anyone at CNC, we had earlier added the Community office to each of our newspapers' free subscription lists, hoping to catch its interest. And as it happened, by the time of the sale, we were finally just breaking even each month, although we had accumulated $300,000 in earlier losses, not including my time.

In the end, CNC liked our product, and the quality of our advertising base, so much that it agreed to pay just over $1 million, plus a generous free-advertising allowance for Cummings Properties' use for decades to come. We would have up to a free full-page ad in each of the three papers each week for as long as I remained active in our business. As of 2016, we still advertise for free in our two remaining former papers and pay a greatly discounted rate to effectively advertise other local interests in a dozen or so of the parent company's other papers.

After twenty years of operating Cummings Properties almost exclusively within the city of Woburn, we had done extremely well. At the same time, before we published the *Advocate* there were few Woburn residents who knew much of anything about us. A large percentage of Woburnites knew only what was said by the naysayers who were so often quoted in the DTC. The *Advocate* routinely wrote about the positive actions and accomplishments of Woburn's other businesses. But readers did come to know our newspaper was a worthwhile public service coming to them free through Cummings Properties for more than three years, and attitudes toward the company seemed to change considerably.

When I look back on this newspaper adventure, my fondest memories are of the talented people I came to know through it. Neil Swidey remained at the *Advocate* long enough to help us build a solid foundation. He left and made a series of impressive moves, ultimately building his career with *The Boston Sunday Globe* and *Boston Globe Magazine*. Today, he is a senior *Globe* writer and has also authored several widely acclaimed books. Neil was followed as editor-in-chief by another highly accomplished Tufts alum, Peter Chianca.

Finally, and not to be overlooked, another prominent staff member at the *Woburn Advocate* was Mark Herlihy, who joined as a primary writer. He worked with at least a dozen other highly qualified full- and part-time reporters and stringers. Like Neil, Mark also excelled academically at Tufts, and he achieved first-team All-America recognition in high hurdles. He went on to earn a PhD in history from Brown University, and upon this writing, he is chair of the Humanities Department and Associate Dean of Arts and Sciences at Endicott College, as well as president of the New England Historical Association. Mark responded enthusiastically when I asked if he would share some quarter-century-old memories of his days with our three newspapers:

Here are a few recollections of my time at the **Woburn Advocate**: *What made the* **Advocate** *successful was that it was a true community newspaper. A lot of community newspapers focus their coverage almost exclusively on* *things like the official business of City Hall and the school department. We certainly covered meetings of the City Council and the School Committee, as well as elections and crime stories—that's important—but we went beyond that. We went out into the community and talked to residents about the impact that events would have on their lives.*

We went into schools and interviewed teachers and students about innovative programs. We found and wrote compelling human-interest stories about people in the city—unsung heroes, new immigrants, activists, individuals with interesting backgrounds, etc. And we put a spotlight on issues that had not been investigated previously.

The Advocate *was also notable for its photography, especially the work of Cheryl Miller and, later, Dan Cummings, whose creative and distinctive shots accompanied articles and were featured weekly in a two-page centerfold photo essay that focused on a theme or an event held in the city. Woburn residents responded positively to the paper, and it caught on quickly. I remember it growing in a span of a few months from thirty-two to forty-eight, and then to sixty-four pages.*

I joined the staff shortly after the paper was launched, selling advertising initially. My understanding was that Bill started the Advocate *to counter what he felt was an anti-business bias of the* Daily Times Chronicle, *which, until the creation of the* Advocate, *had been the town's only newspaper. But Bill realized that for readers to be open to hearing a different message, we had to offer things that readers would find in any other community paper, too—coverage of and commentary on major events, great sports news, plus obituaries, etc.*

And he hired great people to do that. Founding editor Neil Swidey, now a senior writer for Boston Globe Magazine *and a noted book author, was a terrific editor. Neil was also young and inexperienced, but he had high standards and his editing and his way with words gave the paper a certain flair without being pretentious. He made all of us look better. Neil knew the kinds of stories that would resonate with readers, and he encouraged us to go out and get them.*

Joshua Resnek had a talent for writing editorials and columns that were thoughtful and provocative. And he conveyed the pulse of the city and the personalities of its residents and officials in the weekly Around the Town section.

Staff writer and Woburn native Joseph McCool, who would later become a correspondent for the **Manchester Union-Leader,** *and also with a published book to his credit, reported on political developments and crime news in Woburn, and profiled business leaders and entrepreneurs in numerous Executive Corner profiles. Contributing writer Rick Friedman brought his thoughtful knowledge of Woburn history to bear on many memorable stories and columns.*

There were so many others like Marie Lingblom and Gail Carson who also made valuable contributions. It was a terrific team effort.

M.H.

Notwithstanding the two great ongoing rental relationships with Carlson Real Estate and Community Newspaper Company, Dennis' later joining Cummings Properties turned out to be the most significant long-term benefit derived from our three-year newspaper experience. Dennis also ran the newspapers' transition to CNC for one year, as we had agreed, and then, after taking a three-month-long trip around the world with his still new bride, Alicia Angeles Clarke, he returned to Cummings—just as planned, and just as we were taking on a giant new challenge in Beverly, Massachusetts.

❀ *Our experience with the* Woburn Advocate *taught us that an outlandish idea—like a real estate firm starting its own newspapers—can sometimes be the most effective one, especially when seeking to shake an entrenched status quo. An open mind and collaborative atmosphere will leave room for such an idea to emerge, and a thoughtfully assembled supporting cast will help realize it. These together may well also coax out further unexpected dividends—as we did with the important leases, free advertising, and brilliant colleagues we gained through the* Advocate *affair.*

❀ *The most valuable colleagues in any firm are typically those who quickly recognize problems when they occur, and then deal with them.*

❀ *William Faulkner once wrote that Ernest Hemingway "has never been known to use a word that might send a reader to the dictionary." Hemingway shot right back: "Poor Faulkner. Does he really think big emotions come from big words?"*

❀ *A good mentor helps, but most people who do well in business ultimately do so because at some point in their lives they decide what they want, they set goals, and they make up their mind to sacrifice in order to reach them.*

[12]

A Whole Different League

Massachusetts Governor William Weld with Bill Cummings

HAVING RESOLUTELY avoided purchasing any property not in the immediate vicinity of Woburn, I was more than a little surprised when Jamie, in early February 1995, informed me that he would be looking at "somewhat of a monster" of a nearly vacant industrial property in Beverly, on Boston's North Shore. The 100-acre site, known as "The Shoe," had been the world headquarters of the once-proud but now almost-defunct United Shoe Machinery Corporation.

By this time, the former international corporate giant had been all but out of business for more than fifteen years. Effectively, the U.S. government eviscerated it following many decades of protracted antitrust actions in federal courts. There were reportedly attorneys on both sides who spent their entire careers working on nothing but the United Shoe antitrust cases between 1912 and 1979, when the hugely successful Beverly monopoly was finally forced to break itself up.

One intriguing aspect of this case was the unorthodox role played by Louis Brandeis, who in 1916 would become an associate justice of the U.S. Supreme

Court. His brilliant legal career unfolding, Brandeis at one time represented early shoe manufacturers, including United Shoe. His law firm, now Nutter, McClennen & Fish, oversaw the merger that formed United Shoe Machinery Corporation, and Brandeis even joined United's board of directors and served as counsel to the already-giant budding monopoly. Any conflicts of interest notwithstanding, Brandeis was later one of the more notable antagonists to United Shoe while he was on the Supreme Court.

Jamie and I had not known much about it, but the mammoth Beverly property had been on and off the market since 1980. Jamie first described the building as "vacant" and certainly, with all the smashed glass on its vast expanses of window line, it did look the part. The property was so massive, so run-down, and so broken, that all efforts by others to make something worthwhile of it had quickly failed. Meanwhile, the asking price had gradually dropped from $78 million in 1980 all the way down to $10 million in 1995. Broker Bob Cronin told Jamie that he would be willing to present the seller an offer "even as low as $5 million, just to get you guys talking." Jamie convinced me to return to Beverly with him a week or so later.

UP TO THIS POINT, our proudest achievement was probably the 100,000-square-foot office building at 92 Montvale Avenue in Stoneham, only two miles from our Woburn office. We bought it in a distressed sale by Eastland Savings Bank, paying $600,000 for the property in "as-is" condition.

The deal had yielded us a rugged, heavy-steel framework for what would turn out to be a unique upscale office building with an integral parking garage on four floors and a prime location abutting Interstate 93. Almost all the concrete floors were in place for both

| *Rusting steel framework at 92 Montvale Avenue in 1991*   the office and the garage, but the building had none of its exterior walls and windows, and no roof, nor, of course, any interior walls or finishes.

We received no architectural plans from the foreclosing bank, and our only lead on that front had been an angry architect in Lexington who was understandably bitter toward the original builder. In the end, Cummings

Properties' own in-house design staff created a complete set of plans to go with the massive skeleton. They did so within four weeks for about 20 percent of what the as yet unpaid architect demanded for the use of his original plans. Architecturally, the Stoneham building was a full cut above our other properties, and for a long time thereafter it was easily our most impressive structure, but the Beverly property was many orders of magnitude larger and more complex.

WITH THE USMC PROPERTY, Jamie was greatly upping the ante. On a frigid Saturday in February 1995, he and I visited The Shoe, joined by Fred Wilbur and Dennis McClay, who was then our construction superintendent. The property was indeed a monster. *Miles* of hallways and service tunnels crisscrossed through and under the 1.5 million square-foot interior. It was so large that employees in earlier days had regularly used bicycles to deliver mail inside the building. Built in 1903 by Ernest Leslie Ransome, a British engineer, The Shoe was one of the first large reinforced concrete buildings in the world—in fact, until the construction of Boulder Dam, it was reportedly the largest reinforced concrete structure anywhere. In some places, we found concrete walls more than three feet thick, and we would later learn that the first phase of the structure, at the south end, had twisted *square iron* reinforcing rods that were as thick as one inch. Ransome's complex foreshadowed the later notable work of Mies van der Rohe in Detroit.

There were more than 2,000 over-sized windows in these interconnected so-called "day-lit" buildings, almost all of them exactly ten feet square. Most of them were cracked or broken; many were completely smashed out, and the cold February wind streamed straight through. Even so, about thirty small businesses were clustered in areas where the massive oil-fired boilers still kept heat pulsing through ancient steam lines. Because the buildings were constructed before 1934, and because tenants collectively occupied less than 10 percent of the total floor area, the buildings could be treated as abandoned and were therefore eligible for significant federal tax credits. We gradually learned about substantial state and city benefits that were also available if we took on the unenviable task of becoming the property's saviors, disguised as redevelopers.

Jamie wanted to keep us in a strong growth mode, and once I admitted we could do the job, he became intent and determined in a way I had never known him before. Our conversations in early 1995 about the purchase of the Beverly property were some of the most serious and thoughtful meetings we ever had. He was so much the future of the company, and a successful conversion of this colossal asset would really put us in a different league.

WE SOON FORMALIZED what some considered an almost laughable proposal of $500,000 to purchase the entire hundred or so acres of The Shoe, including more than 1.5 million square feet of historic concrete memories. There were no permitting or financing contingencies in the proposal other than the seller's guarantee that after the closing it would cost us no more than $1 million to clear the property of all its petroleum and other contamination issues, as the seller's environmental firm had earlier represented to us would be the case. The seller was an affiliate of The Black & Decker Corporation, and the proposed purchase price was like asking for a gift.

Despite our exceedingly low offer, we believed through March and April 1995, that the deal was going to close on precisely those terms, but the paperwork seemed always a few days away. As is often the case, however, the environmental issues delayed any agreement by many months. Hundreds of voluminous softbound reports from Haley & Aldrich eventually revealed thousands of cubic yards of oil-soaked soil on The Shoe's property, accumulated during United Shoe's more than a century of heavy industrial use. There were some locations where oil had been allowed to slop into the sandy ground "just to get rid of it," as an older retiree from The Shoe later told me.

But we soon found out that there was great community goodwill toward United Shoe's possible successors, and that went a long way in awakening all of us to the real substance and significance of the property. In a communication to the Cummings Executive Committee on March 24, 1995, when we were still expecting each day to close on the purchase, Jamie wrote: "Although it will not negatively impact our staffing level if the Beverly sale does not close, the possible acquisition is a major wild card for the future growth and direction of the company. Also, if a sale is consummated, the project will obviously require great immediate attention on the construction side, and soon thereafter, an on-site leasing and operations presence. I think the odds favor the deal being finalized, but it will be another week or so before anything definitive can be resolved. The major obstacle concerns liability for future discovery of presently unknown environmental contamination (if any)."

IN THE MEANTIME, one of the best examples of our utilizing extra buildability on a newly acquired site arose in April 1995. We purchased a well-located 120,000-square-foot single-story property at 10 Commerce Way, Woburn. An affiliate of New York Life Insurance Company sold us the mostly leased property for a little more than $3 million. Located on a federal Superfund site, as were some of our other Woburn properties, it was only a few hundred yards from the Interstate 95/Washington Street interchange. The property did have upcoming exposure from expiring leases, but we considered that mostly as an opportunity to achieve higher rents. Most important, like so many other properties we have acquired, this one also had marvelous expansion capability, on which we soon built 18 Commerce Way.

This additional structure was designed to fit perfectly in the southeast corner of the existing paved parking lot of the original 10 Commerce Way building. A large water main, along with ample underground telephone, electric, gas,

| 10 Commerce Way, Woburn, after the construction of 18 Commerce Way

and storm drainage, all ran right across the east end of the property. Adequate striped parking already existed, greatly speeding up both the permitting and construction cycle and greatly reducing the construction costs for this new building. We had to do remarkably little excavation, and none of it was deeper than three or four feet. The 18 Commerce Way property was first occupied in early 1996, and it filled rapidly.

Not atypically, 18 Commerce Way shows up on our records as having a zero cost for its land. As I have already recounted, this ongoing philosophy of making judicious use of any extra land for future development has been a key to the firm's success and dates back to the first property we purchased at 10 Henshaw Street. All told, the organization today has built twenty-one major buildings on land for which sellers appeared to have established the price without their or their brokers in any way recognizing the future buildability. In all of these cases, the needed land was effectively free.

We have also taken great advantage of unused buildability when assisting others in solving space needs on their already-owned properties. In addition to donating extra land at the former Choate Hospital for the use of Supportive Living, we helped guide and fund the permanent home for Winchester Community Music School. Also quite locally, I played significant roles in funding, designing, and engineering the major classroom addition at St. Eulalia Church in Winchester. I also did most of the design work for the new sports center at Winchester Country Club, plus a new irrigation pumping station along the second fairway, and the new maintenance building. We have helped to design and fund many other community improvements, including the new public restroom building at Horn Pond in Woburn.

I HAD NEVER DONE significant fundraising for not-for-profit organizations, but in 1997, after Joyce and I strongly encouraged founder Corie Nichols to somehow establish a permanent home for Winchester Community

Music School, I knew we then had to help. Corie and her committee eventually identified the former estate home of the late nationally known comedian Frank Fontaine (a/k/a "Crazy Guggenheim" from the Jackie Gleason Show) as an ideal location for the school. An interesting side story

| *Winchester Community Music School*

here is that my dad, who spent most of his working years as a house painter, single-handedly painted the entire interior and exterior of that structure for the Fontaine family before the family moved in decades earlier. He had previously also painted their former home, on nearby Winthrop Street, Medford.

Cummings Foundation gave the music school $500,000, and that made it easy for me to ask others for similar amounts. I enthusiastically approached only two Winchester friends to request their support, and they both quickly agreed to help. The late Sandra Rogers and J.P. Barger, with his wife, Mary B. Barger, each pledged the same $500,000 amount. I told each of them that I just did not have the time to collect $1,000 from each of 1,000 other friends. As far as I knew then, this endeavor both started and ended my fundraising career with an excellent batting average.

Showing others that you perceive them in the way they hope to be viewed will engender positive feelings and a higher likelihood of a positive result. Bringing together a group of prospective donors and identifying them as "the most visible and generous leaders in a community" will be far more effective in getting their financial support for a good cause than calling them "prospects" for an upcoming campaign. In this case, it took only a tiny group.

Winchester Community Music School has continued to grow and flourish, and it functions as an integral part of the town, with students from Winchester and from all surrounding towns as well. Three of our children attended the school when it was in its early years at what is now the middle school, and it is nice to know that our five-year-old grandson, Gus, is among the hundreds regularly benefiting from classes in the new school.

BY LATE APRIL 1995, we were still interested in The Shoe, especially because there were strong signs that the recently disastrous real estate market was beginning to bounce back. But Black & Decker was now hedging on what was supposed to be its guarantee that all environmental issues could be resolved "for no more than $1 million." When we required that Black & Decker confirm such a broad guarantee in writing, its representatives at first refused.

We were disappointed as the deal all but fizzled out during late spring and early summer, but with the economy still recovering, other active projects were keeping us hopping. Jamie found time to train for and complete his second Boston Marathon in April, yet he stayed in regular contact with Bob Cronin, the broker for The Shoe site.

A Black & Decker on-site property manager in Beverly told us that his firm was losing $40,000 a week on the property, primarily because of its large crew of union-scale maintenance and security staff. It was also pouring money into operating three huge boilers in the power plant to provide heat and hot water for the drafty campus. Miles of ancient steel steam pipes, too, in the many tunnels and under the buildings spewed out energy, with breaches often appearing as fast as the maintenance technicians could correct them. The senescent system would need to be entirely replaced, as would the antiquated electrical distribution and all the HVAC components, and, of course, some 2,000 windows and many *acres* of tired old roof. With clear-eyed knowledge of the unenviable work that awaited us should we acquire The Shoe, we still hoped the deal would be preserved. But we also knew that, with entrepreneurship, not every deal works out.

Hard work, risk-taking, and long hours pretty much define entrepreneurship, along with leadership abilities and surrounding oneself with other smart people who crave being part of a successful and worthwhile firm. Risk-taking should never mean betting the whole firm on any one thing, but being ready to take reasonable risks when we see opportunities with lopsided odds for success, and always-affordable losses should something go wrong.

Entrepreneurs must lead by example and truly be available with an open mind each time there are jobs to be done, including the less attractive ones. They must be constantly looking for and thinking of ways to make the company better and stronger. There are a few incredibly smart people who might be able to create legendary success in a forty-hour work week, but true entrepreneurs will feel deprived if they can't get the benefit of the innovative and extraordinary competitive results that extra effort can bring. And that was our situation.

Meager rents from the few dozen mostly small clients did little to help The Shoe's financial picture, which was bedeviled as well by real estate taxes, liability issues, and other major maintenance expenses. The Black & Decker on-site property manager in the meantime decried his company's resistance to making any new investment in the site to alleviate the city's legitimate concerns about life-safety issues. Although we would never indemnify Black & Decker for environmental issues, we could at least stop its huge monthly losses by taking the property off its hands, and in late August 1995 we resumed direct discussions with Dennis Adams, who was treasurer of Black & Decker.

Finally, instead of our resolving the contamination issue at The Shoe, we agreed to put $1 million cash into an escrow account. Black & Decker would then complete all necessary work and accept responsibility for future issues as well. After that proposed agreement, plus another couple of months, the sale was back on. We would still pay our same initial offer of $500,000, but we were guaranteed a clean hundred-acre property.

One Saturday morning in September, shortly after we had decided to try again to move forward with the purchase, Jamie met on-site with two members of Beverly's Conservation Commission in an effort to learn that board's attitude toward the property. Later, Jamie told me that he was sure the commission leadership would help in any way it could to facilitate a real reclamation of this ugly remnant of Beverly's once-dynamic past, and as it turned out the members were true to their word. We had learned that the two ponds on the property were clean in terms of chemicals, but underwater they were like an uncharted minefield, with all the junk and debris that appeared to have been intentionally discarded into the water during the previous ninety years. In one spot next to the foundry building, there was a major coal spill from a railroad coal car that had somehow, many years earlier, spilled its entire load into Lower Shoe Pond. At that time the Beverly Conservation Commission seemed both sympathetic and supportive.

CONVINCED THAT THE DEAL was almost done, we staged a major media event to announce the sale, in a large on-site tent, just a few days before Beverly's 1995 municipal elections. An enthusiastic crowd of Mayor William Scanlon's supporters, along with dozens of interested city officials, bolstered attendance. Massachusetts Governor William Weld was the keynote speaker. Officials from the city and Black & Decker also addressed the audience. Jamie and I spoke briefly as well, and the transformation was ready to begin.

Despite our decision to pursue this uncertain undertaking, I could not have felt more comfortable about where we were as a company, as I continued to plan my exit strategy with a target of about 2002. That plan mostly consisted of working with Joyce on our still-new family foundation. We had great confidence in the entire organization, especially as the local economy became increasingly active. Cummings Foundation already owned more than half of Cummings Properties' real estate, and certainly by the time of my eventual absence, Jamie and the foundation trustees would be ready to operate all the properties exclusively for the benefit of Cummings Foundation.

Dennis Clarke was due to return to the firm at year's end after his one-year commitment to Fidelity as part of our sale of the newspapers, and his post-wedding trip. By now Jamie and I knew that no one named Cummings was to follow Jamie. Instead, we decided that Dennis should one day become Jamie's successor, perhaps in another ten or fifteen years. Although we never told Dennis anything specifically to that effect, Jamie and I both knew Dennis would be ideal for that role, just as Jamie was perfect following me. Jamie also made it quite clear that he was in no hurry for me to go anywhere while he trained Dennis, completing the second real step in the corporate succession plan.

Although I had expected Dennis to be working closely with me during the earliest stages of the Beverly project, just as he had done in Woburn as general manager of the newspapers, Jamie wanted Dennis with him in Woburn, where the two of them could work side by side, the same way I had mentored Jamie. The extraordinary challenge of getting the colossal Beverly property under control, however, now loomed over us all.

AS THE SHOE PROJECT lumbered along, Joyce and I decided not to postpone a previously scheduled (and much needed) three-week vacation to Australia and New Zealand. We would visit our youngest daughter, Patricia, who was on a Tufts University junior-year-abroad program, studying at Monash University in Melbourne, Australia. Built on a sixteen-hour non-stop flight from Los Angeles to beautiful Sydney, the trip thereafter gave us the best of so many things, like the rain forest, diving on Great Barrier Reef, and climbing Ayers Rock. This visit to Australia was followed by an even more leisurely tour of the North and South Islands of New Zealand. We eventually arrived in Queenstown, New Zealand, which is billed as "the Adventure Capital of the World."

Although Patty and I had talked for more than a year about bungee jumping, I had not purchased tickets in advance. "Are you sure you want to do this?" I asked Patty, just before handing over my credit card for the booking.

After a half-hour ride the next morning, we arrived at the world's first and most infamous bungee-jump site, Kawarau Bridge, in time to stand among the crowd of observers watching three other people fly successively off the bridge before us. Then it was our time to jump. I did not feel one bit fearless, while Patty wasn't at all hesitant. "I love you," she said over her shoulder, and off she flew with near perfect form. My greatest relief was seeing her bounce happily up and down a few times, and watching as she was lowered into a rubber-bottomed raft in the Kawarau River, 150 feet below.

Now it was my turn to show off for my wife and daughter, but climbing onto the jump stand above the railing reminded me of perhaps climbing up on a gallows. I waited four or five seconds but as a cold fear washed over me, decided that I had not flown 12,000 miles to show my wife and daughter that I was a coward. I did a rapid "Three, two, one, jump," and in no time at all the great elastic cord behind me was pulling against my legs, and just as I was about to become wet, the braided rubber cord yanked me ever so softly 100 or so feet back up into the air, almost under the arch in the great old bridge. The three big gentle bounces that followed were even more fun. It was fantastic. In fact, both Patty and I felt that it was the single most exciting thing we had ever done.

Extreme sports seem to rule on New Zealand's South Island. Notwithstanding numerous signs reminding visitors about the inherent risks, local sources gloss over reports of how many people "routinely" die in and around Queenstown engaging in various dangerous offerings. Our sixteen-passenger jet boat pushed every limit later that day, and in one case it cut off the sharp bend in the river by revving up its engine and hurtling entirely out of the water and across a broad sandy beach, two or three feet in the air. What felt like a rip-off as the three of us climbed into that boat turned out to be another thrilling lifetime memory. Patty and Joyce then took the third adventure ride of the day, running off a mountain ledge and hang-gliding with two highly trained guides who kept them riding the strong mountain wind currents for more than thirty minutes.

RETURNING TO MASSACHUSETTS, I found the interior cleanout and new construction in Beverly moving ahead nicely, *well before we owned the site.* The essence of the unusual deal we put together with Black & Decker allowed us to completely take over the property, including the right to negotiate and sign leases, and to begin any necessary or desired construction. All of this began January 2, 1996, four months before the actual transfer of the property title. The final sale of the property needed to wait until after Black & Decker concluded some dealings with its union, which still represented about twenty remaining Beverly maintenance and security workers. The amount of work we did without owning the property was almost bizarre, and something of a risk, but we were confident the deal would go forward, and we had an equitable agreement in place to unwind things in the event anything went seriously wrong.

But then, even as we closed in on actual ownership of

Black & Decker's treasurer, Dennis Adams, left, with Thomas Alperin and Jamie McKeown on October 26, 1995

this enduring piece of North Shore history in April 1996, we still had no idea what we would really do with it. One of our key staff attorneys, David Moynihan, began working with an outstanding Beverly planning official,

The final $500,000 purchase price was less than 1 percent of the original asking price.

Tina Cassidy, putting together what is known in Massachusetts as a tax increment financing agreement, or a TIF. The TIF obligated us to invest at least $13.5 million in the property, to create twenty new full-time jobs, and to refrain from seeking a tax abatement for the excessive real estate taxes, which were based on an imagined property value many times higher than what we actually paid. Years later when Mayor Michael Cahill took over the administration in Beverly, Dennis Clarke was pleased to introduce Ms. Cassidy to Woburn Mayor Scott Galvin, who brought her to Woburn City Hall in a similar management role.

Notwithstanding the size and complexity of the United Shoe property, the agreed broker's commission for the sale was 5 percent of the sales price—even though the final $500,000 purchase price was less than 1 percent of the original asking price—or a broker's bill of a mere $25,000. To our surprise, Black & Decker, on what its treasurer told me was a legal technicality, refused to pay Bob Cronin even this relatively paltry sum. In the end we paid the commission, just to avoid an awkward situation for all.

We completed all our commitments (along with oh-so-many other improvements beneficial to the community) in return for the city's providing us a substantial ten-year reduction on real estate taxes and making us and client firms eligible for some meaningful state benefits as well. With the TIF, we ultimately, and happily, invested $73 million, rather than the promised $13.5 million, to rehabilitate and greatly expand the dilapidated complex.

In addition to our runaway cash investment at The Shoe, Joyce and I personally donated $1 million to build a new teen center building for the Beverly YMCA; we also donated land on opposite ends of our new hundred-acre campus for a new elementary school and for the city's proposed new public safety headquarters. We even gave additional land needed to widen Route 62 and made $2 million of cash contributions to Beverly charities. Far more important, as I write this, we currently provide eighty well-paid full-time jobs at the former United Shoe site, and we have facilitated 5,400 new high-quality jobs provided by Cummings client firms. The impact in Beverly has been truly gigantic.

Jamie and Attorney Moynihan also negotiated a "covenant not to sue" with the Commonwealth, based on newly enacted legislation. Under the agreement, the state guaranteed it would never sue us for any additional environmental contamination found on the property following Black & Decker's cleanup. The covenant might not protect us from any possible federal or third-party claim, but we did have what we believed would be a reliable national firm (now Stanley Black & Decker) standing behind its cleanup of the property. Two decades later, Attorney Moynihan had joined New Hampshire's largest law firm, McLane Law, and was highly instrumental in McLane becoming one of our largest clients at TradeCenter 128 in Woburn.

CUMMINGS PROPERTIES' OFFICIAL arrival at 181 Elliott Street, Beverly, on January 2, 1996, was the start of a brand-new life for what had been widely proclaimed a useless relic of days long past. The former home of United Shoe was finally ready (once again) to become a major economic force on Boston's North Shore. As we were preparing for its return to life, no one, including us, knew where we were going. The $500,000 price to purchase the property, including its two ponds and 1.5 million square feet of solid concrete space, worked out to about eight cents per square foot for the land and the building. *Yes, a purchase price of just eight cents per square foot.*

Just finding our way around the immense facility was a task in itself, with its hundreds of secluded hallways, locked storage areas, and foreboding corners, not to mention the mammoth network of service tunnels carrying many miles of heavy copper cables, water mains, and steam pipes. Every so often, the dark, wet tunnels would open up into wide sepulchral rooms. They reminded me of the catacombs in Paris. We have yet to find much consistent use

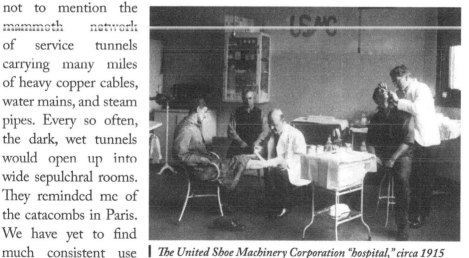

The United Shoe Machinery Corporation "hospital," circa 1915

for these underground spaces, but we are still hopeful that an entrepreneurial employee or client will come up with an imaginative use.

The money we paid up front to Black & Decker to remediate the site was well spent, especially given the large volume of oil in the ground. United Shoe mostly leased its shoe machines, and then as the machines aged, they were returned to the factory by customers from all over the world, either to be updated or scrapped. Routinely, we learned, the old machines were smashed with a large steel ball attached to a railroad crane car (which we also acquired) before being melted down in the on-site foundry. From all we could learn, there was little or no attempt to contain any of the lubricating oil from the machines. For decades, as the old machines were crushed up on the ground before being smelted in the foundry, the oil just "disappeared."

What would we do with this enormous decaying relic from America's golden age of manufacturing? United Shoe had been "the Microsoft of its day." Sixty-four years earlier, *Fortune* magazine had pronounced United Shoe Machinery Corporation "the bluest of blue chip investments." Indeed, the company had been a giant in its day, but by 1996 it was all but dissolved, with only the hulking remainder of its glory days haunting this historic seaside city. There was significant community interest in what we would do with The Shoe, just as there was within our own offices. We had no idea but were determined from the onset that we could not possibly demolish it, as some people thought was our hidden plan. Those people didn't really know us. We felt there was simply too much value in the fine old buildings to blast it all down. Instead, we just nibbled away, establishing footholds of activity. Someday we would connect the dots.

The *Boston Herald* noted our progress and our unique approach in an April 19, 1996, news story: "One major factor in the development of Cummings' business has been its vertically integrated approach, in which all phases of project development are carried out in-house. Recent Cummings coups have included the renovations of the 1.5-million-square-foot United Shoe Machinery Corp in Beverly, and the conversion of the 170,000-square-foot former Northeast TradeCenter in Woburn."

We worked diligently through the summer of 1996 creating well-organized, newly paved parking lots throughout the entire southern half of the campus. Landscaping was another major project. It included planting several hundred deciduous maple, birch, oak, and Bradford pear trees, plus thousands of shrubs of all sorts. Rather than planting maintenance-intensive grass lawns, we relied on hundreds of low shrubs, such as ground-clinging blue rug junipers, that require no sprinklers, little attention, and no bark mulch after a short time. The net effect would be a tidy and beautiful welcome for visitors to the new campus each spring.

Our crew also spent weeks that first summer clearing up the shorelines and dragging dozens of truckloads of junk and debris from the banks and waters of our on-site Upper and Lower Shoe Ponds. Undergrowth, junk, and brush had all but completely blocked any view of the now scenic ponds. We invested more and more to effect beneficial changes and received wide latitude in our extensive work. The relationship with a practical and highly supportive Beverly Conservation Commission at that time was truly outstanding, and we began an almost miraculous transformation.

Close to the concrete-core earthen dam that creates Upper Shoe Pond, an iconic yellow brick chimney towered over the gigantic complex. The corporate USMC initials were set in contrasting dark brown brick on the chimney sides. The 225-foot-tall radial brick structure had an interior diameter of twelve feet at its mouth, where the concrete top ring was seriously spalling following a hundred years of exposure to the elements. The chimney itself was not in any imminent danger of falling, but expensive repairs would have been required to keep it from occasionally (and quite dangerously) shedding small chunks onto the parking lot below, and we had no use for the impressive structure. The day we imploded it, a great carnival atmosphere prevailed, with hundreds of clients and local residents in attendance to witness this exciting highlight of the summer of 1996. In a few thundering instants, the historic USMC trademark no longer loomed over the property.

| *Implosion of The Shoe's 225-foot-tall chimney*

AT NO TIME with Cummings Center, as we would soon call the United Shoe property, did we even pause to consider creating a master plan to lay out in advance where we were going next; we just did it, as the company had done so many times before on so many important but much smaller reclamation projects. Similarly, we had no budget whatsoever for the massive undertaking that had the potential to transform the whole region. If banks or other lenders had been involved in financing, we most certainly would have needed exhaustive detailed plans and budgets, but this project, because of the ongoing environmental issues, would never in those days have been financeable in the first place.

If we had ever engaged any brand of outside architects or designers to accomplish a grand plan ahead of time, we could surely have spent tens of millions of dollars for their efforts, and we would have totally lost two building seasons. Soft costs for all of the pre-construction niceties would have killed us, just trying to figure out the hundred-acre complex.

We had purchased the property at a most propitious time. The great real estate recession was behind us, but the prices of essential materials such as steel, concrete, and drywall had not yet started to skyrocket. It was an exciting time. Anticipating the demand, we rebuilt four cavernous seventy-foot-high warehouse-type spaces, adding three new interstitial concrete floors within each space for another quarter-million square feet of floor space. Other buildings were so much refinished that they were all but unrecognizable. We also demolished more than 100,000 square feet of substandard original construction, which luckily was far from the norm in the otherwise solidly built complex.

We were off and running, and at this early stage it was already obvious to Jamie and everyone else that Cummings Center would become more than even he could have hoped, even though we had only just begun to realize the center's full potential. Following is Jamie's President's Corner feature from the July 1996 issue of our quarterly client newsletter:

What a change a year makes. In the now-rebounding real estate market, many businesses have begun to realize measurable growth and increased potential for future expansion.

Optimism abounds as our region enjoys a stronger economy and as the marketplace shows more willingness to take risks. In real estate, with the surplus of available space in the Boston area rapidly disappearing, future activity will depend mostly on the availability of new space to satisfy growing demand.

Building the first speculative office building in Boston in the past five years, Cummings Properties is forging ahead with this optimism. Our brand-new seven-story, first-class complex at 18 Commerce Way in Woburn represents the company's investment in the future and an overall significant indicator for today's burgeoning economy.

Additional substantial efforts are now being devoted toward the renovation of prime space at TradeCenter 128 (formerly Northeast Trade Center) in Woburn and at the giant new Cummings Center in Beverly. These two facilities combined will provide more than 2 million square feet of multiple-use space for diverse businesses of all sizes.

Providing key access and visibility, abundant on-site parking, nearby amenities and services, full-service leases, and attractive leasing rates, these properties afford ideal opportunities designed to meet the needs of business today.

J.L.M.

"How could they possibly ever fill it all?" was the common refrain around Beverly, but it was happening, and our neighbors were beginning to see it. We had not thought much about the impact our massive restoration would have, but for sure, home values were rising much faster in the Beverly area than in other metropolitan communities. Fortunately, the homes that were selling and the apartments being leased were mostly benefiting long time Beverly property owners, so the complaints about affordability and higher prices never caused too much concern.

By November 1996, businesses were clamoring for space, not only at Cummings Center in Beverly, but also in all the company's other Greater Boston communities. The Cummings Center staff was moving in new clients faster than we ever imagined. Soon, we had seventy newly hired employees of our own in Beverly, just twenty miles away from Woburn. These new colleagues focused exclusively on building and marketing Cummings Center. There were also dozens of mostly small subcontractors helping us complete the total makeover of this giant complex that Jamie had envisioned from the first day he visited the site. At one time, we had *eleven* local electrical contractors working on diverse projects in Beverly, along with eight or nine of our own in-house electricians.

REAL ESTATE developers are sometimes, and sometimes deservedly, maligned for their callous disregard of history. But to fast-forward for a bit, one of the things that makes me most proud about Cummings Center is that people strolling through the hallways of today's sparkling office-and-research park can relive so much of the history of United Shoe Machinery Corporation, one of the true titans of twentieth-century industrial capitalism. Visiting the mammoth engineering marvel that was, at its birth in

Beverly Historical Society

Constructed in 1642, this tidal gristmill was in continuous operation at what is now Cummings Center until 1894

1905, the largest factory in the world, they can see dozens of modern glass display cases filled with memorabilia and mementos from a bygone era of industrial goodwill and plenty.

Before United Shoe assembled its Beverly campus in 1902 and 1903, most of the land, except for the mill site, had been used exclusively for farming. According to area historians, however, part of this historic industrial site is one of the oldest continuously used commercial properties in North America. The city clerk in Salem, Massachusetts, Deborah Berkinshaw, in response to in-house counsel David Moynihan, provided information about the fascinating history of our Beverly site. She sent David certified copies of many old, exquisitely handwritten Salem city records (the land was originally part of Salem), including evidence of a permit for Friend's Mill that was issued "about 1642," she wrote, though the city no longer had the complete record for that period. "The absence of many written records for that decade does not mean that government was suspended or that the construction did not then happen," she clarified in her letter to David.

Dating back to the construction of John Friend's tidal gristmill in the 1640s, what later became the property of United Shoe originally straddled a branch of the Bass River, before the first dam was constructed in the mid-seventeenth century. A second much higher concrete-core dam and a new tidal weir were constructed farther upstream near the center of the campus around 1900 to create Upper Shoe Pond and Lower Shoe Pond. Before the mill was constructed, this inlet was the documented landing area for farmers who traveled back and forth across the Bass River on tiny ferryboats from near the center of Salem. Old Salem records document the ferry service to and from Planters Landing on our property. The ferry service was closely regulated by Salem officials for public safety reasons, even back in the 1640s.

The most prominent of several historic markers identifying the area of Planters Landing is an almost 100-year-old bronze plaque now located on the front lawn of Elliott Landing Condominium, which we opened on the site in November 2016 and which was fully sold (or under agreement) by August 2017. I have sometimes imagined my eight-times-great grandfather, Isaac Cummings, landing in Salem in 1638 and perhaps traveling through this area on Planters Path, before he settled in Ipswich.

At about this same time, in 1643, John Friend's original tidal-powered gristmill was constructed directly on what is now the condominium property (but still closely connected to Cummings Center.) The mill continuously operated there, and then about 200 feet south of Elliott Landing, until the second location burned down around 1889. Dried corn was routinely shipped to Friend's Mill from Long Island, New York, and Newport, Rhode Island. The same ships then carried cargoes of corn meal and dried fish from Beverly to New York City. After the fire, the dock from the gristmill was used in connection with a small foundry, maintaining the continuum of commercial uses until the parcel was purchased by United Shoe around 1902. The submerged wooden piles of the last dock are still readily visible in the river bottom today, at low tide.

SINCE THE EARLIEST days of the company, our leadership team has held Monday night dinner meetings. Monday, November 11, 1996, was no exception; that night we were reviewing a brand-new set of third-quarter operating figures. Our focus then, as now, was on occupancy levels and monthly lease income, rather than net profits, which we simply never track. Our mantra has always been, "If we keep the buildings occupied, the profits will be there," and they always were. The foregoing statement may sound strange to many, but having no outside stockholders to satisfy, we found that it was and is absolutely true.

Everything I did as an entrepreneur has always been so simple and basic. By 1996, when we took over The Shoe property, a dozen great internet firms were bursting forth and beginning to change the entire world. We talked about how exciting it must have been for the whole generation of new computer and electronics entrepreneurs who were coming to the fore then, but no more exciting than it was for us with a real estate boom that defied our imaginations. Our real estate equity just sizzled, and the whole industry in the Northeast was on a roll, unlike anything experienced since the boom years following World War II.

We were also discussing our overall organization's recent much deeper involvement in financial equities investments with Advest under David Leland. Advest would later be acquired by Merrill Lynch, in May 2005, when the account still held only a small fraction of the value to which its assets would later grow.

But the big news this night was that our vacancy factor, calculated to include all buildings in service for more than six months, was under 3 percent for the first time ever. No one was happier to hear this than Jamie, because with my having worked almost totally at Cummings Center for the previous six months, these sparkling leasing figures from Woburn clearly reflected his strong leadership.

❀ *How to create business plans and budgets is surely considered an important aspect of an entrepreneur's education. Interestingly, I have never created either of these "essential" documents. As with our purchase of The Shoe, we have—in all cases— opted to use the time and effort normally required for such planning and put it instead into actually getting started. Although often not possible when a third-party investor is involved, this practice is one of the great benefits of self-financing.*

[13]

The Darkest Days

THE MORNING OF November 13, 1996, at first seemed especially bright and brisk. That was the day we were paving large areas of some of the most visible new parking lots at Cummings Center in preparation for winter. Major excavations for drainage and utility improvements had been underway all summer, and although our construction work goes on reliably year-round, asphalt paving always seems to signal the end of our Boston-area excavation projects until spring.

I was standing that morning exactly where Friend's Grist Mill once stood, near the southwest corner of the new Beverly campus. I had arrived early to be there when the contractor's crew started spreading and rolling out the new surface over the last of the original parking areas being repaved. I took in all I could get of the scent of hot asphalt—such a good smell at the end of another building season. That's when my cell phone began vibrating.

In a heartbeat—that was a phrase Jamie often used to describe how quickly life can change. I thought about that a few minutes later, as I was trying to process this call. It was from Jamie and Denise's next-door neighbor. She tried to remain composed as she told me that Jamie had just been taken from his home to Winchester Hospital after an apparent heart attack. "He was moaning some, but was not otherwise responsive," she said. "You need to come back now." She clearly conveyed the gravity of the situation.

The southbound morning rush-hour traffic leaving Beverly on Route 128 can be slow, but not on this day, and my drive to the Winchester Hospital emergency room was largely unimpeded. Once I arrived at the hospital, the ER desk attendant immediately recognized me. As she walked me into the ER, she told me the worst personal news.

Denise was waiting in a side room with one of her close friends. Both appeared to be in shock. Denise and I embraced for a long time. "Tell me what's happened, Den."

"He is gone," she said. "They did open-heart massage and everything they could, but he is gone."

Twenty minutes after my arrival at the hospital, Jamie's sister, Debbie Laudano, arrived. I knew Debbie well and was closest to the door when she came in. Her heart pounded as she clung to me, hoping that everything was somehow going to be okay. "How can this be?" Debbie said, sobbing, after learning there was nothing more anyone could do. "He was only forty-one." (Jamie's parents experienced their second terrible tragedy when Debbie died from cancer several years later.)

After another hour or so, one of the nurses told us that the last two doctors had left, and that Jamie had been cleaned, if someone wished to go in to see him. Denise did not want to see Jamie in the hospital, but the nurse escorted me to where he was. After asking me to confirm his identity, she stepped outside.

I could barely kneel beside him. *Come back, Jamie, come back!*—a silent scream stuck in my throat. I tried to comprehend the enormity of what had happened. I first held his arm and then his hand. There was no mistaking the significance of his already cold fingers.

WE ALL LEFT the hospital shortly before noon, and I headed directly to our nearby office at 200 West Cummings Park and asked everyone to gather in the leasing department, directly outside Jamie's and my offices. Staff had just started to hear that "Jamie is in the hospital," but no one knew the extent of the situation.

The large open area was packed. My message was brief, and halting, to be sure: "I have the awful duty to tell you that Jamie suffered a heart attack this morning. He managed to complete his usual morning run, and he made it home. Denise thought she had heard him calling and found him just inside their rear entrance. Winchester EMTs responded quickly, but an hour or so later, at 8:40 AM, he was pronounced dead at Winchester Hospital."

There was a dreadful groan from the sixty or so friends and colleagues and an outburst of the rawest of emotions.

Doug Stephens was one of the first to react. As we retreated toward my office, he followed closely behind. "I had them lower all the flags," he said, referring to the dozen or so American flags we flew in prominent locations. We both wiped away tears. Everyone wiped away tears.

The Woburn office, where so many considered Jamie a good friend as well as an admired colleague, was in a state of stunned disbelief following my announcement. But soon the leadership team, spearheaded by Mike Pascavage, Doug, and Dennis, began sorting out what had to be done, such as notifying all staff members, clients, and other key relationships of Jamie's sudden passing. Dennis later told me they felt they were honoring Jamie by doing what needed to be done, in just the manner that Jamie would've expected them to do it, on this challenging and heartbreaking November day.

Joyce was at our Florida condo spending a few days with two of her golfing friends but was unreachable during my twenty-minute drive to the hospital from Beverly. I tried again after the staff meeting and then repeatedly for the next several hours, until we finally connected late in the afternoon. It was a doubly emotional call—I needed her by my side so, so much. Joyce was on a plane early the next morning.

Losing Jamie was more terrible than anything I could have imagined. He had been so much more than a good friend and colleague. Jamie had become a best friend to me and to our whole family, but he was also my successor. We had worked so closely and developed such an extraordinary bond, as I taught him everything over nearly eighteen years. My stomach ached for months with an unshakable agony. And how sad we all felt for Denise and for their young daughters, Molly and Kelly; for Jamie's parents, Connie and Leonard McKeown; and for Debbie and the rest of Jamie's devastated family.

JAMIE'S DEATH WAS covered on the front pages of the Woburn and Winchester newspapers, and as a news story in *The Boston Globe*. The *Winchester Star* reported that more than 2,000 people attended his wake, which continued until well after 11 PM. We were all surprised and deeply touched that honor guards from the *Woburn* Police Department arrived unexpectedly and stood at either side of the Winchester funeral home entrance for almost the entire time. During that evening, Jamie's dad left the funeral home twice when he heard how long the line still was. We later learned that he went to the far end of that line on his own to greet visitors he didn't know, introducing himself and thanking them for coming.

Woburn police motorcycle officers returned the next morning to again honor Jamie by assisting Winchester police in escorting the procession from the funeral home to the church. Three priests presided over his Mass of Christian Burial at St. Eulalia Church, in Winchester. Twenty-four members of the adult choir also surprised us with their gracious presence.

That Saturday morning I delivered the single most important talk of my life. I don't know if it was my prayers beforehand or Joyce standing closely by my side in the pulpit that allowed me to hold myself together through all but the last few words:

Dear Friends,

We came together today in this tremendous outpouring from all over Massachusetts, and from many other states as well, to honor in a singular way one of the finest people ever to live in this community. We came to celebrate Jamie McKeown's life, even though it is hard to even use the word "celebrate" when we feel such an immense sense of tragedy at his passing.

When Denise sat down with Jamie's parents Thursday and selected the hymns in this musical service, they selected those hymns because of their relevance to Jamie, or to their lives together. And as we sing most of these hymns today, we are praying with them.

No person in this church has a better sense of right and wrong than Jamie did, and no man I have ever met cared more about doing "the right thing." Earning the respect of his peers was an overriding tenet of Jamie's being.

Jamie didn't do anything to excess. He loved to run, and ski, and play tennis, and golf and swim, and he did them all well, but each had its limited place—except when he could do them with his family.

How often did Jamie ever get angry? Let me ask you—how many people in this congregation ever saw Jamie get angry, even once? He didn't get peeved or vexed at little things either, and he never pouted, or was snide, or called people names, or even implied them.

Jamie didn't preach, but he led by example. Most of Jamie's friends are better people because of him and because they wanted to earn his approval. I am certainly a better person because of him.

Jamie left us suddenly, but he left with no wrongs uncorrected. He had no fear or premonition of death, but he lived each day as though it could be his last.

We come here today from many Christian traditions, and certainly from other religions as well, but we all celebrate hope, and we celebrate God's boundless love for all. The Lord our God is one, and we know that Jamie is with Him now.

As many of you are aware, Jamie was a private person. He didn't know how to gossip or brag. He was a winner who didn't even think about it, he just did it. Quiet success was his way of life.

Jamie was a wonderful father, son, colleague, brother, and uncle, but Denise always told everyone that he was the best husband who ever lived. How many of his close friends didn't hear, at least once in a while, that our own wives wouldn't mind our "acting a little more like Jamie"? I certainly did.

Twelve years ago, while standing in the front entranceway of Winchester Country Club, just two nights before he was married, Jamie and I had a great talk: "There is nothing I won't do for the rest of my life to try to make Denise happy." He didn't just say that to me, however; he said it as though he was making a promise. We all know that he kept that promise.

When Kelly and Molly came along, Jamie then became the best father any man could be. He learned well from his own great parents, and from many of you, I'm sure.

Watching Jamie for over two decades, and closely working with him for more than seventeen years, I have had the truly unique pleasure of seeing him and knowing him all the way from Woburn Boys "Clubber" to seasoned corporate executive.

I told Jamie many times over the years how proud I was of him and all he had become... I only wish I could have told him, also, how much I loved him.

W.S.C.
11/16/96

NOTHING COULD HAVE prepared me to deal with the shock of Jamie's sudden death. He was a picture of health, and fitness was always on his mind. He exercised almost every day, whether by going on a long run, playing tennis, or putting in an early morning session at Woburn's North Suburban YMCA. Staff at the Y a decade earlier honored him with a specially painted reserved locker in recognition of many things he had personally done to help the YMCA.

From November 13 through most of the next year, there was hardly a single day that I did not feel, at some point, shaken and depressed. I had never been one to reach for drink in times of stress, but just in case, I totally gave up all alcohol for many months.

In the story of this terrible tragedy, it was while doing something Jamie truly loved that his journey on this earth simply ended.

ALTHOUGH JAMIE MADE it home from his morning run that day, I learned many years later that a mutual acquaintance had noticed him earlier that fateful Wednesday morning sitting against a wall along Bacon Street in Winchester as the friend drove by. There was nothing alarming about Jamie's appearance, he told me, but it still seemed odd to see him resting. In hindsight, Jamie must have been in real trouble then. That was shortly before he would have crossed Route 3 and headed up Fernway to be with his family, in the home they had recently built just below the corner of Fernway and Arlington Street.

Jamie was hopeful that he might someday earn a place in Hawaii's Ironman Triathlon, but in the meantime, he said, the Boston Marathon would have to do. His times were not elite, but as his 1996 finish had been better than his previous race, he was hopeful that his 1997 results might be better still. Instead, a fatal heart attack at forty-one years of age ended his life. Every friend he had was saddened. The town was shocked. I was alternatively stricken and devastated.

I could only think how much Jamie had been the future of the company, especially after our own children had made it clear that they did not want careers in real estate. I had known Jamie well for twenty years, and he had reached the point of doing most things he took on either every bit as well as I did them, or better. Together, however, we had been extremely effective in a mutually gratifying relationship.

For several years prior to Jamie's death, my principal interest had increasingly been in solidifying the long-term succession plan, and it had so thoroughly come together. Jamie had progressed so well and was everything I could possibly have hoped for in my successor. Not only was he my successor as president, he would also have been the next chairman before he was fifty. We had talked about it—about my stepping aside. It was too soon then, but we both had presumed by then that Dennis Clarke would move into the presidency when Jamie moved up to chairman, but what now? I fully expected to still be working, only it would have been full-time with Cummings Foundation.

Now, how would I—*we*—ever get through this situation? I knew we would deal with it, somehow. Working with an extraordinary team of colleagues at Cummings Properties, we resolved thousands of situations in our day-to-day activities, usually quite effectively. We almost always achieved good and fair results. But how profoundly I agonized. Losing Jamie was a problem for which there simply was no solution for me.

❀ *Whether due to death, changing market tides, new technology, or myriad other factors, life can change in an instant. To the extent possible, entrepreneurs must prepare themselves for a business' inevitable ups and downs by thinking through a "plan B." Business leaders must be nimble, and they must almost always be ready to adapt to changing circumstances.*

❀ *Creativity is more instinctive than it is learned, and may have little to do with "intellectual intelligence." It is much more a product of how a person thinks about things than it is about what he or she knows, and may be fostered by a liberal education. Infinite curiosity about how things work will be a strong harbinger for creativity.*

❀ *Investors must know all that they can, and must feel good about any investment before committing to it. The best investments, however, will rarely be the ones which everyone else feels good about, too. The smartest investors will make their independent judgments and have the confidence to seize whatever opportunities are available. Feelings and intuition will so often be far more important than calculations. The former United Shoe property required copious intuition.*

A Hole in the World

THE DAYS following the funeral, in November 1996, were grim for everyone who knew and cared for Jamie. We were all particularly concerned for Denise, whose emotional burden included not only her own overwhelming grief but also that of Kelly and Molly. Community support was everywhere, however, and Denise still had her parents close by. They brought enormous personal assistance through the most difficult years. Jamie had provided well for them financially, but there was no easy way to move beyond their collective grief.

Twenty years later, as I was working on this book, I asked Denise to share a few of her thoughts about Jamie. He was loved and respected by so many people, but most really only knew him as a leading business and civic figure. To honor Jamie appropriately here, and at the suggestion of author Bill Novac, I asked Denise to tell about him the way she knew him—as her husband, her soulmate, a father, a man:

> *Bill asked me to write a little something to further describe what Jamie was like in everyday life, besides what he was like at Cummings Properties. Family was so important to Jamie. The memory that really pulls at my*

heart is what an amazing father he was. Jamie was such an avid reader and really believed his children should be too. He was ever the schoolteacher he once aspired to be—so much so that he started reading to Kelly and Molly when they were days old. I remember hearing him reading aloud one day, and I went into the room to see our one-month-old baby lying in his arms while he read Time magazine out loud to her. I laughed and said, 'I don't think she gets it.' But she did. Both the girls must have turned out to have such a love of reading because of all that reading in the beginning. We always had to end the night with a story in bed, or no one would go to sleep. They loved reading and snuggling with their dad. To this day, they are both big readers. It was such a beautiful thing to watch and one of my fondest memories.

Spending time with me and our daughters was always a priority for Jamie. Late-night meetings for work and all the organizations that he volunteered for prevented us from having family time many evenings, but Jamie would balance those nights away with his dedication to us on weekends. On the weekends, he was 100 percent ours. We did things every Saturday and Sunday together as a family. I would steal him away on Saturday nights for our date night. It was important to me that we had a night to ourselves. I'm so glad I did that. We did that almost every Saturday until the weekend just preceding his death, and I shall be forever grateful.

The weekends were always such fun family outings. We always had a fun thing to do with the kids. Whether it be a swim, a bike ride, apple picking, museums, whatever, it was always about the girls. If Jamie wanted to do something for himself such as golf or workout, he would do it early in the morning before the kids woke up, and he would be back in time to be there when they did. They would wake up on Saturdays, get out of bed, go to the railing to look downstairs, and then start yelling, "Daddy, Daddy, come get us." They loved the weekends because they knew Daddy was around all the time to be their playmate. Somehow, I got forgotten, and he was the King. That's okay. I so thoroughly enjoyed it.

Jamie was a lover of sports. Not watching, but doing. He loved to bike and swim, and he ran almost every day. He was so healthy in his eating that his idea of a treat was an apple because it was sweet. He tried to instill these habits in his children. Even as toddlers, our girls went on the back of bikes for bike rides, or in jogging strollers to go for runs with Jamie. We taught them to ski at two years old. It was so important to him that his girls were active with him. He loved to take them swimming, sailing, canoeing. Anything that was moving. He used to be a swim instructor at the Woburn Boys & Girls Club, and he brought our daughters into the pool there at eight months old. Because of all this effort on Jamie's part, the girls were exposed to so many different activities, which they still enjoy as adults.

It is so sad they lost all of that so early, but he made a lifetime of love in the years they had him. That was the thing about Jamie. He lived his life to the fullest. I am grateful now that he was the way he was. We got so much time from him in his short years of fatherhood. The girls were six and eight when Jamie died, but they have memories as if he were here much longer. That comes from his dedication to them and to spending time with them. We have a lifetime of memories.

Jamie loved every day he lived—with his family, with his friends, with his coworkers. Who gets to go to bed every night knowing he did everything just the way he would have wanted that day, with no regrets? Jamie did.

D.P.M.

AFTER JAMIE'S SERVICES, several people commented to me that preparing and delivering the eulogy must have been extraordinarily challenging, and it was. But it was also part of the healing. Our youngest daughter, Patty, who is now a psychologist practicing in California, recently read my notes for this chapter and wrote to me: "I don't know if you want to add it, but I so clearly recall you struggling on the last few words of that eulogy, with Mom closely at your arm." My remembering Jamie that morning on behalf of so many people to whom he meant so much was cathartic to me, and was an essential element of the respect I owed him.

Looking back, my single most difficult task after leaving Winchester Hospital on November 13 was calling all our mutual friends and colleagues together at the office that dreadful morning. My announcement of Jamie's sudden death absolutely stunned the close-knit group. It felt so unfair and unnatural that someone so young and active and fit could so suddenly become only a cherished memory.

After a few months things were better for a while. But then, during the spring of 1997, I began feeling terrible again while trying my damnedest not to let it show. Some days it was extremely hard to focus. There were times when I just had to be alone, and I would drive to some secluded place to walk and think. For nearly all of the seventeen-plus years we worked together, I was teaching and mentoring him, and then we were clearly teaching each other. The loss of his presence was devastating to me, in so many ways.

The emotion was deeper than anything I could ever have imagined experiencing. Unlike the quiet grief upon losing my much-loved parents in 1986 and 1992, and later my sister, Jamie's death moved me to tears so many times. Patty also reminded me of something that Joyce mentioned to Patty at the time: The only thing that could have hurt me more would have been if something terrible had happened to Joyce or to one of our kids.

Despite my emotions over the loss of Jamie, it never occurred to me to seek professional help. I chose not to share much of what was happening, even though talk therapy or medication might have helped me get through the heartache more easily. After many times encouraging business colleagues and others to take advantage of professional counseling to help them through troubling issues, I did not do that in my own case.

The National Institutes of Health website was helpful regarding symptoms of depression, but they just did not fit me. I decided that grief was my problem, with symptoms of sadness certainly—and, in my case, a sense of profound loss. Never feeling hopeless or helpless or in any way incapable of coping with my responsibilities, I clearly did sometimes reveal my sorrow. Those symptoms would and did slowly pass.

Kevin Cummings

| *The main entrance drive into the 2-million-square-foot Cummings Center*

EVEN THOUGH WE were all weighed down with sorrow as we managed our way into 1997, Cummings Properties started gradually recovering its equilibrium—as we knew we had to do. It was helpful that we were all so busy. We carried into the new year the momentum of greatly increased leasing activity from 1996, and our commercial real estate leasing started off strong and remained that way through 1997 and beyond, especially as demand for biotech space was increasingly overflowing out of a greatly overheated Cambridge market. Office colleagues commented several times how much Jamie would have enjoyed this furiously busy period. I thought the same thing as business truly boomed. Each day was exciting and busy, but surely, nothing was the same.

Cummings Center continued to move forward with a mounting volume of activity. Construction costs were piling up more quickly than we ever imagined. "Just like Boston's Big Dig," we joked. But the more we invested to transform that historic complex into a fully restored, first-class business center, the more clients we signed up. Early on, we attracted biotech, medtech, and pharmaceutical start-ups, and Beverly Hospital opened our first walk-in medical clinic there. Many of these new Cummings Center clients became quickly connected to the large and talented North Shore labor pool, and their employees were happier for it. Hundreds of Beverly-area workers no longer had to make the difficult rush-hour trek into Cambridge and Boston, or to the increasingly crowded areas of Burlington, or to the now famous rush-hour gridlock anywhere near Waltham.

We also started signing up dozens of independent medical practices. Area physicians needed a first-class central location to colonize near Beverly Hospital, and the growing reality of significant referral opportunities in Cummings Center became a major draw for an ever-widening base of medical specialties.

We were immediately earning new income from the improvements, and we continued investing more and more. Many of the expenditures generated substantial tax savings, including some major federal abandoned-building tax credits, as the buildings were built before 1934 and had been all but abandoned. Beverly provided us with a unique project on which to spend opportunistically. As a result, we improved and upgraded this vast complex far beyond anything we had imagined. By the end of 2010, we had invested—with no regrets—more than $73 million to improve our half-million-dollar Beverly complex.

UNRELATED TO ANYTHING else, in May 1997 I happily exercised my most enjoyable perk as a trustee at Tufts University. I had attended many Tufts graduations by that time, but this was the best one by far because both our daughters were graduating and I was able to present their degrees. Marilyn graduated from Tufts University School of Medicine while, at about the same time, Patty received her undergraduate degree and conducted the

Bill at Tufts graduation with daughters Marilyn and Patricia

university band. There was a big logistical shuffle for Joyce and me to travel between the ceremonies, but it worked out and was certainly lots of fun.

People can become overwhelmed when good and bad things coincide in their lives, and may feel that they are not grieving properly. But despite Jamie's passing, I was quite able to take in and enjoy the many good things going on in our lives. They were slowly pulling me back to a good place. It was probably close to a year, however, before I stopped feeling a physical ache whenever my thoughts dwelled on Jamie. I credit the marvelous support I received from Joyce and our family as well as from so many colleagues and friends who were universally helpful and supportive.

Coinciding with the first anniversary of Jamie's death, I received a beautifully written anonymous letter from which I have several times directly borrowed when writing to friends and colleagues who are grieving. Instead of advising me to try putting Jamie out of my mind, the letter writer urged me to talk about him often to help preserve the memories. The writer quoted the long-passed German theologian Dietrich Bonhoeffer, who wrote that the loss of people we love creates enormous gaps, but as long as the gaps remain unfilled they preserve bonds between us. "God doesn't fill them, but on the contrary, keeps them empty," he wrote, "and so helps us to keep alive our communion with each other, even at the cost of pain."

The letter gave new meaning to the concept of how much it often helps when people can talk things out. That, of course, is the essence of counseling and therapy, and I was surprised by how much it helped when so many friends, some of whom barely knew Jamie, came by our office over the many months following his funeral. Each time I talked with someone who knew how close we were and recognized how deeply we all missed him, it was uplifting—and that is true even today, more than twenty-two years later.

Although Joyce and I had formed Cummings Foundation ten years before Jamie died, his death was a stark reminder to me that if we were to do meaningful good things, together with the foundation, we really needed to get started. I made fundamental commitments to myself to strengthen the company's executive team, and soon began reassigning more of Jamie's former responsibilities to other members, rather than back to myself.

Jamie and I, but especially Jamie, had already been actively mentoring Dennis. It was so fortuitous that he prevailed in January 1996 when he pushed me repeatedly to make sure that he would be the one who would work most closely with Dennis. Jamie also longed to be in Beverly during the colossal effort there, but he wanted more to coach Dennis in Woburn. We had fully concurred about Dennis' potential just months after Dennis joined us through our *Woburn Advocate* team in June 1992. Jamie readily agreed with me then that Dennis should be groomed for the company's top spot.

During Dennis' year away with Fidelity in 1995, and then with Jamie through most of 1996, he had continued to grow his executive skills. But he had not yet picked up enough to take over Jamie's post when Jamie passed. Nor had there been enough of an opportunity for him to show others in the firm the considerable executive talent that he was rapidly developing. That last issue, it seemed, was especially critical, and Dennis fully realized that his work would be easier in the long run if he did not arouse feelings of resentment among his colleagues.

There had never been even a single moment when I ever thought about hiring anyone from outside the firm. We had several possible successors to Jamie in-house, if one were needed quickly, the most prominent of whom was Mike Pascavage. But after much soul-searching, I decided to wait before taking any steps to directly fill Jamie's position. Jamie would always be my successor and our second president, of course, but here I was now succeeding him.

FRED WILBUR TOOK over more of the management of the Cummings Center construction effort, capably assisted by Bruce Oveson, our newly hired staff architect there. Bruce worked only in Beverly, supervising details to accompany the larger plans produced in our main design headquarters in Woburn. He and several on-site designers in Beverly produced plans for individual fit-ups for smaller prospective tenants, as well as the more detailed plans needed for individual building permits for new clients as they quickly moved in. An important hallmark of our overall approach has been our ability from the company's earliest days to produce and focus on expediting the all-in-house design and paperwork to facilitate prompt, easy leases. That vertical integration was growing rapidly.

> *"The single most important, and generally unrecognized, concrete landmark in this country."*
>
> Ada Louise Huxtable

I have long been a strong champion of our in-house design, but some people and organizations just do not get it. From my earliest active trustee involvement in construction affairs at Tufts, I strongly advocated in favor of the university's hiring on-campus architecture and design professionals. Instead, to this day a constant progression of costly outside architects, designers, and engineers bill Tufts for the vast majority of even its smallest construction and maintenance needs. Universities, in my mind, do not need elite "figurehead" architects; strong on-campus design teams can do so much of the routine work themselves, at a small fraction of the cost.

My viewpoint was vindicated, and then some, in early October of 1997, when *The Wall Street Journal* ran a major feature story on Cummings Center written by its Pulitzer Prize–winning architecture critic Ada Louise Huxtable. We greatly benefited from her abundant praise of Cummings Center, which she described as "the single most important, and generally unrecognized, concrete landmark in this country"—and she raved about our transformation of the property.

Before Ms. Huxtable first called us about writing a feature story, I frankly did not know who she was. When I told Bruce, our new Cummings Center architect, that Ms. Huxtable would be writing an article on all of our Beverly reconstruction, I asked him to tell me about her. Bruce was beside himself. "Bill," he said, "I was *weaned* on Ada Louise Huxtable in architecture school. *Everyone* knows Ada Louise." The winner of the first Pulitzer Prize for Distinguished Criticism, Ada Louise Huxtable was also a recipient of MacArthur and Guggenheim fellowships, and she wrote ten books.

Ada Louise spent a full day with me in August 1997, touring every corner of Cummings Center as part of her research for the article and was in touch for later follow-up. At the time, she was almost fully recovered from a recent hip surgery but was still a little concerned about not overdoing the tour. We resolved that situation nicely, using a golf cart to tour the perimeter of the buildings, our two large ponds, and then the main building itself, where the interior rebuilding was about 80 percent complete. We easily maneuvered

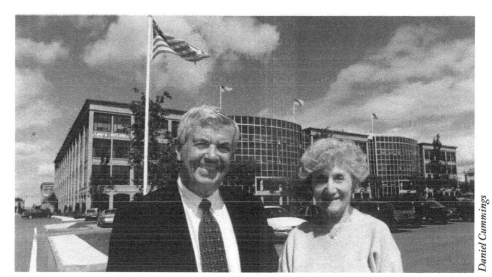

Daniel Cummings

| *Bill Cummings and Pulitzer Prize–winning author Ada Louise Huxtable at Cummings Center, August 1997. "Cummings Center is more than a success story; it is a dream come true"*

the vehicle down the entire length of the wide, quarter-mile-long carpeted main hallways.

During our day together, I learned that this celebrated author and preservationist had earlier written about The Shoe in five different decades—in at least two of her books and in both *The New York Times* and *The Wall Street Journal*. The most prominent architecture critic in the country was delighted that someone was finally making a serious effort to reclaim what she called her "favorite old American building." She had come to know and love The Shoe through the many summers she spent in Marblehead, only a few miles from Cummings Center, and she was highly pleased that we were "getting it right" with the aesthetics that she referred to as "the fourth dimension of architecture."

We all so much appreciated Ms. Huxtable's glowing architectural recognition in the *Journal*. Once again, our entire design and construction teams had distinguished themselves with their dexterity,

> *"Cummings Center is more than a success story; it is a dream come true."*
>
> *Ada Louise Huxtable*

blasting away many layers of grit and destruction, and completely transforming The Shoe. The Huxtable Leisure and Arts feature gave us the most meaningful media coverage we have ever enjoyed: "The Shoe is now Cummings Center," she wrote, "saved, restored and transformed, shrewdly and sympathetically, into nearly 1.4 million square feet of handsome commercial space for business and industry." (Today, Cummings Center contains 2 million square feet.)

We were delighted with the piece and flattered by her effusive comments. She wrote of this pioneering reinforced concrete structure endearingly: "It is a building of outstanding utilitarian beauty. Its stunning glass-walled simplicity, the pleasing proportions based on its structural system, foreshadows the later modular designs of Mies van der Rohe, and one of the basic aesthetic principles of structure to style." She concluded her feature by calling our work "a miraculous rebirth" of The Shoe. "For those who prize an architecture still invisible to many and treated as expendable by most," she wrote, "Cummings Center is more than a success story; it is a dream come true."

Over the next several years, Joyce and I came to know Ada Louise Huxtable fairly well. The summer following the feature article, we were delighted to join her for tea in her charming long-term summer home in Marblehead. She was such a dedicated and fascinating woman and a captivating conversationalist. Another time, we visited her in her winter home at 969 Park Avenue, New York City, accompanied by our daughter Marilyn. I remember Ada Louise being so interested in everything she could learn from Marilyn's opinions about how architectural changes might better accommodate changes in healthcare delivery in New York.

Joyce and I were later pleased to establish a fellowship in honor of Ms. Huxtable at Boston Architectural College, "to pay tribute to Ada Louise's most memorable design leadership career." Subsequently, following a brief note, Ada Louise called to tell us how incredibly moved she

Beverly elementary school students tour Cummings Center, 1999

was by this unexpected tribute. She also reiterated her personal thanks for "so carefully respecting the aesthetics of her forever favorite building" and she again reminded us how important it is to recognize aesthetics as the fourth dimension of architecture.

JAMIE WOULD HAVE been so proud—not just of Ada Louise Huxtable's high praise, but even more so of what Cummings Center has become. Today, the complex is home to more than 700 separate organizations, ranging from traditional business offices to cutting-edge research and technology firms, physicians, dentists, personal services, and even a church. Once again, the entire site is bustling with activity—a vibrant economic engine for Boston's entire North Shore.

With all these tenants, Cummings Center offers an extraordinary array of conveniences at its bustling campus. In addition to the two full-service banks, there are several restaurants, a full-size Merrill Lynch branch, and the sparkling Beverly Athletic Club. Dozens of attorneys and accountants have located within the complex, along with numerous other business and personal amenities, including hair stylists for men and women, a sundry shop, two childcare centers, a U.S. Post Office, a veterinary center, and even a separate doggie daycare. In addition, there is a busy surgical-care center and an outstanding fifteen-bed in-patient rehabilitation hospital.

These key factors, and the center's proximity to nearby Beverly Hospital and North Shore Medical Center in Salem, have been particularly important in attracting the large number of medical, dental, social-service, and other health and wellness practices. In 2017, Cummings Center's vice president and general manager, Steve Drohosky, estimated that we now have more than 200 physicians, dentists, surgeons, psychiatrists, therapists, and wellness practitioners operating daily at Cummings Center.

Each of the four corners of the Cummings Center site now has its own large, multilevel covered parking garage. From two to four stories high, each one is equipped with a major solar-energy system. The northwest parking deck alone, adjacent to 500 Cummings Center, boasts more than 1,700 solar panels. Altogether, the four parking-garage systems include nearly 5,300 solar panels, producing nearly 1.8 million kWh per year of clean electrical energy. With the tax credits and the direct income, the systems were all fully paid off within five years. The "roofs," constructed separately after the garages were built and in use, qualified as solar support structures for substantially better tax treatment.

Irrespective of anyone's concept of global warming, it is an incontrovertible truth that there are finite amounts of fossil fuels, and these are already becoming steadily more difficult to access and harvest. Without new subsidies to offset some of the long-embedded subsidies in effect for fossil fuels and nuclear fuel, it is still difficult to make solar cost-effective in many instances. Solar, wind, and water-source energy are in most cases still more expensive than conventional power, but with greater usage and technological improvements, they are quickly becoming more affordable. And there is enormously greater potential to further reduce our dependency on fossil fuel–produced electricity.

The Shoe's four original concrete buildings work perfectly with our brand-new 500 Cummings Center, an office building we constructed in the northwest quadrant of the campus to provide additional space as we approached capacity in the original Cummings Center buildings. Moving ahead with this 300,000-square-foot structure before we had a need for it proved to be a costly error when the city surprised us by taxing the building based on its cost rather than its rental income. We paid a half-million dollars more than we anticipated when that structure remained mostly vacant for three years. In subsequent new construction in Beverly, we have been much more astute in our timing.

The 500 Cummings Center building overlooks Upper Shoe Pond, providing marvelous scenic views. Aside from the four new parking garages, 500 was the only entirely new structure on the campus until recently, when we built our seventy-three-unit luxury residential condominium.

The Salem News has always been keenly aware of our work in Beverly, and it has often gone out of its way to make complimentary comments about Cummings Center. One such opinion piece, on May 15, 2016, concluded, "Those battling business development in Salem and elsewhere should take a look at the continuing success at Cummings Center in Beverly, which recently, and quietly, celebrated two decades as an economic driver in that city…Working with the city… the company transformed the site into something special. Today it is 90 percent occupied, housing more than 550 business and other organizations, making it the North Shore's largest business park. In recent years, Cummings Center has become a hub for innovation. It's a public private success story that's worth remembering."

And it all began with Jamie telling me he was going to look at "somewhat of a monster" of a property.

ONE ADVANTAGE SMALL companies have, but do not always use, is the capacity to hire a person based on attitude and personality, not just a résumé.

Jamie had absolutely everything I hoped for in a successor, including being a native of Woburn who still lived only a mile from our office. I could give him the experience, but his personality was one of a kind.

In the months and years after his passing, Jamie's memory was honored in many ways. Only four days before he died so suddenly, Jamie had met with Beverly officials to discuss the city's proposed acquisition of several acres of Cummings Center land, on which Beverly's then mayor, William Scanlon, was determined to construct a replacement for the aging McKay Elementary School. Jamie quickly agreed in principle to swapping the old school site for the new land. Then, after Jamie suddenly died, we instead donated the needed land in consideration of the city's naming the new school in Jamie's memory.

There was some political pushback about our proposal to donate the land, but the oddest objection, I thought, came from an unsuccessful repeat mayoral candidate, Phil Dunkelbarger. He made the school naming an issue during his run against incumbent Scanlon. I wanted to laugh

Bill Cummings

| *Beverly's James L. McKeown Elementary School, 1998*

out loud when Dunkelbarger argued that naming the new school "McKeown" would be too difficult for people to pronounce. In any case, the James L. McKeown Elementary School opened for its first students in September 1998.

Somewhat inexplicably, however, and still under the Scanlon administration that built it, the city later decided that it did not need its almost brand-new school after all. It closed the school in 2008, only ten years after its dedication and opening. It was later repurposed for other educational uses.

In 1997, Cummings Foundation established a formal scholarship plan called the McKeown Scholars Program for graduating seniors from nine local high schools. Each community determined its scholarship winners based on the students' performances on a writing assignment, which was graded anonymously by committees of teachers at each high school. The program distributed a total of more than $2 million divided among more than 500 students. Beverly graduates received $430,000 under the program, and Woburn High School graduates received $502,000, before the fund ran itself out in 2015.

Still in 1997, State Representative Carol Donovan, of Woburn, a long-term trustee of Cummings Foundation and a consistent friend and supporter of Jamie's and mine, was also playing her own major role in memorializing Jamie. She and several of her friends in the Massachusetts legislature arranged to name the newly constructed Interstate 93 highway interchange in North Woburn in Jamie's memory. Jamie had been actively involved in lobbying for the creation of that interchange, including at least one personal appearance at a public hearing in the Massachusetts State House.

| *Doug Stephens and Bill Grant, 1998*

Michael Lamothe

In one last tribute, in September 2014 the Woburn Boys & Girls Club announced its name change to the Jamie McKeown Boys & Girls Club, in honor of its cherished former Boy of the Year, board member, and club president.

EVEN AS WE honored Jamie's memory, we also honored his legacy by strengthening our leadership team to meet the challenges of the years ahead. In the summer of 1998 I was delighted to recognize Doug Stephens' twenty-five years of extraordinary loyalty and dedication by appointing him as the company's second-ever executive vice president. Doug had been with me at Cummings Properties since 1973, and before that at Old Medford Foods since 1966. One of the company's best-known faces, Doug directed all of the firm's financial affairs from its single-property beginnings in East Woburn to its then 8 million or so square feet in nine Greater Boston communities, plus its rapidly growing investments in public securities.

In May 1998, William Grant, who had considerable experience as the chief financial officer of two large retail chains, joined the firm as our first CFO. Doug extensively coached and familiarized Bill on Cummings Properties' financial affairs as these continued to grow in complexity. Bill in turn then quickly focused on working with David Leland of Merrill Lynch in managing the burgeoning financial securities of the foundation and ceased working with a small investment-management firm previously used.

Merrill Lynch thereafter took custody of those then-modest assets, and in time David arranged with Merrill to open a highly successful North Shore office in Cummings Center as David and Bill Grant worked ever more closely and effectively. In what seemed like no time at all they grew the securities accounts from tens of millions to more than a billion dollars as Cummings Properties continued to do exceedingly well. David and his wife, Karen, were Winchester neighbors and had been personal friends of Joyce's and mine for many years.

Also that year, we purchased two more somewhat run-down buildings, at 30 and 50 Audubon Road, Wakefield, and another former Cabot, Cabot & Forbes building at 34 Commerce Way, Woburn. We quickly assimilated and leased these properties, converting them from single-user buildings to our typical multi-user buildings. We had fully morphed into a major North Shore developer, but we still had no interests at all in Boston *per se*.

In September 1999, I finally announced the appointments of *two* interim successors to Jamie, naming senior vice president Michael Pascavage and vice president of operations Dennis Clarke to serve as *co-presidents* of Cummings Properties. Although several other in-house candidates were worthy of consideration, Mike and Dennis were the most logical choices. This dynamic team allowed Mike's substantial company experience and management skills

| *Co-presidents Mike Pascavage and Dennis Clarke, outside 92 Montvale Avenue, Stoneham*

to complement Dennis' strong and developing people skills and strategic-management abilities.

"The decision to jointly fill this position also reflects our philosophy regarding teamwork, integrity, and ethics," I said, announcing the promotions. "Mike and Dennis share these traits, as well as a strong personal camaraderie. Their contributions to our company's success, the growing community support we enjoy, and our mission at Cummings Properties are extraordinary. As Dennis and Mike are appointed to this unusual position, where two people share the office of president, they honor the legacy of James L. McKeown." At the center of the company's evolution from an industrial real estate developer into the multi-disciplinary Cummings Properties, Mike continued to direct all design, purchasing, construction, and development efforts.

A Pennsylvania native, Mike earned a bachelor's and a master's degree in architecture from the University of Pennsylvania. Mike also holds an MBA from Northeastern University and is a member of the American Institute of Architects. Dennis, who was thirty-one at the time, is a Winchester native who graduated from Harvard and once served briefly as a licensed commercial insurance broker. Active in both Winchester and Woburn, Dennis became a director of Winchester Chamber of Commerce and had done considerable high-level behind-the-scenes volunteer work with Winchester Hospital.

In 2004, five years after the appointment of Mike and Dennis as co-presidents, I turned over my chairman's position to Mike and, at the same time, appointed Dennis president and CEO, roles each had clearly earned. Managing involves dealing with people and their often widely divergent personalities. Dennis had grown particularly good at this and at reading other people's egos, which is a huge advantage when dealing with generally successful people. These moves allowed me to spend considerably more time with Cummings Foundation.

It was about this same time that Eric Anderson began to emerge as a rising star on the corporate management team, figuring prominently in planning for the future. A 1998 graduate of Colby College, Eric joined the firm in November 1999, first working in leasing and operations at Cummings Center. Single at the time, he lived in a small on-site manager's apartment adjacent to the main Beverly office and was the first resident of the former United Shoe property to ever become a registered voter in Beverly.

A member of the United States Marine Corps Reserve, Eric was called back to active duty after the tragic events of September 11, 2001. He was called again in 2003, after he had transferred to Cummings' operations department in Woburn, where he worked as an associate property manager under Ernie Agresti. During his second call-up, Eric served in Iraq during Operation Iraqi Freedom. He left for active duty shortly after a rousing send-off party at the West Cummings Park office that included an on-site visit by the Woburn High School Jazz Band.

Shortly after his final return from Marine Corps service, Eric was named a division manager in the Woburn Operations Department. He became the

| *Douglas Stephens YMCA of the North Shore Teen Center, Beverly, Massachusetts*

youngest member of the Executive Committee in 2007. In 2013, Eric was selected as one of the "best and brightest of the area's emerging leaders" in *Boston Business Journal's* annual "40 Under 40" feature.

MAY 2004 ALSO MARKED another tragic loss when Douglas Stephens died from pancreatic cancer at age sixty-four. Doug knew every person in the firm as well as or better than I did. He was the "mister nice guy" of our management team who was often able to make the rest of us look good.

Doug warmly touched the lives of everyone with whom he dealt. He and I worked closely together a total of thirty-eight years. In Beverly, the foundation donated $1 million to create the Douglas Stephens YMCA Teen Center in Doug's memory. This brand-new combination teen-recreation-and-childcare center was dedicated in 2004.

❀ *Entrepreneurs must focus not only on what is in front of them right now but also on what their business might become. The present state of a building, product, or company is not nearly as important as its potential. Although we never imagined that The Shoe would land us so prominently on the pages of* The Wall Street Journal, *we knew that the neglected site had enormous promise.*

❀ *"While construction is three-dimensional, architecture is four-dimensional, when we make aesthetics an essential part of each new or ongoing project." A.L.H.*

[15]

Relocating the County Seat

ONE OF THE company's most important and visible developments is TradeCenter 128, a highly prominent office and research complex located broadside to Interstate 95, in Woburn. In October 1995 Jamie had fully negotiated and arranged the purchase of this eighteen-acre former manufacturing site of Sylvania Electric. Barely two miles from our Cummings Park headquarters, this much-abused property, then called Northeast Trade Center, was also only *yards* away from Jamie's childhood home on Pearl Street.

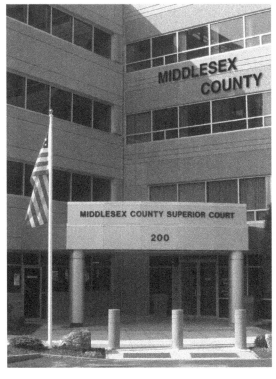

Our internal notes about the project describe that transaction as "likely the best purchase the company ever made." The delay in its major redevelopment was in part because of our later purchase of The Shoe, but it was more significantly due to the extreme political obstacles we were encountering with Woburn's Planning Board and its then highly caustic planning director. With all the political uncertainty and clamor about anything we attempted to build in Woburn during that period, it was just easier for us to invest in Beverly. While we swiftly renovated the existing one-and-a-half-story building at TradeCenter 128, we left the balance of that property unused for ten years while we focused our attention on finishing Cummings Center. The work we did at The Shoe built up Beverly's assessed values by $100 million, greatly benefiting that community for its receptiveness to our responsible redevelopment of the former United Shoe site.

Then, in August 2006, Ernie Agresti, a key member of Cummings Properties' Executive Committee, suggested that we accept an invitation to bid on, design, construct, and lease a "temporary" replacement for the former high-rise Middlesex County Superior Court in Cambridge. Officials had determined that the court's existing building was no longer safe for occupancy, so the commonwealth of Massachusetts needed a new 150,000-square-foot courthouse to be built immediately. I was dubious to say the least. Ernie once claimed to have read a book or two on property development during his student years at Brown University, and I had been under the

| *Ernie Agresti*

impression that he knew what he was doing—until now, when he proposed our TradeCenter 128 as the site of this new "temporary" courthouse.

The state's Division of Capital Assets Management and Maintenance (DCAMM) published exhaustive specs detailing precisely what the court would need, and we not only had the building-site availability but also the in-house financial and design capability to move quickly enough to satisfy DCAMM's highly accelerated timetable. The state wanted all costs incorporated into the rent, but there were numerous aspects of the building interior that needed to be treated as non-standard construction if they were to be amortized into the lease.

For example, our courthouse would have to include an entirely separate parking area and elevator for the exclusive use of judges, and a separate stairway, too, so judges could avoid face-to-face encounters with anyone having business in the court. There were also countless specialized finishes and furniture including judges' benches, jury boxes, built-in seating, individual holding cells on each floor, large holding cells for dozens of male and female detainees, and a sally port on the ground floor. We bid it to make money on the project, but our winning bid to build and lease their temporary courthouse was still dramatically less than the next lowest bid. We also took the extra step with the court's construction specifications to add extensive granite details. We decided that if we got to build the place, we wanted the users to really like it and hopefully remain for many years more than "temporarily."

State officials believed the old Cambridge courthouse might take two years to clean up and modernize, but Ernie had told me DCAMM was confident that if we built a replacement, the renovation of the old courthouse could never be complete in only two years. Furthermore, DCAMM would write requests for proposals in such a way that we could be comfortably responsive. In contrast to the twenty-story building the court was vacating, our building would be only six stories tall, with fourteen courtrooms on its upper four floors. The building could also be readily repurposed for general office or research use if ever that became necessary, reducing some of the risk on our end.

The state agreed to separately amortize the cost of required court-specific furniture, and many special items, such as the extra elevator, extra stairway, and the detention cells, over the first three years, so we were covered for at least this significant part of the up-front investment. Many people still thought we were crazy to risk so much in such a customized structure that could lose its only possible client after just three years. As it turned out, however, the old courthouse was soon deemed too expensive to either repair or tear down. (It was still in place in 2017, appearing to be totally unused and largely unchanged in appearance since 2006, although some commercial redevelopment proposals were still being discussed for it.)

Our proposed new court could be designed to fit extremely well into the building we already had planned for TradeCenter 128, and in a particularly accessible location with free garage parking for visitors and staff. The administrative functions would be on the ground floor, and offices would be on floors two and three. Ernie was right all the way, and instead of preparing a three-year lease, we determined to hold out for a five-year lease with an option to cancel the lease after either three or four years, assuming the old courthouse modernization was completed. And later, when the state extended its lease for seven more years, Ernie's wisdom was even more apparent to all.

There is always a feeling of accomplishment when new clients leave Cambridge for us, but attracting a classic gem of a tenant like the Middlesex County Superior Court was truly special. By any standards, the county seat was effectively moving to Woburn.

Before the "temporary" lease was signed, we already had the building-permit application in process. The permit was promptly issued immediately after Christmas 2006, following direct involvement from Chief Justice for Administration Robert Mulligan. His intervention became appropriate after Woburn's old vocal minority started organizing opposition to the court's moving from Cambridge to Woburn. What was really a magnificent coup for Woburn, as well as for our firm, was barely tolerated by the city's highly controversial building official at that time.

ON JANUARY 2, 2007, we started laying out the entire project's 600,000 square feet of office space, plus a 300,000-square-foot five-story parking garage. Construction of what Cummings Properties perceives as its largest, most prominent, and most intricate new structure began with the driving of the first steel pile the next day. We completed the entire garage and all the exterior walls and floors of three interconnected structures in record time with massive pre-cast concrete panels, including horizontal sections for the garage floors. There were hundreds of truckloads of individually pre-cast concrete panels, support columns and beams, plus the enormous concrete "double tees" for the floors of the garage. It was like the entire project was on steroids.

I marvel at Cummings Properties' longtime structural engineer, Greg Flaherty, who has designed the concrete foundations and steel framework for all our new buildings since 1998. Greg once admitted to me how nervous he feels every time the large construction cranes pull in, followed by trailers loaded with steel beams. And no wonder: Every piece of steel has to click precisely into place in each enormous three-dimensional jigsaw puzzle we build. Any left-out or mis-cut beam during the typical two- to ten-week erection process

| *Greg Flaherty on site*

can cause chaos, but that has never happened. Greg views a plan for every single piece beforehand, and he just does not miss. Our largest built-from-scratch structure at TradeCenter 128 started out in a frozen windswept field, and not a single beam or bolt hole had to be corrected or altered.

Greg's work style, which features his marvelous concentration and attention to the smallest detail, needs to be the exact opposite of mine—I constantly balance multiple major priorities simultaneously. I would not be one bit successful if I had to do Greg's rigidly focused work. Knowing that about myself has been important and has certainly never hurt Greg's job security. Managers must learn about the abilities of all their staff members, and they must certainly know and work within their own abilities. Valued employees so often fail in their positions because they have been advanced one step beyond their ability or their willingness to perform a given job at the required level.

This will often lead to worker and management dissatisfaction, and even to fully preventable terminations. It can often work out well to restructure a position, presumably with lower compensation, when a well-qualified, able worker simply needs fewer hours, or less responsibility than originally agreed upon or expected. Salvaging such a team member can keep someone gainfully (and often more happily) employed for everyone's benefit.

To ensure that we were ready on our end, we worked until well after nightfall on December 31, 2007, completing the final touches of the courthouse carpeting before celebrating the New Year. The court took a little time moving in, as we imagined it would, in part because we surprised virtually everyone with our speedy delivery, and the state was not quite prepared to start its big move. There was a long way to go with the balance of the building at 300 and 400 TradeCenter 128, but the court building was fully complete, and all we needed was an occupancy permit from the building commissioner, which we received in a timely manner.

| *Greg Ahearn*

Bob Venezia, who had joined us originally as a master electrician, retired as Cummings Properties' senior field management official during the TradeCenter 128 project, and Gregory Ahearn, a master plumber and fifteen-year company veteran, succeeded Bob as our general field manager. Both Greg and his predecessor happened to be graduates of Woburn High School. Greg moved into the superintendent's role directly from his former position as an associate division manager, skipping over the division-manager level in the process. Subsequently, he was named vice president of field operations and became a member of the Executive Committee in September 2011.

OUR DESIGN TEAM, with no outside engineering or architectural assistance except for the design of the pre-cast concrete, completed this gemstone among our properties: TradeCenter 128. As with all our structures, we designed this extraordinary 900,000-square-foot office complex (with garage) entirely in-house, and then as always we were our own general contractor. Mike Pascavage was the original managing architect, of course, with Greg Flaherty as the senior structural engineer for the entire complex.

We probably made a few errors during the TradeCenter project, but I personally made the most costly one when I looked at the total size of the

| *Aerial view of TradeCenter 128, facing Interstate 95 in Woburn*

complex and decided that our plans called for too many parking spaces. Without really studying the situation, I arbitrarily reduced the size of the precast concrete parking garage from six stories to five, just before the deadline, thinking that we were saving perhaps a half-million dollars. It was less than a year later that we built a small additional garage to "put back" the spaces I earlier rejected—at a substantially greater cost than that of the original garage plan. It is important for managers at any level to be aware of all errors, but it is even more important for them to own up to their own.

IN OCTOBER 2008, our entire staff was shocked when Mike Pascavage was recruited to leave the company for the second time. He had served eighteen years during his second stint, most recently as chairman, and he left, with nothing less than mutual best wishes, to join the Swedish construction giant Skanska International. In a way, we were perhaps even a little proud that a world-class powerhouse with tens of thousands of employees would come to a comparatively tiny firm like ours to supplement its top executives.

Although Mike's colleagues and I were sad about his departure, he once confided to me that he had a dream and a vision about someday altering the Boston skyline. I told Mike several times that we had no difficulty understanding that dream, or why he might take the chance he did, even in what turned out to be such economically perilous times. Mostly, I was relieved to learn from Mike that he had not been looking for another job, nor did he leave because of any unhappiness with our firm.

For two years thereafter, Mike led Skanska's efforts to develop office buildings for Skanska's own account in Boston, but his new employment began at almost exactly the same time as the great real estate bust of late 2008. By the time Mike left Skanska, we had already filled his complicated role with us. Wishing to send a message about how well we thought of Mike, however, I invited him to serve as a trustee of Cummings Foundation.

Several years after he left Cummings, Mike then founded his own architectural-services firm, also here in Woburn. We were pleased to provide complimentary accommodations for him at TradeCenter 128, where a prominent lobby plaque identifies Mike as chief architect of the complex. We were delighted when, in 2016, the directors of the newly named McKeown Boys & Girls Club selected Mike's firm to design and oversee the development of the club's new $10 million structure.

For this book, I asked Mike to share some more of his most pertinent reflections concerning his two decades of important leadership positions with Cummings Properties. Because Mike was so integral to our entire operation for such a long time, I shall, with great thanks, use much of his response here:

> *The most striking recollection of my time at CPL is of the people who made up the company. Cummings employees ultimately were a true reflection of the work ethic and attitude that started at the top. Many folks cycled through, and the self-selection process generally weeded out those who did not fit the mold. I take pride in having known every employee in the company (over 260 at the time) and to this day still recognize and care about the CPL employees I encounter.*

| *Michael Pascavage*

> *There is no question as to the impact that you, personally, Bill, had on me throughout my career. My growth in the organization was measured, culminating in significant authority and responsibility, only after having been vetted through every conceivable design, development, construction, personnel, and cultural aspect of your personal philosophy.*
>
> *Relative to individuals, working alongside Jamie McKeown was a true highlight—vibrant, smart, charismatic, and holding your highest confidence, he was the gateway to the future. To now have the opportunity, as its independent architect, to recast the former Woburn Boys & Girls Club facility in his name and memory is truly special. Doug Stephens, totally understated,*

but truly loyal, dedicated and a saint in his own right, is similarly missed.

On the field side, Rick Freeman stands out as such a positive force in CPL's growth. Jim Trudeau, Mike Aveni, and Jim Gillette, and others who continue to be the bedrock of CPL's production, made every day a pleasure to come to work.

My initial Cummings involvement blended well with my personal work ethic and approach. While oft overused, the firm was truly a 'hands-on' organization. Complete involvement in every minute decision, direction, and process insured the success of each effort. The Cummings attitude of 'do-it-yourself' across all corporate functions was key. We did not rely on third-party consultants to do critical path components of the work that were both time sensitive and expensive.

The total immersion of all the company resources in charting a path through the myriad issues presented at the massive Cummings Center undertaking is tops on my list. From the purchase offer and acceptance of a $500,000 bid for a 2-million-square-foot hulk, to the $90 million investment required to effect its ultimate transformation, this was a fantastic project.

Our weekly Saturday walk-throughs together charted the course for the next week as we gradually figured out what markets developed. We could never imagine at the time this would become the diverse, self-contained full-service microcosm of commercial development that it is today. A stellar feature review in The Wall Street Journal from Ada Louise Huxtable, and multiple industry awards, were just deserts for this spectacular transformation.

Being in control of your own destiny in every aspect of the development process was, I believe, the key ingredient to CPL success. Controlling the design, financing, construction, legal, leasing, and property-management aspects of the total real estate process was truly unique in the field and continues to be a defining premise of CPL. It became our calling card for uniqueness in the industry.

The significant developments we put together define a career's worth of projects. Each was an independent effort with a combination of right place, right time, and total dedication of all resources to the project success. These projects became as much a labor of love.

Bill, the biggest, always understated, achievement of your career has been the establishment of Cummings Foundation. It needs no endorsement from me, I just want to say thank you for the trust you had in me to allow me to serve for a time on the Board of Directors of this amazing new Massachusetts institution. It continues to serve so many organizations that will most benefit from the largesse, and I am most proud of the involvement I had with CF.

M.H.P.

After a year-long closing of Woburn's now Jamie McKeown Boys and Girls Club, Joyce and I were so pleased to see the totally rebuilt club operating again directly next to Place Lane Condominium, in September 2016. Still serving such a broad base of primarily Woburn families, and now with a fine new regulation-size swimming pool, it seems so fitting that the directors voted to rename the club in Jamie's honor.

Although Cummings Foundation has since made more than $200 million in grants of $100,000 or more, the Foundation's first $100,000 grant was presented by Jamie to the former Woburn Boys Club in 1989 (photo on page 106).

ONE OF THE MOST endearing and enduring aspects of our organization is the outstanding level of corporate respect within. Throughout the company, the pride and loyalty of the staff are obvious at every turn. The single most apparent sentiment from our most experienced colleagues is how greatly they value the friendly collegial environment of the entire firm. Our team members have heard many times that solid professional and personal ethics must absolutely define how we do business, and for the vast majority of times they do. Staff have also heard how important it is that we think of corporate and individual success as a lifetime journey and not a destination.

Among our early decisions about TradeCenter 128 was that we needed a full-service, white-tablecloth restaurant to serve both our own local business community and the general population along Route 128/I-95. It was not the Company's plan to become involved with operating any such venture on-site, but when no viable prospects emerged with the interest and ability to build a premier restaurant on our timetable, we moved forward and opened a first-class destination restaurant on our own. We called it Beacon Grille. Desiring to give the restaurant a Boston theme, which was already implied in the "Beacon" name, the Cummings in-house design team created oversized Boston photo art, including my favorite picture of Boston's Leonard Zakim Bunker Hill Bridge, taken from Bunker Hill by our son Kevin.

As a company, we thoroughly enjoyed working out all the complicated details for the complete build-out of this 300-seat restaurant prior to its opening in January 2010. Our staffing issues at Beacon Grille, however, were in stark contrast to my decades of personnel experience at Cummings Properties, where our management team has always been so strong. We recently calculated that the thirty or so people filling our highest management and executive positions at Cummings

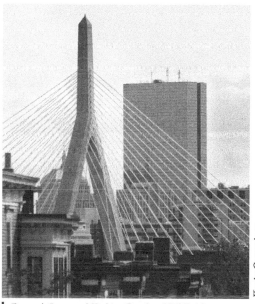

| Boston's Leonard Zakim Bunker Hill Bridge

Kevin Cummings

Properties have an average seniority of more than twenty-one years with the firm. Our nine most senior field managers average slightly more than twenty-six years. At the restaurant, however, for one good reason or another, it seemed no one on the management team lasted much more than a single year.

With this contrast in mind, and the chronic Beacon Grille issues so disproportionally occupying our senior corporate management time, we were clearly ready, after three years, to sell the restaurant. In traditional terms, the restaurant had been an unqualified success. With annual sales having grown to $4.5 million in 2012, we proved that TradeCenter 128 was a viable site for a first-class dining venue. But selling it would relieve us of a significant distraction and perpetual angst about what *might* happen next at Beacon. Fortunately, nothing serious ever went wrong, but for years we were concerned that our collective inability to recruit and retain the right staff might somehow cause us great embarrassment, or worse. My personal track record in management selection at Beacon was dismal at best.

So, we all felt great when Nick Varano, sole owner of The Varano Group, agreed to buy us out. Nick had built a great name with his high-end Strega restaurants in Boston, and now he wanted his first suburban presence. He was as motivated to buy Beacon as we were to sell it. No matter how well it was doing, and how proud we were of the overall project, it was time to turn it over to some real professionals.

Kevin Kelly

| *Nick Varano with Bill Cummings, May 2013*

But even though we had a firm oral agreement with Nick, he came in near the end of the process with a push for us to either reduce the price by $300,000 or lose the deal. We certainly could have agreed to his price, after a "split the difference" proposal didn't work, because Nick was pretty convincing with his "last and final" statement: "Take it or leave it," he said, "but I'm out the door if you don't take it now." And we did want Strega there.

Then I remembered how much Nick had sometimes talked about gambling. "Instead of splitting the difference," I said, "how about we toss a coin to decide?" Nick immediately agreed.

I reached in my pocket and pulled out a coin and flipped it. Nick called "Tails" with the coin in the air. The $300,000 coin landed heads up.

The sale to The Varano Group closed in May 2013, and Strega Prime opened, with its brand-new glitzy décor and considerably fancier menu, to great acclaim in early August. For those who want and can afford the flourish and frills of such high-end dining, Strega Prime at 400 TradeCenter 128, like Boston's Strega restaurants, is always a sure bet for a memorable meal.

BEYOND THE excitement and occasional exasperations of permitting and constructing TradeCenter 128, there was the challenge in an exceedingly slow market for leasing it all out—that is, the remaining half-million square feet not leased to the court. As has always been our custom, we built the balance of the complex entirely "on spec," with no clients or even prospective clients for any of it.

I have long believed that most people who get things done have to be inherently gamblers of a sort. They sometimes come up short, because there are downturns in any game. Such people, if they are smart, will usually have a reasonable fallback position, and in the long run they will rarely lose, unless they walk off the field. TradeCenter 128 was such a gamble, especially the courthouse building. In the end, however, this gamble paid brilliant dividends.

With its unique three-story archway between its 300 and 400 wings, TradeCenter 128 is distinctive, and the structure deserves all the acclaim it has received for its fine in-house architectural design. Despite the financial crisis in 2008, the building began filling immediately after it was ready for move-ins, undoubtedly benefiting from our creative marketing.

Michael Lamothe

One of our central marketing objectives is always to bring amenities—banks, health clubs, restaurants, dry cleaners, childcare centers, and the like—to each major building complex as soon as possible. These make a campus highly attractive to many prospective clients, because they and their employees have access to so much more than merely a place to work.

Amenity-rich TradeCenter 128 has a large YMCA daycare as well as My Montessori School on campus, and direct-to-door MBTA bus service to and from the Wellington "Orange Line" station in the historic Boston rapid transit (subway) system. In addition to its upscale Strega Prime steak house, it has a busy Dunkin' Donuts, plus a terrific sandwich shop and an excellent small gift shop in the central lobby. There are also a thousand fully covered free garage parking spaces. The complex is additionally home to a large number of medical and legal practices, and, of course, the fourteen courtrooms of the Middlesex County Superior Court at the far northern end of the campus.

Another major point that helps us when we are negotiating with prospective clients is the uncommonly strong financial condition of Cummings Properties and the foundation that has come to own so many Cummings buildings.

Described by many in the industry as one of the most financially solid real estate firms in New England, Cummings Properties has often been informally identified as the "owner and operator" of millions of square feet of mostly office and research space in ten metropolitan Boston communities, with headquarters in Woburn. In reality, Cummings Properties, as our operating entity, has never owned *any* real estate or much of anything else besides tools, service vehicles, and an enormous collection of heavy-duty snow equipment. All land and buildings have, for the most part, been owned by separate corporate entities, more and more of which are themselves now owned by Cummings Foundation, and all are debt-free.

The separate entities have mostly to do with limiting exposure in the event of any sort of catastrophic liability claim. If, for instance, an accident occurred involving an underinsured vehicle carrying dangerous cargo onto one of our properties, separate ownership of adjacent lots could keep one property owner from becoming exposed to claims against another property owner.

SINCE 2007, our in-house legal department has been directed by Craig Ziady, our senior vice president and general counsel. Craig was another highly serendipitous personal connection I made through Winchester Country Club. Before Craig and his wife, Joan, joined WCC, I met them, in my role as a director of the club, during their membership-application process. Craig and Joan were both working at a major Boston law firm, where Craig had made a name for himself as a highly successful environmental and real estate litigator.

| *Craig Ziady*

Craig told me during his interview at the club that he might sometime explore professional opportunities outside the city. Shortly after the family joined the club, he responded favorably to my invitation to also consider joining Cummings Properties, and since June 2007, we have had a marvelous relationship. Interestingly, Cummings Properties typically has more than a dozen full-time attorneys, with all but four of them filling important management roles *outside* the legal department. Our legal department also serves Cummings Foundation on a strictly *pro bono* basis. IRS regulations prohibit payments from the foundation to any related for-profit entity, no matter how reasonable the payments might be.

We try hard to avoid legal skirmishes unless absolutely necessary, and we strive for clear and thoughtful documents, letters, and emails. Communication is imperative, and those with the greatest literary skills tend to be the most effective communicators. True empathy toward others, as well as to their needs, desires, and personal dignity, will also enable good entrepreneurs to communicate effectively. Entrepreneurs who do well rely on facts to support their points, and they will expect others to do the same.

When court proceedings are necessary—and they seem to most frequently develop when client firms cannot meet their rent obligations—it is helpful to have a solid in-house legal team. With literally thousands of client firms, we tend to see the same fact patterns repeat themselves, and there are many major benefits to always having the same legal team for each case.

We have argued more than a few precedent-setting legal issues, however, and our in-house team has done outstandingly well. Susan Brand, during her eighteen years as counsel and general counsel, had several notable and significant cases, including her only trip to the Massachusetts Supreme Judicial Court (SJC): Cummings Properties, LLC v. National Communications Corp. The SJC, of its own volition, selected that case after we first won in the trial court but then lost in the Massachusetts Appeals Court. The SJC determined that an accelerated rent provision negotiated in a commercial lease between sophisticated parties was an enforceable liquidated-damages clause, and the ruling has since been cited effectively in other cases. An unrelated but analogous case held the holder of a New England Patriots luxury box ticket contract liable for the full multi-year contract amount after an earlier default. Several other in-house legal cases, including two others before the SJC, have established significant real estate precedents in Massachusetts courts.

In another precedent-setting case for our legal department, our senior litigator, Joseph Mingolla, spent years finally earning a win on an important right-of-way case. Effectively, he established in the Massachusetts Supreme Judicial Court that the rights of an owner of "registered land" in Massachusetts are similar to those associated with unregistered land when it comes to adjusting or relocating a recorded right of way. In both situations the rights to use a right of way may be changed but the beneficiaries of the rights must not be materially disadvantaged.

| *Joseph Mingolla*

One more significant Cummings case, also in the SJC, established the rights of landowners and tenants to protect both parties with insurance against losses or claims including those that might allege negligence by the owner/lessor of the property.

AFTER HAVING INSTALLED and benefited from video-recording devices at many of our properties, we first installed cameras in a systematic way at TradeCenter 128. This was partly due to our involvement with the elaborate camera systems in the Middlesex County Superior Court building, where the State reportedly installed about 300 digital recording cameras. We initially planned 200 cameras for the rest of the TradeCenter 128 complex but ended up operating a total of almost 300 interior digital cameras ourselves, plus another twenty exterior cameras.

There have been numerous times when video from the garage or parking-lot cameras have dramatically contradicted drivers' testimonies in automobile mishaps. In one memorable video clip, an alleged victim of a trip-and-fall injury is seen intentionally banging her knee against a car bumper before sitting down on a curbstone between two parked vehicles. Then she starts yelling for someone walking toward her to "call an ambulance."

One of our earliest successes with exterior video involved footage of two felony suspects stopping in front of a remote trash dumpster to discard items linked to a crime. After being alerted by Cummings watch staff, police checked the trash container and found freshly bloodied clothes. Prosecutors were able to use the video as conclusive evidence in an attempted-murder case in a nearby town. The video cameras have come into play in literally dozens of incidents, fully justifying our expenditures of several hundred thousand dollars on the system.

| *Father David O'Leary*

AS THE YEARS have passed, Joyce and I have been fortunate enough to become increasingly involved in hugely satisfying situations and causes—many of which have nothing whatsoever to do with the company or the foundation. As a trustee *emeritus* of Tufts University, for instance, I somehow became the designated emissary for a significant church issue, one that again involved obtaining an unusual approval from the Archdiocese of Boston. This time, Tufts sought to have Father David O'Leary appointed by the diocese to serve a ten-year term as the *university* chaplain. Father O'Leary would become what appears to have been the first American Roman Catholic priest to officially serve in a nondenominational religious role at a public or other non-secular university. Father O'Leary held a doctorate in philosophy and had earlier served as Tufts' Catholic chaplain. Following a long line of largely, if not exclusively, Unitarian Universalist clergy in that role, this highly respected Roman Catholic priest contributed much to the university community during his ten-year appointment.

During this same period, and without any prior discussion with Tufts officials, Joyce and I funded the Cummings Chair in Entrepreneurship in the Economics Department at Tufts. The funds are used to support an eminent scholar who is what I call "an all-star academic economist." When that Cummings Chair eventually became vacant through a retirement, and was left unfilled for more than a year, however, it was transferred at our request to School of Engineering at Tufts, in 2017.

Joyce and I also decided it was time to downsize from our large Fernway home, where we had lived for twenty-five years. In November 2003, we moved from Myopia Hill to a more modest home in the not-so-elegantly-named Winchester Flats. Denise McKeown was our broker, during her affiliation with Winchester's Century 21 Fortin Real Estate. The "Fortin" in that firm is the son of my Tufts classmate and long-term TWA pilot, Richard Fortin, whom we frequently see in Florida. Shortly after Denise managed our new home purchase, we were delighted that she joined the Cummings team on the management and leasing staff of our TradeCenter 128 Executive Office Suites.

Our new house lot is comfortably one-tenth the size of our former two-acre lot on "the Hill." While this home is better suited to our current needs, I do miss the sweeping view from our bedroom window at Fernway, which looked out over Boston and allowed us to see flights arriving at Logan International Airport. We donated the Fernway home to Cummings Foundation, which quickly sold it to a Bermudian couple for use as their off-island summer home in the United States—but then they deeded it back to the foundation three years later, in lieu of foreclosure. When Winchester's brokerage community seemed to tire of showing the home after the first sale fell through, the foundation signed with a Cambridge broker to represent it. The Cambridge broker then rather ironically sold the home to a Winchester couple, who were themselves represented by a broker from Concord, Massachusetts.

ONE ESPECIALLY LONG-ENDURING and enriching activity for Joyce and me has been what we call our SHARE Group, a small community discussion group that first emerged out of a larger program at Winchester's St. Eulalia Church in 1976. After originally coming together for ten weekly meetings that fall, we and eight other Winchester couples changed things to a monthly format, except during July and August, and we have never stopped meeting. Each couple hosts one of the meetings and selects the discussion topic and facilitates the discussion, most often with a short reading assignment for all.

During the four decades that Joyce and I pretty much grew old with members of the SHARE Group, we also found great enjoyment regularly playing duplicate bridge with seven other couples. We have never kept records

Lloyd Franke

| *Joyce and Bill with their SHARE Group, 2016*

but have played our favorite card game with our Winchester Duplicate Bridge Club once a month for about thirty-four years. This was always a friendly, casual group, though it did include two "life masters"—Althea Shirley and Anne Nevins. But we are all at least somewhat competent players and provide one another with much intellectual stimulation.

When Joyce and I are at our condo on Singer Island, Florida, during the winter, we play in games sanctioned by the American Contract Bridge League. We also sometimes play as often as once a week at what has become the largest duplicate bridge club in New England. The Bridge Spot, at 400 West Cummings Park, Woburn, is certainly convenient, and it offers an extremely friendly and well-run game for duplicate players of all levels. The proprietor, Dean Panagopoulos, an MIT grad, has a lighthearted sign near the entry reading: "No Grouches Allowed." Dean and his predecessors, Dennis and Jackie Dawson, have provided bridge competition in Cummings Park for more than forty years.

Deal-making in business can be quite similar to playing chess, or bridge, or billiards, in terms of knowing how and when to take advantage of situations as they develop. A little bluffing—not lying—is often part of any serious game and must be anticipated. And like experts at chess, bridge, or billiards, the negotiating expert is always thinking ahead to the next move or the next turn.

Bridge is great training for business. Duplicate bridge at a competitive level opens and expands one's mind in a meaningful way. The process of writing and self-publishing this autobiography probably also accomplished somewhat the same thing as bridge, but without the competitive camaraderie. Both, however, have had a noticeable and highly positive effect on me by energizing my memory to create reliable accounts, in some cases dating back more than seventy years.

ONE OF THE most meaningful of all our many international trips was my second and Joyce's first visit to Israel, in 2009, when we joined a superb Tufts University Travel-Learn group for two weeks in Israel and Jordan. I had made a limited visit to Israel in 1964, as part of my solo

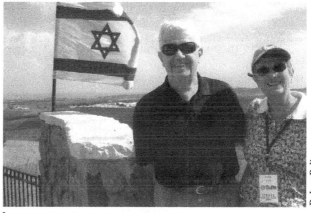
Joyce and Bill at Golan Heights, 2009

Robert Belin

adventure around Europe and the Mediterranean, but this later trip was planned to give us a real sense of the immense importance of the region from the earliest of recorded times, particularly its spectacular role in the development of world civilizations.

Our bus tour looped clockwise through Israel, beginning northward along the coast from Tel Aviv, and included a multi-day stay in and around a large kibbutz with many farming and dairy operations as well as a fascinating furniture factory. These days, the kibbutz also makes highly customized wood pews and other seating for churches and synagogues all over the world. We visited vast areas of carefully planted and irrigated new pine forests around the kibbutz, learning how they are reforesting several other species, as well.

Our crossing of the Sea of Galilee, visits to the areas along the Jordan River, and learning about the massive reforestation efforts were all interesting and educational, as were our attempts to understand the complicated water issues associated with the Jordan. We saw up-close that this river is but a narrow stream and only a few inches deep at the point where it enters the Dead Sea. At that exact location, I easily stepped across the five-foot-wide river without getting my shoes wet.

Every day, we enjoyed sites of biblical history and came to better

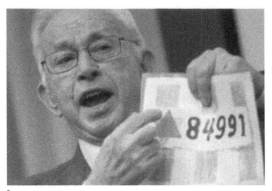

| *Eliezer Ayalon, 2010*

understand places and events that would have taken years of study to truly comprehend. We read literature provided by the Tufts Travel-Learn office, but a book given to us by our son-in-law, Jason, stood out from the rest. We both found *History of Modern Israel*, by Colin Shindler, to be superb and particularly useful, placing so much of what we saw and witnessed in the context of what Israel is today. Beginning well before the 1948 founding of the state of Israel, Shindler's detailed account provides magnificent insights.

Although *History of Modern Israel* provides some details about the Palestinian issues in Israel, more current sources like Jewishvoiceforpeace.org advocate strongly against human rights violations there against Palestinians. Decade after decade of international talks have gone nowhere through 2018, and President Trump's move to recognize a Jewish Jerusalem as the capital city of Israel may have greatly set back whatever progress there might have been.

One issue that particularly fascinated me concerned the potential good that would come from a replenishment of the Dead Sea, the so-called "Red to Dead" project to use siphon lines to bring billions of gallons of water to slowly refill the Dead Sea and use up at least a tiny part of our growing surplus of sea water.

One of the most surprising aspects of our 2009 visit along the Jordan River was the extent to which the "average people" in the regions we visited appeared to fully embrace the notion of peaceful coexistence and mutual support. Tourism benefits both lands enormously, and both peoples seem intent on preserving cooperative policies. More moderate voices in Israel are working toward more equitable solutions with the Palestinians, but that will take enormous efforts.

Near the end of our journey, just before we crossed into Jordan for a fascinating stop in the ancient carved city of Petra, we visited Yad Vashem, the Holocaust museum in Jerusalem. Following a four-hour tour, our forty-person group met Holocaust survivor Eliezer Ayalon for a moving ninety-minute talk about his experiences in five concentration camps. Joyce and I consider ourselves fairly well read and thought we knew quite a bit about the Holocaust. After touring Yad Vashem and hearing Elie, we realized how little we really knew.

He told a riveting story of arriving in Israel as a survivor, but being suspected by some of being a Nazi collaborator. Many mistreated him, as they simply would not accept that he survived the Nazi horrors without conspiring with the despicable regime. He learned quickly that, even as he began to locate family members in this new land, he had to fabricate an entirely different story about how he got to Israel.

We later came to three powerful realizations: First, the lessons of the Holocaust are far too vital to be forgotten or denied. Second, genocides are still occurring throughout the world. And finally, thinking people cannot simply sit quietly and let more genocides happen. While flying home, Joyce and I determined almost simultaneously, "We have to do something."

Paul Vyriotes

Tufts students fill the auditorium for a Cummings Foundation talk about the Holocaust

ONE OF OUR first steps after returning to Boston was to invite Elie Ayalon to Massachusetts. Joyce and I had learned so much from him and were so grateful for our ten days in Israel. We wanted to help him share his experience with others. We met with Tufts president Larry Bacow, who lost family members in concentration camps, and with longtime friend Rabbi Jeffrey Summit of Tufts Hillel. Together, we arranged for Elie to come and speak to Tufts students, which he did in 2010. That was the beginning of Tufts' interfaith Cummings/Hillel Program for Holocaust and Genocide Education. Elie stayed two nights in our home and was almost ecstatic when I knocked on his door the first morning with his first cup of coffee. During his visit, he met and spoke with two large groups at Tufts, and he particularly enjoyed meeting informally with many active and acutely interested students before and after his formal presentations.

Following Mr. Ayalon's visit, the foundation established two long-term programs in Holocaust and genocide education, each with a $1 million commitment. One of these was at Tufts University and the other at Salem

State University with Professors Robert McAndrews and Chris Mauriello. We also began supporting substantial programming at the United States Holocaust Memorial Museum in Washington, D.C., at about this same time.

The Cummings/Hillel program at Tufts is directed primarily by students, who received constant early support from Rabbi Summit. It offers film screenings, discussion groups, and panel presentations by local survivors of contemporary genocides. Tufts also sponsors annual travel-learning opportunities, which have included trips to the Holocaust museum in Washington, D.C., and many more-distant trips by both schools, including trips to the Kigali Genocide Memorial Centre in Rwanda. Our earliest interest in Rwanda arose from our support of Tufts students who traveled to Agahoza Shalom Youth Village in Rwanda. We learned so much about the Village which was originally founded to help high school-aged victims of the terrible Rwandan Genocide of 1994.

"Bill and Joyce's commitment transcends particular religious affiliation," Rabbi Summit noted in a May 2014 *Chronicle of Philanthropy* article. "To join hands across religious traditions to look at these issues is extremely important." Convinced that real change can come from the next generation of world citizens, we created and then formalized our programs. It is our hope that through academic courses, immersion-travel experiences, meetings with genocide survivors, and much more, these students will be sensitized to the early warning signs of genocide and become strong and passionate enough to stand up against genocidal forces.

❈ *Inherently risky, serious entrepreneurship is not for the cautious or faint-hearted. To be successful in business, it may be necessary to gamble a bit, as we did so many times while bidding for building the courthouse, buying Choate Hospital, opening a 300-seat restaurant, and flipping a $300,000 coin. Dozens and dozens of times, we have purchased existing commercial buildings, or we have constructed brand-new buildings, with not even a hint of who their clients might be. Bear in mind, however, that none of these were reckless gambles made without thought. Rather they were calculated risks that we could afford to lose if things did not go our way.*

❈ *A solid new business will usually make many more friends when it comes across to others as the little guy just trying to get by, rather than bragging about how great it is. Running the competition down, or talking about putting someone else out of business can be the most fatal mistake of them all.*

[16]

Cummings Foundation Matures

Michael Lamothe (alt-red)

FIRST FOUNDED AS Cummings Properties Foundation, Inc., in 1986, our foundation was created to become a meaningful philanthropic presence, hopefully during our lifetimes. We expressly organized it to "give back" within the communities where Cummings Properties does business and where most of its employees and clients live. In large part these communities were the source from which our assets were derived.

Although Cummings Foundation's first $100,000 gift was made to the Woburn Boys Club, as described earlier, it was a quarter century later that we established our first programmatic plan for giving. Joyce and I determined that if we worked first at building an endowment for this new financial entity, we might be able to create a truly meaningful organization by the end of our productive years. And that was exactly what we set out to do.

There were, of course, many other things we were able to quietly support as we chose to, and did, but mostly we worked to create a substantial net worth for the foundation, and we handled our ongoing philanthropy through personal funds, or through Cummings Properties, as time went on. The largest of these efforts was a $50 million commitment to support and actually take over what then became the Cummings School of Veterinary Medicine at Tufts University.

In business, I always sought to surround myself with people who were smarter than I am and who brought diverse experiences and perspectives to their work. Cummings Properties owes its success largely to the synergies resulting from dozens of talented, caring, honest individuals working so beautifully together. Joyce and I approached the foundation in a similar way, inviting trusted friends and respected community leaders to serve as trustees, with a strong majority being *non*-family.

Our daughters, Marilyn and Patricia, are trustees without limit of time, as are Joyce and I, and Marilyn's husband, Jason Morris, a Yale and Harvard Medical School graduate who is chair of the Department of Natural Sciences at Fordham University. Other trustees serve three-year terms but are eligible for multiple reappointments. No trustees receive any compensation or financial advantage of any sort in return for their generous service.

As of 2017, the ten non-family trustees of Cummings Foundation include my Medford High School and Tufts friend Dr. Joseph Abate, retired Massachusetts Supreme Judicial Court justice Margot Botsford, former state representatives Paul Casey and Carol Donovan, Cummings School of Veterinary Medicine dean Dr. Deborah Kochevar, Tufts University president Dr. Anthony Monaco, and retired *Boston Globe* president Richard Ockerbloom. Our newest independent trustees are a preeminent gynecologic oncologist and Winchester friend, Dr. Arlan "Skip" Fuller; a retired managing partner of Wellington Management Company, Laurie Gabriel; and Tufts University provost Dr. David Harris.

Under its longstanding executive director, Joel B. Swets, Cummings Foundation also benefits greatly from *pro bono* management help from its trustees, from Cummings family members, and from many colleagues of Cummings Properties. Joyce Vyriotes, the long-term communications director for Cummings Properties

Foundation executive director Joel Swets with pro bono *deputy director Joyce Vyriotes, 2015*

and a 1996 graduate of Mount Holyoke College, also serves as the *pro bono* deputy director of the foundation. Joel, a 1976 graduate of Colby College, is also a graduate of Suffolk University Law School.

In addition, Cummings Foundation benefits magnificently from more than fifty otherwise unaffiliated volunteer professionals and others who assist so diligently in reading and processing many hundreds of grant applications. Other volunteers also conduct site visits with many grant recipients.

"The plan for the grant-making foundation was to depersonalize the giving side and to gradually move all that activity away from Joyce and me," I told a reporter for "Chronicle," a popular Boston news television series, in December 2011. "It works so much better now that we have some organized systems in place. We have determined we must soon get beyond our personal involvement, because we are surely not going to be here fifty years from now." We are both still feeling great, but our runway is, of course, becoming ever shorter.

ONE OF THE FOUNDATION'S most significant relationships began with a rather plebeian meal. In early 2002, when former Tufts president Lawrence Bacow was still the new guy on Tufts' campus (a role he is now reprising at Harvard University), he invited me to join him for lunch. By that time, Joyce and I were significant donors to my alma mater, having recently endowed the Cummings Family Chair in Entrepreneurship. I remember going to that lunch visit with a self-satisfied sense of "immunity" from any kind of solicitation.

| *Lawrence Bacow*

Although we were initially going to dine at Boston's Four Seasons Hotel, I suggested the on-campus Dewick Dining Hall instead. That particular student venue had served many times as a convenient testing site for me two decades prior, when I was developing Old Medford beverage bases, and Tufts Dining Service has been one of Old Medford's first new college accounts. It would be a nostalgic treat for me to have lunch there with Tufts' new president. Because there was no agenda for that "get acquainted" meeting, I could particularly enjoy what we now refer to as our "veggie burger lunch."

But following that casual meal, we had one of the most instantly productive advancement conversations any two people could imagine. After walking back up the hill to Larry's office in Ballou Hall, out of nowhere he and I scoped out a "what if" agreement for Cummings Foundation to first *purchase* the School of Veterinary Medicine from Tufts and then hire the university to run it for us. The foundation would effectively adopt the educational component of the school, which is located in North Grafton, and then invest $50 million to significantly stabilize its future growth.

The school, which had recently taken a major wallop in its contracted annual state appropriation, stood to benefit greatly from the foundation's financial assistance, as well as from some occasional management and consulting participation of the sort we could readily supply. The school would also be renamed Cummings School of Veterinary Medicine, and its teaching component would be legally merged into the foundation.

This now thirty-five-year-old school of veterinary medicine, the only such school in New England, was building a magnificent reputation for itself, but the severe budget constraints were limiting its further improvement.

Neither Larry nor I anticipated this complicated proposal, and yet it came together in substance in about forty minutes. Tufts' trustees effortlessly approved the agreement in principle, but it then took close to a year and a half before all the required regulatory and accrediting approvals came through. In the end, however, the basic understanding was almost exactly as Larry and I had arranged it following that fortuitous meal.

Most unusually, attorney Michael Bohnen of the Boston law firm Nutter, McClennen & Fish represented both the university and the foundation in the $50 million transaction, handling not only the acquisition agreement itself, but also the federal tax and regulatory considerations, for both entities, as well as the naming of the Cummings School. President Bacow went on in October 2018 to later become president of Harvard University.

I happened to bump into Tufts' venerable Professor Sol Gittleman shortly after my get-together with President Bacow, and when we discussed the pending Cummings School grants he was truly ecstatic. Along with my late classmate Dr. Tom Murnane, Sol had made quite an effort over many years to softly encourage us to expand our philanthropy with Tufts. A longtime Winchester resident, Sol was the archetypical "professor about town" and still is a nationally renowned and beloved ambassador for the university.

The trustees soon announced our $50 million commitment as Tufts' largest gift ever, and it has since grown to almost $80 million. It was also the first naming gift for a veterinary school in the United States. In 2005, we were told that our gift helped to inspire an even more innovative $100 million gift from fellow Tufts alumni and fellow Giving Pledge members Pam and Pierre

Omidyar, the 1995 founders of eBay. That wonderful contribution made us feel even better.

The agreement with Tufts University that resulted in the renaming of what is now the Cummings School of Veterinary Medicine was highly original and unusual in other respects too. In that situation, Cummings Foundation was beginning to dramatically grow its net worth, and it determined to also grow its operational side beyond the scope of its not-for-profit assisted living facilities. To continue to qualify as an operating foundation, current IRS regulations require that we *spend* approximately 4.25 percent of our endowment value each year. The intention of the regulation is to ensure that the foundation substantially conducts its exempt activities *directly*, rather than through grants to other organizations.

Joyce and I have directly collaborated with the school on several major projects in Rwanda. One of the most significant projects has been helping Cummings School introduce the One Health concept promoted by United States Agency for International Development throughout Africa, including at the University of Global Health Equity (UGHE) in Rwanda.

AFTER FORTY YEARS in commercial real estate, I came to a point where Cummings Foundation was now occupying the majority of my time and attention. Cummings Properties, under Dennis Clarke's capable leadership, meanwhile is operating quite successfully without anything like my daily involvement. Eric Anderson became our third-ever executive vice president in 2013, and the Executive Committee is growing steadily stronger. Joyce's and my early involvement in Rwanda was central in distancing or removing me from my desk at West Cummings Park—so much so that even when I am in the office now, I can sometimes be there a full day without my desk phone ringing a single time. (Writing and rewriting this book has also taken all of its fair share of my time.)

| *Dean Deborah Kochevar*

Not long after our relationship with Cummings School began, its dean of nearly ten years, Dr. Philip C. Kosch, stepped down. Since then, we have greatly enjoyed working with Dean Deborah Kochevar, who is an extremely bright and down-to-earth scholar and leader. Only the fourth woman in the United States to head a veterinary college, Dean Kochevar came to Cummings School from Texas A&M University, where she served as associate dean.

Debbie, as we know her, has been a true partner,

Andy Cunningham and Beth Mellor

Joyce and Bill Cummings delivering the commencement address for the tenth class to graduate from the Cummings School of Veterinary Medicine, May 2015

both at the North Grafton campus and in relation to our mutual work in Rwanda. She has also served as a trustee of Cummings Foundation. Joyce and I were delighted when she invited us to jointly address the tenth commencement class from Cummings School *per se* in 2015.

EACH YEAR, THE FOUNDATION receives hundreds of letters of inquiry for the annual *$100K for 100* grants program. In 2017, it received a record-breaking 597 submissions. Applicants are narrowed down in a three-stage process, and 100 winners each receive a grant of $100,000. Most of the program's annual 100 grants of $100,000 go to small nonprofits, and an extra proportion of the awards goes to urban areas such as Lowell, Lawrence, Dorchester, South Boston, Roxbury, and Lynn, since opportunities to make a meaningful difference are most significant in these places. We especially avoid making grants to applicants whose assets already dwarf our own.

The foundation has now established major donor relationships with close to a thousand local organizations—all in eastern Massachusetts—and has made cumulative grants to them totaling more than $200 million. Improving access to better educational opportunities is an important cause to us, as are initiatives concerning genocide, homophobia, job training, recidivism, and bullying. Programs supporting English skills for inclusion and assimilation and those promoting better writing and computing skills also rank high in our minds. There is an extensive list of the highly diverse grant winners on Cummings Foundation's website.

Joyce and I determined that becoming personally "connected" with any portion of so many different organizations would greatly impede our personal and family lifestyle, as we receive so many hundreds of invitations to attend these organizations' events each year. Although we once made most grants anonymously, the Cummings name has gradually become well-known in Greater Boston, though the foundation is still able to operate with its minimal staff and a rapidly growing group of dedicated and enthusiastic volunteers who help in many phases of the grant-making process. In recent years, attorney Robert Keefe of Boston law firm WilmerHale, close Tufts friend Susan Solomont, and Paul Lohnes of Massachusetts Charitable Mechanic Association have taken leadership roles organizing and assisting with the work of more than sixty volunteers each year.

WHILE THE VAST majority of the mostly small charities supported by the foundation's *$100K for 100* program were previously unknown to Joyce or me, every so often we personally add a grant recipient that is "close to home" for us. One such grantee was the Royall House and Slave Quarters on Main Street, Medford, which has lately been diligently unearthing parts of Medford's long-hidden colonial history.

It is little known, for instance, that Massachusetts was the first American colony to pass laws *legalizing* slavery, in 1641, and that African and, for a while, Native American slaves were kept throughout the colony. Indeed, one of the largest slave populations in Massachusetts was reportedly at the Isaac Royall House and Slave Quarters, where as many as forty slaves were held. This is perhaps not surprising, because Medford was famous for its clipper ships and its Old Medford rum, two of the essential legs in the "triangle trade" between Africa, the Caribbean, and Boston. In the late colonial days, however, there was apparently a rampant epidemic of amnesia throughout Massachusetts, at least regarding slavery in the region. *Ten Hills Farm*, by C. S. Manegold, offers remarkable insight about Massachusetts slavery.

Seventy years ago, I was taught in junior high school by teachers, who probably believed what they taught us, about the Royall House being part of the Underground Railway that harbored escaped slaves on their way to Canada. In recent years, instead, the management team of Royall House and Slave Quarters has been doing a remarkable job telling the fascinating albeit long-hidden true story about the horrors of slavery in the Boston area. It has been special to include the Royall House in our grant programs. There has been a particular interest in reaching middle school students from the entire region, with substantial funding from the foundation.

EVEN THOUGH WE have no business interests directly in Lynn, Joyce and I began working closely with Catholic Charities in relation to its English language program there. We established it as one of the first eastern Massachusetts organizations to receive what we now call a ten-year $1 million Sustaining Grant from the foundation. Not surprisingly, the Catholic Charities program brought us in contact with Cardinal Sean O'Malley.

While Joyce and I were enjoying a perfectly delightful dinner with His Eminence in 2014 at Winchester Country Club, he mentioned in passing

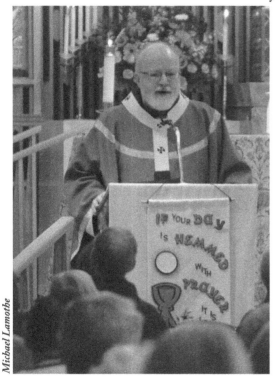

Michael Lamothe

that he had recently said Mass at Tufts. I told him about the arrangements I had made more than fifty years earlier with his distant predecessor, Cardinal Richard Cushing, to have the first-ever Catholic Mass on the Tufts campus. The service, held in Cohen Auditorium, was in connection with the 1957 regional convention of the former National Newman Club Federation. We joked that if I had not secured that approval back then, Cardinal O'Malley might not have been able to say Mass at Tufts in 2014.

His Eminence then celebrated the fiftieth anniversary of the Sisters of the Good Shepherd's residence in Marlborough by saying a Mass

Cardinal Sean O'Malley speaks during the daily Mass, New Horizons, Marlborough

for the Sisters and other New Horizons residents in January 2015. (Some of the Sisters housed at New Horizons taught in the Madonna Hall girls' boarding school, which operated at that location from 1963 to 1993.) Although it is nonsectarian, New Horizons offers daily Catholic Mass in its beautiful on-site chapel, plus weekly Jewish and Protestant services. Following the service, the Cardinal spent an additional hour visiting individually with all interested residents. We have come to know Cardinal O'Malley fairly well, especially through New Horizons and the work of the foundation, and hold him in extraordinarily high regard. He is an excellent listener and seems interested in wanting to know what people think as well as what they think about. We have enjoyed several extended quiet conversations concerning possible economical initiatives in Greater Boston.

In 2016, the foundation announced and funded a formal new program to identify an undetermined number of local charities to which we have begun awarding Sustaining Grants of as much as $1 million each, spread over ten years. The first recipients of these grants included CommonWealth Kitchen and Generations Incorporated, of Boston, Girls Incorporated of Greater Lowell, Lawrence CommunityWorks, and United Teen Equality Center of Lowell. This expansion of the Sustaining Grants, along with the *$100K for 100* program, brings our pre-programmed annual commitments to a total of $25 million in Eastern Massachusetts.

In 2017 and 2018, we began selecting dozens of other previous Cummings Foundation grant winners that collectively will share this additional $15 million or more each year in ten-year Sustaining Grants. Other diverse recipients of early Sustaining Grants of $1 million include Supportive Living, Inc., Winchester MultiCultural Network, and Boston VNA Hospice, as well as the Cummings/Hillel Program in Genocide Education at Tufts University and the similar program in Holocaust and genocide education at Salem State University. Most of the Sustaining Grants will be for ten years at $20,000, $25,000, or $33,000 per year.

Through Sustaining Grants, we shall help address the dearth of long-term financial support for nonprofits, especially smaller organizations. After learning of CommonWealth Kitchen's Sustaining Grant, Jen Faigel, its executive director, was quoted in a Boston newspaper saying, "This kind of resource is a real game-changer for an organization like ours. It's the kind of support that instills confidence in other funders. It's exciting how much this will accelerate us to the next level."

While the *$100K for 100* grant decisions are based primarily on written applications and online research, we wanted to get to know organizations on a deeper level before awarding Sustaining Grants. We are fortunate to now have a thirty-four-person committee of mostly retired professionals performing regularly scheduled site visits. Each charity in contention for one of these ten-year Sustaining Grants receives two site visits by pairs of committee members before they are selected. Recruiting diverse volunteers from among Greater Boston's professional community has helped us so much in making excellent philanthropic decisions. The foundation's volunteer force is now directly responsible for making the majority of all awards in this $25-million annual disbursement of funds. We were delighted that Massachusetts' enormously popular Governor Charlie Baker attended the celebration to honor the May 2018 grant recipients.

Many much larger grants of as much as $15 million and $20 million have recently also been made to Partners In Health, Boston; Tufts University; Lahey Health; Jamie McKeown Boys & Girls Club in Woburn; Salem State University; and Boston Museum of Science.

THE FOUNDATION now owns a substantial majority of all the buildings Cummings Properties operates, but , by law, the company is not allowed to receive any remuneration or fees from the foundation for any of its "in-kind" services. The comparison has been made with the Newman's Own food-products brand, which also reportedly uses 100 percent of all its profits to support charitable work. That's the case here, including all sales proceeds from this book.

Cummings Properties effectively provides Cummings Foundation with a sizable trust from which it writes grants and makes donations to a vast variety of highly diverse organizations that improve their respective communities. The company also often makes substantial grants in its own name (and outside the foundation), especially when it happens to have a business relationship with prospective grant recipients located within a building owned by the for-profit element of the organization. The focus on local donations is similar to Cummings Properties' business strategy of soliciting small local businesses as clients. The organizations that receive grants from Cummings Foundation tend to be institutions for which each dollar is crucial to their operating budgets.

The company has identified a critical interdependence between our business and its community: the stronger the community, the stronger the potential success for business. We believe any successful business has a responsibility to contribute to the strength of its community by helping to care for people who live there and patronize the business.

Although a business can invigorate a community merely by its presence, by paying its taxes and by contributing financially to the economy of a municipality, Cummings Foundation was created to truly enhance the communities where the Company has thrived for forty-five years. Through the two New Horizons residences, Cummings School of Veterinary Medicine, and significant support for multitudes of other resources, Cummings Foundation is now a major benefactor of people all over northeast Massachusetts.

Even though the original intention of Cummings Foundation was to stay local, Joyce's and my belief in the goodness of *all* humanity has also led us and the foundation to support genocide education, prevention, and recovery, especially relating to the Holocaust and the Rwandan genocide.

Our work with Partners In Health and the brand-new University of Global Health Equity, in Rwanda, is greatly improving health options and expanding the education of citizens across Rwanda and soon, we expect, all of Africa. Joyce and I have both been abundantly blessed with extraordinarily good health. I cannot remember ever taking a weekday off and hanging around the house not feeling well. With the exception of a couple of hernia repairs, plus two outpatient surgeries for cataracts, and a malignant melanoma fifteen years ago, I have needed almost no sick days over the past half-century, and I am so grateful for that. This has surely heightened our interest in wanting to help in our own small way to provide and ensure good healthcare for others.

Many small projects the foundation has undertaken have grown much larger than expected. Together, those small projects resulted in a huge difference in the quality of life for hundreds of thousands of people. Similarly, Cummings Properties started from a recognition that the unused land of Old Medford Foods should be something more. Meanwhile, we have tended to specialize in the small clients that might—and in many cases do—grow and expand. Small is not insignificant. Collectively, the impact from the organic growth of our leasing clients as well as our philanthropic clients has been gigantic.

❋ *As much as entrepreneurs might like to think they are going it alone (or that their teams are going it alone), companies do not exist in bubbles; they coexist as part of communities. In the spirit of the saying, "A rising tide lifts all boats," remember that money spent improving the lives of local residents will pay dividends by enhancing the entire community as a place to live, visit, and do business.*

❋ *A "transformative" gift is of such a magnitude that it will often result in a meaningful change in even the goals and aspirations of the receiving entity.*

❋ *Managers must constantly optimize combinations of quality and cost, and they must constantly teach others how to do the same. Well-trained, caring, long-term colleagues who understand what their company is all about and who want it to be a great firm are the greatest asset in any firm.*

❋ *All successful businesses have a responsibility to contribute to the strength of their communities by helping to care for people who live there and patronize these firms.*

[17]

Not a "Billionaires Club"

Joyce and Bill during a Guadalupe sailing vacation

IN EARLY 2011, JOYCE and I began to greatly broaden our philanthropic commitment when we joined the Giving Pledge, the international organization founded in 2010 by Bill and Melinda Gates and Warren Buffett. There are numerous excellent groups around the United States and abroad dedicated to high-level philanthropy, but we have never become involved with any others.

Neither Cummings Foundation nor Cummings Properties has enough staff members for them to be joiners or to attend non-essential meetings or events. In the forty-five-year history of Cummings Properties, we also almost never needed to attend conventions, trade shows, or similar gatherings. Joyce and I have traveled extensively all over the world for personal enrichment and enjoyment, and now for philanthropic purposes, but business travel *per se* has been all but nonexistent.

The Giving Pledge is loosely organized and except for occasional references to the three "founders," I have never seen or heard of any member of the group holding a title. Neither have we ever heard of votes being taken for any purpose, and there are no dues or membership fees. All these aspects help to make the group unlike any "club" we have ever known.

The group does not promote any particular charities or causes, and it was not set up to organize joint or collective contributions. It also appears to be entirely non political, although we, along with the Gates, Warren Buffett, and two dozen or so other Giving Pledge members, did meet with President Obama in the White House, in July 2011. For two hours, the President chaired the meeting, which included considerable give-and-take discussion about how philanthropies might better work with government agencies to accomplish more.

SHORTLY AFTER BECOMING Giving Pledge members, Joyce and I attended the first annual meeting, which brought together dozens of billionaires as guests of a delightful southern resort. It was startling to realize that every participant in the hall had not only the interest but also the desire *and the ability* to meaningfully improve the lives of *millions* of people. Bill and Melinda have likely already *saved* millions of lives through philanthropy. Looking over the large group of guests, we realized that while we fully qualified as members, we were among the "poorest" members there.

Although the participants tend to be extremely pleasant and friendly, it would be wrong to think of the Giving Pledge as a social organization. Its sole purpose is to promote philanthropy and share knowledge, techniques, and strategies for making a positive impact in our varied world. To that end, there is an annual meeting each spring and occasional regional meetings dedicated to specific topics. The meetings often feature member-led panels.

These events, as well as periodic communications from the Giving Pledge, are extraordinarily well planned and implemented. The Bill and Melinda Gates Foundation capably arranges activities, and numerous members serve as hosts, speakers, and facilitators, rather than employing outside speakers. The annual gatherings are typically hardworking two-day, three-night meetings, with full agendas from 7 AM through after-dinner hours. As I write this, Joyce and I have attended all but one of the Giving Pledge's first eight annual meetings. The members, each one an all-star of world philanthropy, participate to discuss and learn about philanthropy and have little time for amenities. Not that we have sacrificed in any way—the accommodations, service, and cuisine at each meeting have been beyond superb.

Some of the more well-known Giving Pledge members who joined early included: AOL founders, Steve and Jean Case, Chuck Feeney of Duty Free Shops, Ted Turner, George Lucas, Carl Icahn, Lyda Hill, David Rubenstein,

Elie and Edyth Broad, and eBay's Pierre and Pam Omidyar. Also, Jeff Skoll, Mark Zuckerberg and Priscilla Chan, and former New York mayor, Michael Bloomberg, as well as T. Boone Pickins, David Rockefeller, and Jon Huntsman.

Bill and Melinda Gates and Warren Buffett are an impressive trio, and before they leave this earth, they will likely find ways to save and then meaningfully improve more lives than any other three people now living. We have found them to be as genuinely smart, friendly, and caring as they are rich and powerful, whatever "powerful" means.

A national news source once quoted Bill when he jokingly bragged that he was valedictorian of his Harvard class—"the dropout class." From reading Warren's biography from a quarter-century ago, I learned that my earliest background is in many ways similar to parts of his, particularly our

| *Framed photo hanging in Bill's hotel room in Virunga National Park, near the northern edge of Rwanda*

predilections for self-made part-time jobs. And we tell strikingly similar stories about being rejected by Harvard Business School. I have heard that at one time the only plaque on Warren's office wall was the one he received years ago for completing a Dale Carnegie course. My office wall, on the other hand, is loaded with family pictures and other memorabilia, but they do not include even a single photo autographed by anyone.

In January 2012, during our first visit to Rwanda, we enjoyed a good example of how well-known Bill and Melinda Gates are in so many corners of the world. The majority of that trip was dedicated to foundation business, but we took two days to visit the highly endangered mountain gorillas in Virunga National Park, which required several hours of exceedingly bumpy driving north of Kigali. As we were settling into our mountain hotel, some familiar faces in a framed photo caught our eyes. Hanging right there in George Washington-slept-here style was a nice picture of past hotel guests Bill and Melinda, flanked by Dr. Paul Farmer, second from the left, and some others we did not know.

We should not have been too surprised to learn that Bill and Melinda had visited this place, as we were well aware of their many philanthropic interests in Rwanda. Looking back, I remember the private conversation with Bill Gates during the 2012 annual gathering of the Giving Pledge that gave us the reassurance we needed to commit to making a significant charitable investment in Rwanda. We were in the earliest stages of discussing—with Boston-based Partners In Health—what would eventually become the first outpatient center for cancer treatments anywhere in Rwanda. We had little experience with international philanthropy, but after the informal chat with Bill, we felt confident that Rwanda would be the ideal place for us to try to make a meaningful impact. And Joyce and I had already decided that Partners In Health was the perfect partner with which to do it.

This anecdote demonstrates what I think many Giving Pledge members find to be the most beneficial aspect of the organization: the opportunity to learn from others' experiences. As is shown on its website and elsewhere, the Giving Pledge has grown from about seventy American members to a roster, as of mid-2017, of more than 160 members from fourteen countries. Joyce and I were delighted when three additional couples from Massachusetts appeared on the published list of members. Most members are well-known, either regionally or nationally, and almost all are interesting and smart, and much like "regular" people. They demonstrate what appears to be a great and genuine care and concern for doing important, good things for the world.

Warren Buffett, in particular, was a helpful sounding board for me as I struggled with being simultaneously engaged in the seemingly contradictory activities of making money and giving it away. From my earliest days, my parents instilled in me the importance of *saving* money. And having run businesses for so long, I know all too well how difficult it can be to earn a dollar. Yet, no one needs to look hard to see the urgent needs in our own community and throughout the world that will benefit from our financial support. Warren readily related to the mental tug-of-war inherent in concurrently

An illustration to describe conflicting feelings about generating money and distributing at the same time

managing enormous assets and doing massive grant making.

Warren's solution, as he publicly shared in 2006, was to pick one primary activity: running his business. He effectively delegated much of the giving-it-away part to Bill and Melinda Gates, donating upwards of $30 *billion* worth of Berkshire Hathaway stock to *their* foundation, according to a June 26, 2006, *Wall Street Journal* article.

Joyce and I do not see ourselves sunsetting or outsourcing our philanthropy. The act of giving hard-earned dollars to help improve other people's lives fulfills me not only as a human being but also as a son. My parents and Joyce's parents were intimately acquainted with both sides of that equation—the discipline and ingenuity necessary to earn a dollar and the selflessness to help others in any way they could. Collectively, they are at the root of my story. Nevertheless, it was reassuring to hear Warren's perspective, and we hold him in extraordinarily high regard.

Another Giving Pledge member whose work I greatly admire is Michael Bloomberg, the former mayor of New York City and founder of the eponymously named global financial data and media company. Michael is also a former resident of Medford and a fellow graduate of Medford High School. While our alma mater recently noted that two of its graduates went on to become members of this unique group, it is unlikely that many other public high schools will ever make the same observation. His Honor was two years behind me at Medford High. We did not know each other at all at the time, but we lived two miles apart and had friends in common.

Medford also has at least one more less-direct tie to the Giving Pledge: Tufts University graduates Pam and Pierre Omidyar who hung around Medford for four years as Tufts undergraduates. After studying computer science at Tufts, Pierre went on to found the groundbreaking online auction company eBay. Although this talented and generous couple attended Tufts three decades after I did, our paths crossed in later years at trustee meetings and during major university events, including at Tufts' European campus in Talloires, France. Bloomberg, both of the Omidyars, Joyce and I all hold honorary degrees from Tufts and continue to be involved with and supportive of the institution that played such significant roles during our formative years. The Omidyars' $100 million grant to Tufts, in 2005, is still the university's largest-ever single grant.

Until we joined the Giving Pledge, Joyce and I had done most of our giving quietly; even our major philanthropic activities were known only in a relatively small geographic area. We have never been a part of Boston society circles, and rather than attending fundraising galas or museum openings, we far more often spent our evenings with the same friends we have enjoyed since our kids and theirs were all in their infancies. Our lives are much the same today, except that our participation in the Giving Pledge and other foundation-related activities does provide some fascinating experiences.

When *The Boston Globe* ran a front-page story in 2011 about our joining the Giving Pledge, the response was overwhelmingly positive, although all the attention was a bit embarrassing. There followed exceedingly kind notes from strangers and friends alike, including many friends who were greatly surprised by the revelation. Most of our friends pretty much knew that we were comfortable financially, but none had guessed that our assets or those of the foundation had grown enough to put us in this particular company.

Although membership in the Giving Pledge comes with no requirements beyond committing at least half of one's wealth for philanthropic purposes, members often help educate potential new members about the organization and its activities. As the first Massachusetts couple to join, Joyce and I were pleased to co-host an intimate dinner with Bill

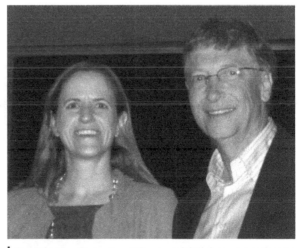

Dr. Marilyn Cummings Morris and Bill Gates, immediately following 2012 Giving Pledge dinner

Gates for some Boston-area residents whose assets were believed to meet the billion-dollar threshold. Given that Joyce and I were not well-acquainted with any other people who fit this description, the Giving Pledge provided a prospective guest list, and we assisted by providing a great venue and making personal phone calls to follow up on formal invitations. This dinner, in February 2012, took place during the time when we owned and operated Beacon Grille Restaurant (now Strega Prime) at our TradeCenter 128 office campus in Woburn.

By the time the Giving Pledge dinner came together, Joyce had already made plans to be with friends in Florida. Our eldest daughter, Marilyn, therefore served as my co-host, driving from New York to help me welcome Bill Gates, his staff members, and our local guests, which included one Boston couple who did later join the Giving Pledge.

As one might imagine, everyone present was extremely interested in what Bill Gates had to say. He openly shared his and Melinda's thinking about many aspects of philanthropy, but he also showed much attention and genuine interest in every other guest's charitable activities and thoughts about how to make the largest impact through giving.

BOLSTERED WITH encouraging information from Giving Pledge associates, we began our first Rwandan trip in Kigali in 2012. Kigali is a modern city in the center of a landlocked sub-Saharan country about the size of Vermont. There is a rapidly growing airport and major roads leading out of the city in several directions, but even some of these spoke roads soon run out of pavement, and the country has little yet in the way of connecting highways.

Our good friends Alice and Dr. Arlan (Skip) Fuller joined us for this first trip, after learning that we planned to include a visit to Rwanda's Volcanoes National Park for up-close encounters with families of the rare mountain gorillas. In addition to visiting Agahozo-Shalom Youth Village and the gorillas, we toured two rural hospitals operated by Partners In Health, the Boston-based organization founded by Dr. Paul Farmer, Ophelia Dahl, and others. Coincidentally, Joyce and I had the pleasure of meeting Paul for the first time a few days before this trip, during a lunch in Boston arranged by PIH trustee

Bill took this photo of a 700-pound silverback in the wild from about nine feet away

and philanthropist Jack Connors.

There are reportedly fewer than 800 mountain gorillas in the world. All are now highly protected, and most dwell in the contiguous national parks of Rwanda, Uganda, and the Democratic Republic of Congo. These parks meet on the side of a high volcano in the Virunga Mountains, north of Kigali. The gorillas typically roam at high altitudes, eating as much as seventy-five pounds of vegetation daily. Another smaller population of gorillas inhabits the Bwindi Impenetrable Forest. Eighteen individually named mountain-gorilla families reside in Rwanda, and fourteen of them are acclimated to humans. We visited the Ugenda family on Friday and the Sabyinyo family on Saturday.

Our first trek to visit with the gorillas began after our Land Rover bumped us violently up to about 6,000 feet above sea level. Then we climbed to a spot at more than 8,000 feet, where, higher up than our guide expected to find them, the guide's scout located the family we would visit that day. We had already become somewhat acclimated to the lower oxygen level because all of Rwanda is high above sea level, so the altitude did not seem to be much of an additional factor for any of our eight-person group.

The adult gorillas were ready for a rest, but several babies were crawling around over the adults. The dominant silverback lay still for quite a while, but eventually he rolled around and let one of the youngsters know he was in no mood to be bothered. We were remarkably close and able to get terrific photos, but after exactly one hour, we were required to leave promptly.

THIS BOOK CANNOT begin to devote appropriate space or attention to the historical and political events surrounding the horrendous Rwandan genocide. Instead, here is just a bit of context for our trip to Rwanda, and Cummings Foundation's philanthropy there: The genocide officially began in April 1994, although sporadic massacres had been occurring for several years prior, and it lasted for 100 days, during which the Tutsi people of Rwanda were singled out for death. Altogether, the horrifying atrocities claimed

Skulls of victims killed in a Kigali church are lined up and displayed on steel racks

the lives of more than 800,000 Rwandans.

In 2001, the Rwandan government invited Aegis Trust, a charity dedicated to the prediction, prevention, and ultimately, elimination of genocide, to establish a memorial and museum in partnership with the Kigali City Council. The memorial opened in 2004, at the time of the tenth anniversary of the genocide. More than 250,000 victims of the genocide were buried on the museum grounds, many in respectful glass-topped crypts surrounded by beautiful gardens.

The museum's main exhibit tells the history of Rwanda leading up to the genocide, and it catalogues the details of the genocide through personal testimonies, photographs, videos, and artifacts. There is also a small room dedicated to children, the most innocent victims of the genocide. On another floor, the exhibit "Wasted Lives" reflects on other genocides of the past, including the massacres in Armenia, southwest Africa, Bosnia, and Cambodia, and of course, the Holocaust.

The day after visiting Kigali Genocide Memorial, we toured Kigali and also traveled out of the city to visit two former churches where thousands of people had sought refuge during the massacres. When there were troubles in 1959, the church supposedly protected anyone who was able to get to it, but not so in 1994. Many priests and ministers had reportedly left the country and were simply not there to provide sanctuary. Emotionally, this was the single most difficult part of the trip.

At the two former churches, we viewed walls gruesomely splattered with blood, where babies had reportedly been thrown against the walls to kill them. Each church also has hundreds of victims' bloody clothes, turned brown with time and carefully laid out

> *The Holocaust is the most readily recognized example of genocide, and the most atrocious outbreak of this recurring madness...*

on pews and kneelers. Even altar cloths were heavily stained with splashed blood. We repeatedly heard stories of women who were raped and then further violated with poles thrust into their sex organs. Like in a horrific nightmare, rows and rows of skulls are displayed on steel racks with piles of the victims' other bones just beneath. "This one was killed by a machete," the guides pointed out. "This one by a club..."

The Holocaust is the most readily recognized example of genocide and the most atrocious outbreak of this recurring madness that has infected our world throughout history. But from the tribal groups in Darfur today to Rwanda and Armenia to the Native Americans during the European colonization of the Americas, and even long before that, history provides all too many examples of the persecution, displacement, and murder of entire populations.

IN 2007, in Rubona, Rwanda, Anne Heyman, a South African-born woman from Long Island, New York, and her family began building what would become a wonderful residential high school called Agahozo-Shalom Youth Village. They used basic, quality materials and good workmanship, and the complex is beautiful in its no-frills simplicity. In 2008, it opened with one class of 125 students and added similar-sized classes each of the next three years. By 2012, it was at its full occupancy of 500 students as a marvelous four-year facility for the most needy young people in the country. Anne, who died in a tragic equestrian accident in Florida in 2014, and her husband, Seth Merrin, had three young adult children.

Agahozo-Shalom means "a place to dry one's tears in peace." In one way or another, most of its students are victims of the 1994 Rwandan genocide, but all are now selected because they are among the country's most vulnerable children. Joyce and I and the Fullers spent three nights in the guesthouse there.

The "mayor" in each of Rwanda's thirty districts submits to the school a list of the ten most vulnerable children between the ages of fifteen and nineteen in the district, from which a list of 300 children is created. The list

| *Agahozo-Shalom Youth Village was established in Rwanda by Anne Heyman in 2007*

is culled to around 200, at which point "home" visits are made to determine which children will be chosen to attend Agahozo-Shalom. "Home" is in quotation marks because some have no family and are living on the streets. Others have no parents but live with a relative. Some have one parent, often a mother who has HIV from being raped during the genocide. (The HIV rate in Rwanda is substantial but still reportedly among the lowest in Africa.)

Still other prospective students are effectively heads of households, taking care of younger siblings. Most new students pick up some English before they arrive, but all are soon fluent.

The 2,000 daily meals served in the single large dining room, designed to hold the entire school population, are an excellent example of the school's efficient and organized operation. The students, all of whom appear to be quite happy, healthy, and well-mannered, eat together at long tables that each seat twenty people. They enter the dining room, serve themselves family style from huge containers of rice and vegetables (refilled by student runners), clear their plates, wipe the tables, and depart, all in well under an hour. Much of the food at Agahozo-Shalom is grown on its own farm. At the time we visited, there were no freezers and only two small reach-in refrigerators. Food was cooked in great oversized pots, over wood fires.

While many of the school's graduates go on to college, including some who have already come to the United States and Canada, the overriding goal is to give students tools to be responsible citizens with the ability to earn a living, be good parents, think straight, and contribute to a peaceful society.

Throughout the country, there is a fervent policy not only of reconciliation but also of retraining people to not blindly follow anyone. Still, the question remains: How much will it take to change a culture that condoned the massacre of hundreds upon hundreds of thousands of friends, neighbors, and even family members in the horrific genocide of 1994? How will Rwandans eventually overcome this disastrous tragedy?

Founder Anne Heyman visited Salem State University with Joyce and me in early 2014 to meet with Salem's then-president Patricia Meservey. With President Meservey's magnificent support, that university sent its first faculty-led groups of students to Rwanda in 2015 and 2016. They were based most of the time at Agahozo-Shalom Youth Village. Like ten classes of Tufts students during the prior decade, most of the Salem State students come back with enormous gratitude for (and a new perspective on) all they have back home, accompanied by a remarkably increased interest in helping others less fortunate than themselves.

ON ONE OF our mornings in Kigali, Joyce wrote, "Looking out the hotel window at a beautiful large swimming pool, listening to soothing sounds of a fountain, drinking in the clean air, and enjoying large tropical plants… This is the way God intended Rwanda to be." From its 1994 image as the worst country on earth, Rwanda has come magnificently far. There

| *Joyce and Bill Cummings with Alice Fuller in a rural Rwandan village*

Arlan Fuller, Jr.

are many organizations with smart, energetic, dedicated people who are working hard every day to help return Rwanda to its natural beauty and its peaceful way of life. Partners In Health is one of the most important and effective such organizations.

Dr. Paul Farmer, Ophelia Dahl, Dr. Jim Yong Kim, Thomas J. White, and Todd McCormack all worked to found PIH in 1987, originally to support schools and healthcare in Haiti. Although well-known for its ongoing work there through Tracy Kidder's renowned best-selling book *Mountains Beyond Mountains*, PIH has expanded its services throughout the world, creating medical centers in the United States, Russia, Peru, Mexico, Guatemala, and several African countries. We visited two of the three PIH hospitals in Rwanda.

Rwinkwavu Hospital, the first Rwandan PIH hospital, was launched in April 2005, when the Rwandan government's health officials asked PIH to replicate the work it was doing in Haiti. When Dr. Farmer went to Rwanda to scout potential locations, he declared one of the sites too nice and asked to visit instead the most impoverished area in Rwanda. Rwinkwavu was it.

We had a morning meeting at Rwinkwavu Hospital with all levels of the hospital management and healthcare providers and received an extensive tour of the facility. In the afternoon, we went with a nurse and social worker for some home visits. It took more than an hour to get to the first village, far off the paved road, where the many children who greeted us all wanted the wazungu ("white people") to take their photos. The kids were excited when they saw their pictures on a digital camera.

Butaro Hospital, in northern Rwanda, was built through a collaboration between PIH, Rwanda's Ministry of Health, and private North American financial contributions. The flagship 150-bed facility is the first permanent hospital in Burera District, which previously had only one doctor to serve more than 300,000 people. Plans are underway to make Butaro Hospital the cancer center for the entire country and the hospital component of the new medical university.

Dr. Peter Drobac,* the former director for PIH in Rwanda, who also holds an appointment at Brigham and Women's Hospital in Boston, described the neonatal intensive-care unit at Butaro as just one example of the new services the hospital is now offering. "Prematurity and low birth weight are incredibly common here because of malnutrition, malaria, and other factors associated with poverty," Dr. Drobac said. "Even babies born full-term frequently look like preemies, and many babies are still dying. Although we now have incubators and other equipment, simple things can also be done to prevent these deaths."

| Dr. Peter Drobac

In 2013 Cummings Foundation built the first outpatient cancer clinic in the country, adjacent to Butaro Hospital. A year later we would be highly instrumental in working with PIH to begin the first phase of University of Global Health Equity there as well.

❋ *To accelerate the learning process, seek out opportunities to learn from the experiences of others. Joining the Giving Pledge allowed Joyce and me to hear about different philanthropic practices and philosophies, albeit often from vastly different perspectives. Although what works for other members—even Warren Buffett—may not work for us, being aware of the many possible paths helps us to make better, more confident decisions.*

❋ *Most people do not lack the strength to succeed, nearly as often as they lack the will.*

---

* *Dr. Drobac and his wife, Dr. Neo Tapela, and their two young daughters left PIH in October 2017 for England, where Peter became director of the Skoll Center for Social Entrepreneurship at The University of Oxford. I was honored in late 2018 to accept a speaking engagement at the Saïd Business School Entrepreneurship Forum in March 2019.*

[18]

Real-Life Monopoly

MORE THAN FORTY years ago, a highly successful real estate friend from Reading, Massachusetts, gave me a copy of Bill Zeckendorf's 1970 autobiography, *Zeckendorf: The Autobiography of the Man Who Played a Real-life Game of Monopoly and Won (and Lost) the Largest Real Estate Empire in History.* My friend inscribed the book "Bill – Wish you a portion of this success, but a more successful ending. s/Don Dolben."

Michael Lamothe

Cummings Properties' new (July 2018) president, Eric Anderson (left), founder Bill Cummings, and chairman, Dennis Clarke (seated)

The Zeckendorf book, written with Edward McCreary, describes Zeckendorf as "a Monopoly tycoon," and by all standards, he likely was. When Dennis Clarke committed us in 2011 to purchasing the fifty-four-acre former headquarters of Parker Brothers and Atari games, before I ever saw it, we effectively acquired the local-area legacy of this famed Massachusetts firm. We would be successors, in a way, to a choice bit of the iconic and most genuine Monopoly patrimony, on Dunham Road in Beverly.

Although I was never even close to being a failure as real estate moguls go, I would also never have tried to emulate Mr. Zeckendorf's spectacular career, even if I did have the brains or the opportunity. Furthermore, the older I grew, the less important it seemed to accumulate more square feet. On the other hand, I still enjoy the game of Monopoly, and as a firm we greatly enjoyed the opportunity to play real-life Monopoly in Beverly, and what an opportunity that was. At first, we joked about calling it "Ultra Monopoly."

With massive unlocked potential and 760 feet of frontage abutting Massachusetts' famed Technology Highway (Route 128), just off exit 19, this project let me play yet again with real-life Erector sets and Tonka trucks—hundreds of them. We may soon have a major hotel on a new main street named Boardwalk Drive. Founded in Massachusetts in 1883, Parker Brothers was a family-owned company that General Mills purchased in 1968 and operated as a subsidiary for several decades. Later it was purchased by Tonka, and then Hasbro.

Purchasing this site was the sweetheart deal that Dennis, in his tenure as president and CEO of Cummings Properties, found and determined we could not pass up. It truly was a unique opportunity to purchase an existing 100,000-square-foot first-class office building on

| *The former Parker Brothers headquarters at 50 Dunham Road*

fifty-four bucolic and conveniently located acres. This lone structure was neatly centered among the tall trees, hills, and streams and overlooked beautiful Norwood Pond.

Eastern Bank facilitated the transaction by signing off on a deeply discounted short sale, thus waiving its mortgage loan balance on the property. The asset, with its almost empty building, was lovely, but as with The Shoe, there had supposedly been no other interested buyers for years. Luckily, we were able to do another all-cash close for a rock-bottom $2.3 million purchase price in December 2011. The property had stunning but totally unrecognized additional buildability for about eight large office or other light-industrial buildings. The most important and difficult and expensive project was creating a gorgeous "shovel-ready" five-acre site at the top of West Hill after we removed a heavy forest of fifty- and sixty-foot-tall pine trees, and leveled the hill off at thirty-two feet below its original peak elevation.

Real estate investors will do well to remember that December is the best time to be looking for deals on problem real estate. Banks are much more motivated to rid their balance sheets of loans gone bad before each calendar year ends, often giving buyers who offer no-nonsense purchase proposals much improved buying opportunities. The cost for financial institutions to maintain under-producing assets on their books can be truly staggering. Fast, decisive moves can consummate such transactions and secure the most attractive deals. Having the ability to do all-cash proposals, as we always have done, or at least having enough cash to qualify for a conventional mortgage, can put any buyer in a great position.

Somewhat ironically, within six months of our purchasing the Dunham Road property, the largest tenant by far, Fantastic Sams, moved out, but it moved only three miles to our Cummings Center. Then, about one month later, Cummings Center general manager Steve Drohosky convinced a major Cummings Center client, Microline Surgical, to expand at what we now call Dunham Ridge, and we were off. Moving to Dunham allowed Microline Surgical to double its office and light-manufacturing footprint to a total of 68,000 square feet, and to do so in just the idyllic country setting it sought.

WHEN OUR DEVELOPMENT TEAM first arrived at Dunham Road, we were surprised to learn about some exceedingly limiting wetlands restrictions at what we otherwise found to be an ideal new location. The Beverly Conservation Commission, in our opinion, had mistakenly and somewhat arbitrarily classified several large areas of the Dunham property as "vernal pools," a type of protected seasonal wetland. What we viewed as commission's overreaching measures totally confounded our initial long-term development thoughts. After being rebuffed during meetings with the commission, we took the matter to Essex County Superior Court but lost. The court effectively ruled that irrespective of the wording of Beverly's wetlands regulation, it was the intent of the conservation commission regulations that mattered and not the

Stephen Drohosky

Jonathan "Bo" Lamb

exact wording of the published regulation. More specifically, the court determined that several wet areas on the property did not have to completely dry up each summer to be classified as vernal pools, even if the plain English of Beverly's regulations clearly stated otherwise. There was abundant evidence proving that the supposed vernal pools retained water year-round and, therefore, were not vernal pools, but our position was totally rejected.

One of our top in-house attorneys, Jonathan "Bo" Lamb, immediately appealed the case in the higher Massachusetts Appeals Court, however, and in April 2015, a portion of the Superior Court's decision was quickly reversed in our favor. In a summary decision, Judges Green, Wolohojian, and Blake remanded the case back to the Beverly commission for further proceedings after finding that its omission of a portion of its own regulation was in error as a matter of law. Most importantly, the Appeals Court rejected the Superior Court's view that even though the Beverly regulations may have been intended to have a different effect, the clear language of the written document could be interpreted only in accord with the common and customary use of the English language.

Not surprisingly, a senior engineering official who had recently left the city's employment thereafter appeared to take on a retaliatory attitude unlike anything we had encountered before. Although the conservation commission itself responded appropriately enough, the engineer demonstrated an adversarial approach, several times delaying approvals or even disapproving other unrelated site activities.

Nevertheless, following this important Appeals Court decision, Dunham Road became dramatically more developable and is already delivering meaningfully increased municipal real estate taxes, even without much rental income. Indeed, construction is underway for a new large office and research structure at 48 Dunham Ridge. Altogether, the 54-acre site will support several hundred thousand square feet of additional mid-rise buildings.

Still a giant factor in the success of the company is our ability to occasionally acquire occupied but undeveloped or grossly underdeveloped properties and then build one or more new buildings adjacent. New space created in this manner—often with effectively no cost for the land and with adequate utilities, parking and other amenities available at little or no additional cost—have helped us build dozens of new buildings and additions at a fraction of the usual cost. This has been the ongoing and hugely successful operational mode of Cummings Properties, greatly benefiting several host cities.

UNUSED BUILDABILITY has thus been a common denominator among so many of our real estate transactions for four decades. Such buildability is among the most significant features real estate developers should seek, yet it is so often ignored. What "extras" are there that other prospective buyers may have overlooked? The value implications of unused or underused land can be astonishing and can make a dramatic difference in the long-term success of any real estate investment.

> *"Unused buildability" has thus been a common denominator among so many of our real estate transactions for four decades.*

We had expected to lie low for a while after almost completing the highly successful development of Cummings Center in about 2010. Yet, here we are into the present day with two new Cummings Center buildings recently developed or under development and four more large structures in design or in progress at Dunham Ridge. Though acquiring the property that would become Dunham Ridge seriously postponed my *emeritus* phase with the company, it gave us a tremendous opportunity. Dennis found such a good deal that was totally

| *Bill at the future site of 52 Dunham Ridge, August 2015*

overlooked by others in the marketplace. Plus, how many builders have the opportunity to redevelop and likely build a real life hotel on the property where Monopoly grew and thrived?

Putting aside much of my personal work at Cummings Foundation, I had what will probably be my last big fling of fieldwork during the summer of 2015 at Dunham Road. We had trucks, bulldozers, a giant rock crusher, and huge excavators going in every direction as we totally reordered almost thirty acres for these new projects. I have taken no salary from any source for eleven years now; my work at Dunham has been a labor of love, with all corporate profit, in one way or another, benefiting Cummings Foundation.

We blasted untold thousands of tons of granite, and then excavated and crushed the broken granite every day for a month. This would have been a small project for a big land-development company, perhaps, but it was quite significant for us. Doing it all in-house with our own team of a dozen staff members, a few small subcontractors, and lots of heavy-duty rental equipment was perfect. From my view, I had a bonus vacation playing with all the equipment for a whole season. To boot, I lost a beneficial dozen pounds during the process. I chased earth-moving equipment all over the site from 7:01 AM every day and loved every minute of it.

Reportedly the largest taxpayer in Beverly, we are as concerned as every appointed or elected official should be about Beverly's fiscal health and about building the tax base of the city. Once it became obvious that key members of Beverly's municipal leadership might be intent on throwing up roadblocks, however, the time had come to reduce our efforts in Beverly.

We seek cooperative, open relationships with local administrators, and we work with our host communities in a mutually respectful manner. Going to court to establish such relationships is not the perfect outcome for us, and certainly not for the municipality, either. Making use of the court system is, however, sometimes a necessity.

Recognizing that we might be creating more commercial space than greater Beverly needs, we decided to build only one or two more office buildings at Dunham Ridge for our own account. Although 100 percent of profits earned by Cummings Properties eventually goes to support the philanthropic work of Cummings Foundation too, all buildings owned by either entity still pay their full fair share of real estate taxes in each host community. We also work to donate earnings to the best charities in the communities where the buildings are located, especially when we are not pressured to do so. We remain careful about *not* donating when it becomes clear that it might appear that we are attempting to win imbalance in any community by making large contributions.

For the remainder of the beautiful Dunham property, we now expect to sell or lease most parcels for independent, freestanding businesses. Indeed, in February 2017, we sold off the newly laid-out 54 Dunham Ridge parcel to Vitality Senior Living. The six-acre portion is expected to be developed in 2019 or so as an upscale, independent memory-care and assisted living complex with approximately 118 units. Vitality is a new national chain of memory-care and assisted living homes being developed by affiliates of the Gary and Mary West Foundation. In connection with that broker-free sale we were pleased to arrange a direct 1031 Exchange with Boston Properties to acquire our first office building in Andover.

THE ELLIOTT LANDING condominium project, meanwhile, is one of our latest major building developments. The seventy-three-home property is located in Beverly at the extreme southwest corner of Cummings Center. Although we had always expected that this now ninety-acre site would continue to be redeveloped entirely for commercial and public-service uses (including, we thought, a hotel), we determined in 2014 that adding high-

| *Elliott Landing condominium at Cummings Center, Beverly, 2017*

end residences to Cummings Center would work especially well.

With thoughts of providing good housing in areas convenient to workplaces and public transportation, we determined that luxury residential units are the perfect bookend for the south side of Cummings Center. Already being recognized as an established Beverly community, Cummings Center, after twenty years, had everything but residents. But now, the new condominiums have brought in about 140 new Beverly citizens to enjoy magnificent water views over the Bass River to the south and Cummings Center's own urban environment to the north.

We already had the steel piles and concrete foundation in the ground when we decided to give up plans for a Cummings Center hotel, and it was not difficult to enlarge the footprint and build the six-story condominium building instead. Although I did not realize it at the time, my last-minute decision to add two feet to the new building's ground-floor elevation, in anticipation of global warming, proved to be highly beneficial when it came time to certify that we were not in a defined flood zone. Selling the Elliott Landing homes as condominiums was, of course, consistent with beginning to reduce our commitment to and our exposure in Beverly.

About half of the Elliott Landing buyers are retirement-age couples or individuals who are downsizing from large local homes they no longer need. The other half are people of all other ages, some of whom are now walking to their work in Cummings Center or to nearby MBTA stops. The lack of grounds maintenance required by owners is highly appealing to those no longer interested in cutting grass, raking leaves, and shoveling snow.

Highly attractive also to many buyers at Elliott Landing is the Cummings Center neighborhood itself, which has a half-dozen good dining options, two of which include full-service lounges, and the eighteen-hole Beverly Golf and Tennis Club. There is a mile-long circular walkway, with twenty-four cast-aluminum historic markers, around our two beautiful on-site ponds, plus Beverly Athletic Club and several smaller fitness facilities. Cummings Center's robust health and wellness community includes approximately twenty distinct medical specialties which also appeal to local residents.

We decided to provide housing, rather than more office space or a hotel, on this newly laid-out lot after determining that Cummings Center, like Dunham Ridge, has enough office space. Building more offices there would further delay our ability to enjoy a fully leased office complex. In fact, across most of Beverly, there is no longer an insatiable need for more office, laboratory, or marketing space, and if we continued to build commercial space, we would soon be competing mostly with ourselves and hurting other commercial owners, too.

ONE COMMON MISCONCEPTION about relieving Greater Boston's housing shortage is that it makes a great difference what type of housing is built in any community. With Greater Boston's chronic shortage, new housing units at any level will ultimately benefit *all* levels of housing needs. Even the most expensive new units will help to free up other less expensive housing, thus trickling down to lower housing costs for even the least affluent buyers. The seventy-three Elliott Landing homes sold out at prices from around $400,000 to just over $800,000.

Construction of Elliott Landing went along exceedingly well, and we moved in the first residents during Thanksgiving week 2016, just thirty years after we completed our much larger Place Lane Condominium in Woburn. As of August 2017, all the Elliott Landing homes were sold or were under written agreement. Cummings Center is now truly Beverly's newest neighborhood and, as our sales theme states, thousands of people now "Live, Work, and Play in Cummings Center."

Work on a much smaller building for housing at 33 Balch Street, at the opposite end of the property, is separately pending municipal approval as I complete this chapter. Building housing at the otherwise unused areas at each end of Cummings Center seems to be the correct approach to finishing those two areas, which have now been totally repurposed twenty years after we acquired the property.

According to knowledgeable members of the Beverly Historical Society, the seventy-three Elliott Landing homes are located exactly where the original Friend's Grist Mill stood during the 1650s, when this area of Beverly was a part of the city of Salem. We celebrated the history of this seventeenth-century mill that launched an uninterrupted series of commercial uses for the site that is now Cummings Center. An actual millstone believed to be from Friend's Mill and on loan from Beverly Historic Commission, is prominently displayed along the walking trail adjacent to Acapulco's Restaurant.

Cummings Properties' management was pleased to host the 2015 Tide Mill Institute Conference in the Community Conference Room at Cummings Center. John Goff, a local representative of the Tide Mill Institute, recently discovered an additional millstone from Friend's Mill at the edge of Bass River, partially buried just above the high-water line.

| *Tide Mill Institute Conference, 2015 at Cummings Center*

This newly discovered stone is visible near the terminus of the crosswalk, fewer than 100 yards from Elliott Landing.

❀ *Whether writing a book, developing a piece of land, or doing any number of other activities, a fresh set of eyes is invaluable. Do not simply accept someone else's assessment (or maybe even the general consensus) without looking more closely for what others might have overlooked. Consider, too, how the source of any advice might be burdened with latent or outright biases, and remember that not all opinions should be given the same weight. Seek out the unused buildability in your area of work.*

❀ *Acquiring commercial properties with "unused buildability" have been an oft-repeated theme in this book for real estate success. With the cost of purchasing and developing land typically representing 20 to 40 percent of a building project's total cost, buying a property capable of supporting additional square feet can be like finding free money.*

[19]

Back to Africa

An intrepid Dr. Skip Fuller was first jumping into Devil's Pool at the top edge of the breathtaking 1,000 foot-high Victoria Falls, in the Zambezi River, 2013

AFTER OUR FIRST exciting and highly successful trip to Rwanda, Joyce and I were delighted to return in August 2013, again with the Fullers, for an even more stirring and productive visit.

On this journey, we took a more scenic route to Rwanda, from London via South Africa, and then enjoyed three days at Victoria Falls on the border of Zambia and Zimbabwe on the Zambezi River. After observing the majestic mile-long falls from all the conventional viewing trails, and then from a helicopter, Alice, Skip, and I were signed up for a guided water-level view from Devil's Pool *in the water* directly at the upper edge of the falls. This is surely one of the most dangerous tourist attractions in the world, and we knew it.

From late August through January, a few tourists are able to travel by boat every hour or so across the open water to Livingston Island at the upper edge of Victoria Falls. Our guide's sixteen-foot-long aluminum boat had a new-looking single outboard motor, but anyone who has spent any time around small boats knows that outboards will sometimes stop running at inopportune times. Possible motor failure was the first real danger of the day.

Once there, we were required to hike upstream along the edge of the Zambezi River from Livingston Island. Then we swam to an outcropping of ledge just above the edge of the falls, near the midpoint of this spectacular natural wonder. The greatest danger during the swim seemed to me to be the possibility of becoming mesmerized by the fast downstream flow and missing the tiny island. Although neither guide asked if anyone wanted to back out, he did ask us a second time if we still self-identified as "strong swimmers." I wondered what that question really meant in a life-or-death setting like this one, but after a vigorous swim across the rapidly moving current, we all scrambled safely onto the rock near the center of the falls.

At that point, there was nothing to do but throw all caution to the wind and leap into the deep, water-filled depression. The pool itself is about thirty feet square and perhaps twenty feet deep. The natural rock formation defined the outer edge of Devil's Pool and the edge of the chasm wall and was about eighteen inches thick. While resting in the water on the top of this shallow lip of rock, we leaned out, oh so carefully, and looked 1,000 feet straight down into the thundering mist.

After the visit to the pool, with millions of tons of water cascading down all around us, we swam safely back across where the

The awe and majesty of this gem of south-central Africa were breathtaking. We did it because it was there.

current was slow, and then the guides escorted us individually to where Joyce held our wallets and watches, on Livingston Island. Dozens of people have reportedly been swept over the falls to horrific deaths over the last fifty years, including one guide who had died just a year earlier. Three elephants were swept over the year before. In one manner or another the deceased tourists had been doing exactly the same thing we were doing. This was adventure tourism at its most extreme, with no expectation of safety for anyone. The awe and majesty of this gem of south-central Africa were breathtaking.

Bungee jumping in Queenstown, New Zealand, a decade earlier was more scary, but swimming at the brink of Victoria Falls was by far the most dangerous thing any of us had ever done, or ever will do again.

We timed the rest of this second African journey to coincide with the dedication of Butaro Ambulatory Cancer Center. During our visit the previous year, Joyce and I had committed several million dollars to fund the construction of this important new center. Although Rwanda had made impressive strides in healthcare since the genocide, the foundation's new facility was still the first outpatient cancer-treatment clinic in the country.

The New Times, Rwanda

Shown at the Butaro Outpatient Center are (left to right): Burera Mayor Samuel Sembagare, Joyce Cummings, Patricia Campbell, Bill Cummings, Dr. Paul Farmer, and Dr. Agnes Binagwaho

We spent considerable time during this dedication visit becoming better acquainted with representatives of PIH and the government of Rwanda. Paul Farmer and his wife, Didi, hosted a lovely dinner in their Kigali home. We also greatly enjoyed the company of Dr. Peter Drobac and his wife, Dr. Neo Tapela, who lived then in Botswana with their two young children. We were also honored to share an elegant lunch with Paul, Peter, and their wives at the Kigali home of His Excellency, President Paul Kagame, and Madam First Lady Jeannette Kagame. I continue to exchange occasional emails with President Kagame, and we were delighted to see him again in 2014 at Tufts University, where he lectured and spent time with students. Later, I spent a morning with him in Boston, in February 2016.

Over a short few months, we came to know and highly respect Paul Farmer and his truly remarkable organization, which was then regularly operating in eight countries around the world. Likewise, we admired President Kagame for how well he used his keen intellect and business mindset to completely turn around the economy of his country and the quality of life of its citizens. Any political leader trying to prevent a country from annihilating itself has a moral obligation to fairly use all power at his disposal to restore order. Kagame must be admired and honored for his work.

While some may portray President Kagame as a tyrant, he is the one who suppressed the madness of a whole nation going insane at the same time. He has proven to be a smart, courageous, and highly effective president. Rwanda managed to find a heroic and trustworthy leader with great competence who also appears to be creating an honest and graft-free society. Those who would malign President Kagame for his desperately needed strong methods in stopping an unfathomable genocide, in my opinion, do him and the republic a great disservice. Another great book by Tracy Kidder, *Strength in What Remains*, is certainly an outstanding resource for understanding how the great genocide materialized and was then brought under control by Kagame and other leaders. I asked President Kagame what he thought about *Strength in What Remains*, and he told me he did not agree with Kidder on everything he wrote, but on balance, His Excellency was "glad he wrote the book."

OUR 2013 TRIP to Africa was most notable for providing an opportunity for Joyce and me to spawn the notion that the significant upgrades under discussion for Rwanda's health sciences schools could become something much greater. A fortuitous conversation developed in Kigali during a meeting billed as an Oral Health Stakeholders Meeting, a session that brought us together with Rwandan experts in the field of dentistry and healthcare delivery, along with Dr. Drobac and several key educators from National University of Rwanda, Tufts University, and Harvard University. In addition to Peter, and Skip and Alice Fuller, Joyce and I were joined during this meeting by Tufts University's executive vice president, Patricia Campbell, and Dr. John Morgan of Tufts University School of Dentistry. Most significantly, John had been conducting a review of Tufts' involvements in Tanzania and elsewhere that included an epic study of African dental health (which was completed in 2016).

Earlier this same day, Cummings Foundation had offered to assist in building a dental clinic in Butaro, in the same area where the foundation had funded the outpatient cancer clinic. Upon learning that a new medical school was now under consideration, however, we set aside the dental school offer. We suggested to the group of distinguished attendees that, with the backing of the renowned PIH organization, Cummings Foundation would like to help develop a world-class pan-African—not just Rwandan—multidisciplinary medical university in

UNIVERSITY OF
Global Health
EQUITY

Rwanda. The whole concept of the new international health sciences university first materialized that afternoon during a ninety-minute meeting.

After we returned to Boston, our overwhelmingly positive experiences in Rwanda, combined with our confidence in PIH's ability to work well with President Kagame's administration to bring about meaningful change, prompted us to move forward quickly.

A few weeks later, on October 4, 2013, Joyce and I reached out to several interested parties at PIH and Tufts, as well as in Rwanda, to confirm our thoughts on what we first called Pan-African Colleges of Health Sciences. We envisioned a university that would attract the best students from all over Africa—and well beyond—and that would help Rwanda fulfill its potential to become an economic and educational hub for Africa.

By early 2014, we formalized our offer of a $15 million matching gift from Cummings Foundation to build the first phase of a major new health sciences university. Beyond the condition that matching funds be raised, we specified only three contingencies: The new university would not bear the name of any person, now or in the future; the Rwandan government would assemble and provide all needed land; and everything needed for the construction and continuation of the new school would be free of value-added or sales taxes.

The enthusiastically received report immediately generated these responses from Partners In Health: "What a great vision," said co-founder Dr. Paul Farmer, "and one that squares with the Rwandan vision of pulling people up by building a 'knowledge' economy while delivering care—and what better way to promote peace, justice, and development in the region."

Ophelia Dahl, PIH co-founder and board chair, wrote, "This will be transformative in ways we cannot yet even imagine."

Shortly thereafter, Skip Fuller, who had by then become a foundation trustee, and I traveled to Seattle and personally petitioned for the matching grant from the Bill and Melinda Gates Foundation on behalf of PIH to fully fund the first phase of what was ultimately named and accredited as University of Global Health Equity. Phase I of this new university will open in rural Butaro in September 2018. In the meantime, the new university has conferred its first master's degrees in Global Health Delivery. UGHE graduated its first class of master's degree recipients in May 2017.

Phase I of the main UGHE campus is almost complete, and is adjacent

UGHE's main campus, under construction in Butaro, was designed by Shepley Bulfinch, the firm founded by the original designer of the Woburn Public Library

to a beautiful valley and directly across from Butaro Hospital and the Butaro Outpatient Cancer Clinic. When the UGHE project is complete, a ninety-acre campus will feature classrooms, labs, housing, food service, sports, visitor housing, and other amenities. The university will grow in phases, eventually creating an academic community of more than a thousand Rwandan and international students, faculty, and staff. It will also have a smaller city campus in Masaka, near Kigali and the new international air hub already planned there. The government of Rwanda has enthusiastically supported UGHE from its earliest phases. Government officials recognize its potential to provide high-quality education and a well-trained healthcare workforce. This fine new school will also help bolster Rwanda's international standing and attract businesses to locate or invest within its borders, all while strengthening its economy. Rwanda seems to be the perfect nation in which to locate UGHE.

The Rwandan government acquired the land for the new campus on UGHE's behalf, and while its construction is moving rapidly, the government is making major much-needed improvements to the surrounding infrastructure. We anticipate that the enhancements to the area, along with the construction-related and educational activities taking place at the new campus, will greatly benefit the entire Butaro region in the form of job opportunities, vocational training, and higher living standards. A new national highway is also now nearing completion from Kigali to Butaro, near one of Rwanda's most stunningly beautiful lakes areas.

Former Rwandan Minister of Health Dr. Agnes Binagwaho, who has done so much to help her nation become a recognized healthcare leader for all of Africa, is vice chancellor. Dr. Hellen Amuguni, DVM, PhD, MA, of

Cummings School of Veterinary Medicine, is the first Tufts addition to the fledgling UGHE staff in Rwanda. As soon as the new campus is operational, the school will train physicians, dentists, nurses, post-graduate veterinarians, public-health workers, and other healthcare practitioners.

UGHE will be much more than an African version of a Western medical school. It has been conceived as a fully accredited groundbreaking international university. It will teach not only the science of healthcare, but also the *delivery* of it, even in the world's poorest regions. Often overlooked by teaching institutions, remote healthcare delivery requires a

good understanding of applicable social forces, the ability to marshal political will, and the capacity to manage and refine dynamic, multifaceted operations.

There will be a strong emphasis from the beginning on the concept of "One Health." This interdisciplinary approach focuses on the linkages between animal, environmental, and human health, and it will encourage far greater collaboration and cooperation among all different types of healthcare providers. This starts

| Dr. Hellen Amuguni

with common classes to teach basic sciences to all students so that there is a uniform core of knowledge, which is terribly lacking in many societies. With a goal of improving health outcomes by emphasizing practical solutions, One Health breaks down the traditional boundaries between academic disciplines. With One Health as a foundational element of UGHE, students will have the core competency and biosocial approaches to solve and plan for the most critical and emerging global health challenges.

UGHE will train clinician-leaders who will be uniquely qualified to narrow the gap between knowledge and implementation. Its novel approach, however, has required rethinking every aspect of a university, from its curriculum to its research priorities to the location and design of its campus. In a May 2014 email to me, Dr. Farmer wrote, "We're all so excited about the idea of this whole new type of 'foreign aid,' one that focuses on real delivery and on real capacity building. And this 'One Health' notion is going to move all of this forward in Rwanda and beyond."

UGHE will take on great inequities and will attempt to lessen the deepest of them in some of the farthest corners of the world.

While PIH immersed itself in research and the early planning for UGHE in 2014, West Africa was devastated by a massive and deadly Ebola epidemic. Dr. Farmer told me that, at one point, he could not return to his family in Rwanda for seven months because he had so frequently been in and out of Ebola-affected regions of Africa. Because of weak and, in some cases, non-existent healthcare delivery systems, the disease spread rapidly from country to country, creating what started out to be one of the worst public-health catastrophes of our time. This tragedy highlighted the urgent need to train health professionals how to build and sustain effective and equitable health systems.

THERE ARE NO LIVES THAT ARE NOT WORTH SAVING, yet there are still so many millions of preventable deaths each year. In many remote areas of the world, with appalling disparities, even the most basic of medical services will make enormous life-and-death differences.

| *Joyce Cummings and Dr. Paul Farmer, 2014*

Aside from its work already in helping to launch UGHE, Bill and Melinda Gates Foundation is achieving magnificent international improvements, and the graduates of UGHE will soon be offering their services in a worldwide market. Rwandans are busily reconstructing a beautiful and brave nation as they continue to resurrect it from the catastrophe of genocide.

❀ *Entrepreneurs cannot become so enamored with one idea that they miss a greater opportunity. Joyce and I walked into that Kigali meeting with the idea of supporting a dental clinic. Because we listened—really listened—to a conversation about Rwanda's broader healthcare needs, however, we left the meeting with the beginnings of a bigger idea that quickly turned into a major new international university.*

[20]

Building the Future

Joyce and Bill speak to a delighted crowd of grant winners at the June 2015 Grantee Celebration, held in the Atrium Lobby at TradeCenter 128, Woburn

UNLIKE A TYPICAL grant-making foundation, operating foundations (including most hospitals and schools) are required to concentrate the vast majority of their *expenditures* on the entities they operate. Indeed, the combined expenditures of Cummings Foundation's four operating divisions form the basis for a cap on its uncommitted holdings.

Cummings Foundation added its most recent operating division, Cummings Institute for World Justice, in February 2011. The original intended purpose of Cummings Institute for World Justice was to operate educational programs in genocide prevention and social justice, but this division was eventually re-purposed as a grant maker in support of these and other efforts. In 2012, we began committing $10 million per year to local charities with our signature *$100K for 100* program. In 2016, we committed an additional $10 million annually in ongoing ten-year Sustaining Grants.

These programs primarily support small and medium-sized charities, because they mostly do not enjoy the stable donor bases and endowments that support so many larger institutions in the Boston area. "The little guy needs our money," Joyce explained in 2014 to a news reporter who had asked why national organizations don't typically receive funding from the foundation. "We want our $100,000 grants to go where they can really make a difference."

Nonprofit organizations learn about the grant process and apply through the foundation's website (CummingsFoundation.org). Applicants first submit a Letter of Inquiry. Then, executive director Joel Swets and deputy director Joyce Vyriotes work with three different committees made up of about forty-five carefully selected volunteers to review proposals. They first verify which applicants appear to meet all requirements as posted on the foundation's website. In 2017, nearly 600 applicants preliminarily qualified through the computer screening for the *$100K for 100*.

All qualified applicants are then sequentially reviewed, and the number is reduced by two standing committees of experienced and dedicated volunteers. The committees award as many as half of each year's grants to previous grant winners, but at least half the grants are awarded to newly selected organizations. The committees ultimately present what they determine to be the 100 best applications to ten four-person final-selection committees of additional volunteers. Each of those committees then selects half of its ten applicants to be *$100K for 100* grant winners.

The highly impressive list of volunteers includes college presidents, a retired Massachusetts Supreme Judicial Court justice, a former White House staffer, newspaper publishers, community activists, well-known area writers, and even other local philanthropists. Three of the four members of each final-selection committee are "community members," and the fourth member is often an employee of Cummings Properties, from any level in the firm.

Many committee members tell us they had no idea how difficult it would be to give money away because the needs presented are so compelling. They tell us how challenged they were to make the final decisions and, across the board, they want to continue working with the foundation on a volunteer basis. Company employees, too, have enjoyed outside camaraderie they might otherwise not have experienced, and they are eager to tell others about their role in the process. This has proven to be a marvelous way to build understanding about what the foundation does.

Some of Cummings Properties' in-house staff at 2017 Grant Awards night

Given the small size and relatively limited budgets of so many of our grant recipients, most of the uniform $100,000 awards are disbursed over periods of two to four years. This longer-term support provides some stability, allowing organizations time to develop additional funding sources and avoid a "bolus" effect, in which the sharp drop-off after a large front-loaded grant leaves the organization in a difficult position.

As Joyce told a reporter, we are reaching local organizations for which $100,000 will be much more than a drop in the bucket. In this respect, we are succeeding. After sending award letters each year, the foundation is awash with phone calls, emails, social-media shout-outs, and letters of gratitude. A word we hear from many grant winners is "transformative," and that is exactly what we want to be. We want to provide the support necessary for hands-on grassroots organizations to reach the next level and to help them make larger impacts on the community. At the same time, many of these smaller organizations have reported that their Cummings grant has helped them secure funding from other foundations.

ALL PROFITS EARNED by Cummings Properties are for the exclusive benefit of the foundation, as are all earnings from any personal investments. Except for our personal belongings that will go to family members, any and all real estate and remaining financial assets will eventually go to the foundation. Our children and grandchildren have no need for anything more. Joyce and I are pleased and proud that all of our children have been totally supportive of our contributions to the foundation.

Rather than being just a place for our extra earnings, or a place where our net worth will go when Joyce and I reach our journey's end, Cummings Foundation gives us many extra reasons—or perhaps excuses—to continue working. I stopped drawing a salary in 2006, but the foundation is my justification to keep on building, both literally and figuratively. From an administrative perspective, as of 2017, Cummings Foundation has extraordinarily low overhead, thanks in part to so much *pro bono* help. No trustee earns any compensation, and only one-third of the trustees are related in any way to the Cummings family or the company. The foundation still has only one paid administrative employee, and the administrative expenses of Cummings Foundation average much less than 1 percent of its annual income, and include no expenses for travel.

> *No trustee earns any compensation, and only one-third of the trustees are related in any way to the Cummings family or the company.*

The most dramatic change from my previous work schedule is that I now routinely average fifty or so hours in the office each week (when I am in town), as opposed to sixty or more. Since 2008, however, I have also managed to take ten to twelve weeks of vacation every year, including time that Joyce and I dedicate to foundation work, which sometimes involves visits to remote places.

Among the most rewarding aspects of our foundation work are the frequent opportunities to help connect like-minded nonprofits that can work synergistically to benefit the communities they serve. We are so delighted about the valuable relationships Partners In Health is already creating with Cummings School of Veterinary Medicine and with Agahozo-Shalom Youth Village. We find it quite fitting that University of Global Health Equity, at its beginnings, is already partnering with these tremendous organizations, too.

Billions of dollars have been invested by so many in medical infrastructure throughout Africa, including mega-sized hospitals in many major cities. UGHE, with no billions but perhaps about $200 million starting out, will teach effective healthcare for some of the most underserved areas of Africa and the world. Indeed, its greatest emphasis, as already noted, will be on healthcare delivery, including to many of the planet's most remote areas.

THE SOURCE OF most of Cummings Foundation's assets has been internal, including the remarkable returns from its equity investments with the guidance of the foundation's *pro bono* CFO, Bill Grant, and David Leland of Merrill Lynch, a chartered Advisor in Philanthropy. Bill and David were extraordinarily effective for decades in handling almost all of the combined Cummings investments.

| *David Leland and Bill Grant, 2017*

As a director of wealth management and a certified specialist in foundation investing, David operated from a new large Merrill Lynch office at Cummings Center in Beverly, which he helped lobby for and develop.

We were shocked and deeply saddened in January 2017, when David was diagnosed with esophageal cancer. And, despite a valiant fight and the best available care, he succumbed to the disease a few short months later, on May 4, 2017. David was a trusted, beloved, and extraordinarily important part of the Cummings organization. He helped to build and then service $1 billion of Cummings' securities, accumulated since the foundation's earliest days. Aside from much smaller investments through Commonfund and Goldman Sachs, Merrill Lynch held the vast majority of all Cummings financial investments. David and Bill increased the value of our invested funds by several hundred million dollars. We could not have been more pleased, and we fully expect to continue working with the Leland Group in Merrill's Beverly office.

Right up until a few days before his death, this master investor continued his daily supervision of his Merrill Lynch investment practice from his hospital bed at Massachusetts General Hospital. David played such a major role in our lives as he constantly strengthened the foundation. Thanks so much to David, the foundation now has the ability to meaningfully help people in need, all over this world. I was so moved to learn after his death that David was having the last of an early proof of this book read to him at Mass General Hospital.

Like the passing of Jamie McKeown and Doug Stephens, this was so much more than the loss of a close business colleague, as David and his wife, Karen, and Joyce and I were also close as couples. That overlapping relationship was mostly through Winchester Country Club, where for decades we played golf and did so many other activities together. David's parents were our friends before we knew David and Karen. We also shared such fond memories from time with David and Karen, and sometimes Bill and Kathy Grant, at the Wianno Club in Osterville, on Cape Cod, where we all happened to be non-resident members.

This relationship with the Lelands was so much like our relationships with Doug and Carrol, and then with Jamie and Denise. Because of these unusually close connections, my sense of any business loss has been overshadowed in each case by profound and enduring personal sorrow. The compounded emotional effect from all three deaths, though spread over twenty years, has sometimes been quite cumulative.

Jamie, Doug, and David were all totally supportive of everything Joyce and I hoped to do, or were already doing, with Cummings Foundation. As we go on establishing partners for sustainable giving, we shall do so in their collective memory. We shall also continue recognizing the wonderful current Cummings staff, in whose honor we shall also continue to move the foundation forward. There is so much more we can do, and so much we will do to use these funds wisely.

❀ *Surrounding myself with smart outspoken professionals has always served me well. By enlisting assistance from dozens of highly accomplished volunteers, the foundation is greatly benefiting from the thinking of some of the most qualified members of our local communities. In 2017 and 2018, volunteers made the majority of all final grant-winner selections.*

❀ *Despite the best computers, the best decisions will always come down to careful personal observation and intuitive business judgment.*

[21]

Setting a Better Pace

AFTER JOYCE and I met, and then married in 1966, our early vacations were limited, but they included a dozen great family trips to places throughout the Caribbean, and in Bermuda and South America. We also enjoyed several wonderful multi-week shunpiking trips to Great Britain and the rest of Europe, navigating back roads, usually with only a single night's hotel reservation to start each adventure. In between these many special vacations, however, I was always overly busy with mostly sixty-hour work weeks.

More recently, with our four children all off on their own, of course, we arranged a self-guided trip with seven other mostly Winchester friends to Dubai, United Arab Emirates, and Egypt. In Dubai, we saw unimaginable new growth everywhere. I could not get over the stunningly unique and even fanciful buildings throughout the entire downtown. Anchored by Burj Khalifa, which stands more than a *half mile* tall, these structures represented a staggering variety of designs, and my enthusiasm to see every one of them amused all present. I was like a kid let loose at a carnival.

That trip continued with four or five nights on the Nile River, starting just below the two-mile-long Aswan High Dam. We traveled on the river all the way to Cairo, with many cultural visits each day and enormous exposure to the fascinating history of that area at every stop along the way. There appeared to be no end to the wonders we saw of that ancient world, as each stop seemed even more outstanding than the last.

We organized another special journey with a different hometown group to Iceland, where, among other activities, we golfed through the bubbling hot springs outside Reykjavik. This trip also amounted to a Winchester Country Club trip, and even today, we often reminisce at the club about that little adventure.

Joyce and I traveled alone, for a change, to China for three weeks, including four captivating nights on the Yangtze River, in October 1998. When we signed up for an escorted tour, the operators advertised that no more than fifteen travelers would be permitted. Upon our arrival in Beijing, however, we were met by a driver in a Mercedes and a fine English-speaking guide who informed us that we would be the *only* people on the tour for our entire itinerary—and off we went.

An early 2013 trip to Myanmar (formerly Burma)—a country that had been mostly closed to Americans for many years—and Thailand was strictly for tourism. The welcome for Americans in this distant land nestled between China and India could not have been warmer. The Myanmar trip nicely rounded out our other trans-Pacific trips to Hawaii, Australia and New Zealand.

We did other Tufts Travel-Learn trips to the Greek Islands, Turkey, and India. Joyce also traveled, without me, to India, with our daughter Patty to South Africa, and with Patty and our daughter Marilyn to Alaska. Joyce and I returned to South America with another Tufts Travel-Learn trip, this time exploring the biodiversity of the mighty upper Amazon River, some 2,000 miles inland, sometimes trekking far into the forest. Flying into Iquitos, Peru, from Lima, we boarded our nineteen-passenger ship in what is the world's largest metropolis not accessible by roadways. This is a major city with boulevards and buses and 180,000 people, but everything, even the buses, came to the city via the river or the city's small airport. We recently counted up our visits in seventy-four foreign nations, to date.

THE MAJOR CHANGE in my work life after age seventy-two or so was a significant alteration in our yearly routine. After purchasing our modest beachfront Reaches Condominium in Singer Island, Florida, in 1988, we finally began to use it regularly after the year 2000, and now we manage about three months there each winter, with lots of additional travel.

We have also enjoyed some great ocean-sailing weeks, always with no captain or crew. Our first such trip, in 1995, was a sailing and scuba-diving adventure in the British Virgin Islands with our dear friends and former Winchester neighbors Nancy and Chat Watts. May is a perfect time to sail in the Caribbean, and we enjoyed a delightful week in a bareboat charter from The Moorings. We had a great week of island-hopping, scuba-exploring, reef-snorkeling, and fancy island dining, at least for most of our evening meals. Some delightfully mellow local rum helped set the tone for dinners once we were safely anchored each evening.

Bill preparing for a deep-water wreck dive off Jost Van Dyke, in the British Virgin Islands, with Chat Watts

After the British Virgin Islands, we sailed with another Winchester couple, Laura and Bill Shea, on two bareboat charters. On the last day of our first trip with the Sheas, an unexpected squall quickly engulfed us. Sailing off Guadeloupe near the center of the Leeward Islands, we were suddenly all alone on an angry sea. There were no other boats in sight, and our marine radio was useless behind the nearby mountains off the northeastern coast of Grande Terre. With no radio contact, we had no way of knowing what we were in for.

For almost two hours a vicious windstorm whipped the Caribbean into a frenzy as our sailboat heeled hard on the port gunwale, and the sea rose higher and higher. Off our port side, the surf crashed onto a ten-mile-long stretch of jagged barrier reef. Along the coast there was no harbor or other refuge anywhere within reach, and we were soaked with repeated explosions of salt spray. There were plenty of reasons to be scared, and we all were.

I had much earlier partially reefed the mainsail, but now it needed to go lower. I clutched whatever I could and inched my way out of the cockpit and reefed it to about a third of its usual size. Earlier I had tried to furl the jib, but the line controlling it had somehow jammed into the side of a broken brass pulley that was well beyond my reach. We had no chance of repairing it then, because with one slip, I could be instantly overboard. We had practiced man-overboard drills, but Joyce, Laura and Bill would not have had the slightest chance of getting to me if I had gone overboard. I would surely have been torn apart on the reef.

Just then, an extra-strong gust grabbed the still-extended jib and instantly rent the sail in half while our tiny boat continued to slip sideways toward the treacherous reef. Ever closer, the jagged reef appeared ready to devour the whole boat and grind us up with it. Finally, I was able to cut loose half of the jib, which flew away with a giant whoosh, but the other half was still attached at the top of the mast—flying straight out, perpendicular to the horizon, if there was one.

By then, I had already started the engine to try controlling our fate. With most of the jib gone and the smaller piece more or less out of the way, we finally began to make a little headway into the wind, but we were still in mortal danger. Only a few hundred yards from the jagged outcroppings, I pushed the diesel engine almost to its limit, and then I shoved the throttle to its absolute maximum output. The RPM gauge was solidly in the red danger zone, but I knew that if our boat had been blown onto the reef, the condition of the engine would have mattered little. With extra engine help and the wind beginning to relax ever so slightly, we gradually inched our way back on course.

At one point Laura, a Canadian by birth, started to sing, "O Canada. Our home and native land. True patriot love, in all thy sons command..." I was reminded of the *Titanic* story about how the ship's band bravely played *Nearer My God to Thee* as the stern lifted high before plunging to the bottom of the North Atlantic. For us, however, the wind eventually just stopped as quickly as it had started, and we were soon back in port for our final night, no worse off except for our lost jib sail.

In 2013, we and other friends chartered a fifty-foot bareboat catamaran sailboat with four sleek double-bed cabins for a week. We sailed with Dennis Clarke's parents, Nancy and Dick Clarke; Tufts friends Jane and Dr. Mark Hirsh, from Boston; and Tufts classmate Dr. Bob Belin and his wife, Jo, from Lexington, Kentucky. They joined us on a trip to and around the French island of St. Martin, including the Dutch half known as St. Maarten, and neighboring islands for another great but generally quiet adventure.

We must be getting really old now, considering our most recent bareboat charter, in September 2017, was aboard a grand sixty-foot-long, four-bedroom houseboat on the Erie Canal. Joining us were two Winchester couples, Dr. Ric and Judy Bush and Dr. Denis and Joan Byrne—all fairly serious bridge players. It was a four-day weekend of marvelous dining, camaraderie, and bridge games along the Lakes Seneca and Cayuga branch of the Erie Canal. The early morning smell of cooked bacon wafting in from the galley was always so welcome. The people with whom Joyce and I most often do things are our many, many good friends from the last fifty or so years.

Joyce and I celebrated our fiftieth wedding anniversary in August 2016. For our anniversary trip to Amsterdam, Venice, and the Dalmatian Coast, we broke our self-imposed ban and purchased business-class airline tickets for the first time ever. Joyce said she deserved special treatment after putting up with me for fifty years. Just before our trip, the entire family gathered at a unique family vacation inn called East Hill Farm, in Troy, New Hampshire, to celebrate our first half-century.

We also traveled to Tufts' European campus in Talloires, France, that summer for an intensive session titled What Happens Next?, which addressed questions important at the "older and wiser stage" of attendees' lives. This was a special collaboration between Tufts' Rabbi Summit and Rev. William "Scotty" McLennan, a former chaplain at Tufts and now a retired dean for

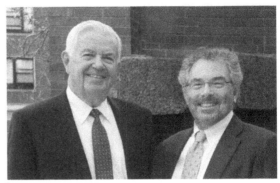

| *Bill with Rabbi Jeffrey Summit of Tufts University*

religious life at Stanford. "What happens next?" is a question that Joyce and I have long tried to help answer in a positive way, for ourselves, our colleagues, and our community.

ABOUT 60 PERCENT of the real estate Cummings Properties manages is the commercial property Joyce and I donated to Cummings Foundation. The company receives no fees for its management work on behalf of the foundation, yet the Cummings staff who assist, on a *pro bono* basis, in the management of the foundation-owned properties have a clear fiduciary responsibility to manage them to the best of their ability and solely in the best interests of the foundation. A foundation-owned maintenance firm also employs a significant crew to service its buildings.

Cummings Properties now has a well-established corporate culture. To help prospective new colleagues better understand this culture and, more importantly, to encourage them to think beforehand about whether it would be a good match for their personal working styles, we created a carefully worded Corporate Philosophy document. If we think employment candidates might have special potential with our team, we often give them a copy of the Corporate Philosophy and invite them to come back to learn more if they remain interested after considering its contents.

The outline of our corporate environment describes in some detail the sense of urgency with which most of the staff try to stay ahead of our competitors, and also the type of work ethic expected. After outlining what some find to be the more challenging aspects of our work, the sheet describes some of the work of the foundation. Since 2010, Cummings Foundation has been the sole financial beneficiary of all that the company does. The document goes on to describe some of the special benefits of joining our truly outstanding team of colleagues.

Interestingly, whenever we have asked staff what they like most about working at Cummings Properties, the dominant response for decades has been "the people." Employees genuinely like their colleagues to a remarkable level, and this more than anything else may be why people work here as long as they do. We will soon have a dozen members in the company's super special 40 Year Club, and currently the average tenure of our employees is about eleven years. Our eight-person Executive Committee tops out with an average seniority of twenty-three years and, incidentally, a total of twenty-four children. Somewhat of an oddity today, all eight of these long-term leaders are still married to their first spouse.

As a privately held, nearly half-century-old firm, we are extraordinarily fortunate to have so many team members who have chosen careers with us. We benefit immensely from the continuity of experienced staff who have learned "the Cummings Way." As it becomes better known how much good Cummings Foundation can accomplish, prospective employees who want to benefit more than just themselves and their own families are becoming increasingly interested in working with Cummings Properties.

New employees often tell me they were attracted to the company because they knew about our charitable purposes. The foundation's signature *$100K for 100* program celebrated its sixth year in 2017, but our far smaller Employee Directed Giving program, offered through Cummings Properties, seems to have become the most universally popular employee benefit we have ever provided. I think staff like it even better than casual Fridays. Each Thanksgiving since 2012, in addition to receiving a fresh or frozen turkey, all of our 400-plus regular full-time colleagues at Cummings and New Horizons have been invited to select an organization to receive $1,000 from the company. Participants are encouraged to think locally, and the recipients include many schools and PTOs, as well as youth sports organizations, Boy and Girl Scout troops, and animal shelters—in other words, nonprofits with which families are directly involved.

The following quote comes from *Quartz*, an online magazine that called the program bottom-up giving: "One employee donated her Employee Directed Giving funds to a local social service agency after her teenage daughter was heartbroken to learn that her best friend's family was relying on its soup kitchen to eat." We also especially liked the story about a librarian bursting into tears when Eric and Kari Anderson's two young children, Clara and Caden, presented her with their $1,000 check to support their local library. The librarian thought they were bringing her a holiday card.

We have heard many more stories about employees talking with their entire families to decide what charity they want to support and then often going as a family to present the check. Not every eligible employee has taken advantage of the program, but we do get more than 90 percent participation. These modest checks have now been gratefully received by thousands of mostly small or even tiny groups that had no idea anything was coming.

❀ *Becoming a successful entrepreneur often requires much more time and hard work than most people are willing to give. Those who do put in the effort and achieve prosperity, however, should reap some of the rewards. Make time for the pursuits (other than business) that fuel you. For me, they have always been primarily family, travel, community good, and philanthropy.*

❀ *Regardless of their stage in life or career, entrepreneurs always keep an eye out for the next great opportunity, though perhaps unconsciously at times. Because of this predilection, most will probably never truly retire. Their focuses and roles, however, may change over time—sometimes in unexpected ways, like with our decision to take a public stance on the contentious 2016 election.*

[22]

New Directions

Greater Boston Chamber of Commerce

| *Bill and Joyce accepting induction into the Academy of Distinguished Bostonians, 2017*

BECAUSE CUMMINGS Properties and Cummings Foundation are positioned well to survive Joyce and me, it seems important to tell their story for the ultimate benefit of those who will follow. This book does much of that, as will the wonderful cadre of colleagues and others who do so much to guide and support both entities through each day. The book has also proven to be extremely beneficial to me in trying to order some details of my life for the possible benefit of those who will later lead these organizations.

As I finish this concluding chapter in early 2018, Joyce is now seventy-six, and I reached the magic four-score and one years. Our five terrific grandchildren are everything we might want to brag about and then some. Our fondest hope is that we are able to live long enough to know them all as young adults, God willing. Sonia and Nate Morris, in New York, are the oldest, with Sonia, now fourteen. Nate, who is thirteen, recently completed an extremely long walk—from New Rochelle, New York, to Boston with his mom. Gus Cummings, in Winchester, has just started kindergarten, while Patricia's preschool daughters, Isabel and Valerie Cummings, are busy learning what life is all about from their two moms, Patty and Jadine Louie, who relocated from San Francisco to New Rochelle, New York in 2018.

None of our children, or their spouses, has ever expressed interest in taking management roles in either the company or the foundation, although there has been some thought about the possibility that one or more might later become more involved in Cummings Foundation. Third-generation involvement could still happen, but that possibility has not yet made it to my wish list.

THERE IS NO REASON for any of us to try to change who we are just because we become good (or lucky) at whatever we do in life. Any and all talents we have we are given, and what we do with those talents tells the most about who and what we are. Certainly, our occasional exposure to the Giving Pledge environment has caused Joyce and me to think more about who we want to be. We hope and believe we have been able to comfortably stay almost exactly the same as we always have been.

I have now grown fully complacent about not retiring, although I will someday turn over my office. The notion of Joyce and me taking off and traveling somewhere about twelve weeks each year is working out well, although that time is at least partially occupied with foundation-related activities. The foundation work, however, is something we do and enjoy together. I have worked my way out of most board and other positions that I greatly enjoyed for many years, but others have since represented the firm well. Dennis Clarke has been in leadership roles with Winchester Hospital and is just finishing up as board chair with the Massachusetts chapter of NAIOP after having served as its president, while Bill Grant has served effectively on the board of Associated Industries of Massachusetts for nine years.

While spending the vast majority of my career creating things, I also collected so many experiences along the way. I frequently went out of my way to encounter people, things, and events outside of my regular realm. Exploring the innards of the old Charlestown Penitentiary and the Pennsylvania coal mine, and biking around Damascus during a revolution, and deep-water wreck-diving off Cyprus were all prime. Swimming to the frightening edge of Victoria Falls, and bungee jumping with Patty in New Zealand were also among the best. And at this later stage in life, Joyce and I are enormously proud and grateful to still be part of the lives of our four children and five grandchildren.

After we revived Old Medford Foods and turned it into a thriving business, we launched Cummings Properties and our three newspapers. We developed Place Lane Condominium, we established and built Cummings Foundation to serve and help support the many communities that contributed to Cummings Properties' success. I had help from so many as we rebuilt or erected building after building, starting with our first construction projects on Henshaw Street in 1966.

Seeing opportunity in the oversized Henshaw Street lot was the first step in Cummings Properties' successful history. Each new client, building, employee, and manager has been another block or beam that strengthened and sustained the business. After more than forty-five years of building, Cummings Properties can point to achievements that are more than outsized for the small local firm we have always been. With such capable staff and future leadership now in place, the firm will be prosperous for many decades to come.

First, we made and saved $1 million, and now the foundation has already given away $200 million. Nothing I have ever done has been massively successful, but I have built successful businesses and run many successful organizations. Collectively, these entities have provided or facilitated thousands of new

| *Bill with Dr. Bob Shirley at Winchester Country Club*

jobs and greatly aided local economies. Along the way, I have had great fun and fulfillment, and Joyce and I together are now gaining much satisfaction by giving away more and more, and trying to make a success of that, too.

Trying also to make a little more room in my life, I started giving up golf after 2010. Although I was never all that good, I had immeasurable fun playing golf for close to 40 years, as has Joyce, who is still playing. My most memorable experiences came from winning several three-day member-guest elimination tournaments at Winchester Country Club, all a decade apart. The first two wins were with Jamie McKeown and then Don Lewis. The last was with the late Dr. Bob Shirley of Braeburn Country Club. Bob sank a huge 60-foot curving playoff putt with a green-side crowd of at least 100 other members. Bob's sensational putt across the ninth green turned out to be the last shot of the tournament, and the overall win in one of my (and his) last "serious" golf games.

DURING 2016, Joyce and I spoke together before large Boston-area audiences during four widely differing events. The first of these was in May at the John F. Kennedy Presidential Library and Museum, where we received the Compassion and Justice Award from Catholic Charities of Boston, presented by Cardinal Sean O'Malley. The following month, we and New England Patriots owner Robert Kraft were honored to accept Friends of Israel citations, presented by Robert Lappin, a longtime Massachusetts sponsor of Operation Birthright.

We also addressed four hundred guests during the annual celebration of Cummings Foundation's *$100K for 100* program, when we announced the recipients of that year's $10 million in local grants. Finally, Joyce and I also received honorary doctorates from Endicott College in 2016 and delivered our third joint commencement address to several thousand attendees.

This was at a time when obdurate speakers were saturating the airwaves and elsewhere copycatting Donald Trump during the 2016 presidential campaign, and his ideas were spreading like measles. There was a common element to all four of our 2016 talks. At each one, Joyce and I spoke out in opposition to the profound increase in prejudice and violence in the United States by extremist elements. While there appears to be an alarming dearth of honest, selfless leaders of either party in government circles today, we view this rapidly increasing violence being fueled, and even promoted, by an anti-American election strategy of Trump.

President Trump knows that millions of Americans are disillusioned by the actions or inaction of many of the nation's political leaders, of both parties, and that there is an enormous faction of disgruntled citizens contesting a deeply entrenched federal bureaucracy. This disaffected portion of our citizenry, in our opinion, was shamelessly courted by the outrageous behavior of the Trump campaign, which promised discontented voters anything they wanted to hear, while railing against gun control, immigrants, and all available scapegoats.

The Endicott College commencement address that Joyce and I made was prominently referenced in a *Boston Globe* story by Sacha Pfeiffer on June 16, 2016. This was just before historian Ken Burns famously unloaded on Donald Trump during Stanford University's 2016 commencement. Joyce and I spoke the previous day about the election year's terrible political discourse. We discussed what so many people around the world see as Trump's hateful anti-immigrant, anti-Hispanic, and anti-gay platform, which at various times even declined to disavow racist and anti-Semitic extremists.

Joyce and I are not openly political, but we felt compelled to speak up. It was never a political issue we were addressing. Indeed, over many decades I have never financially supported Democratic candidates for the Presidency, but have several times supported Republicans. This situation for us was a moral imperative in every sense of the word.

During our 2016 *$100K for 100* event, one of the award winners scored a rousing audience response. She jumped up while Joyce was speaking and loudly shouted, "Joyce for president!" Here are a few of the common elements in our 2016 addresses:

> *Although Joyce and I have been active in philanthropy for many years, we have never considered ourselves political activists, and we have never spoken publicly for or against particular causes or issues, and certainly not for or against any political candidate. That changed in recent months, however, as we became greatly alarmed with Donald Trump's sudden prominence as a presidential candidate.*
>
> *Some people see great similarity between this candidate's derisive appeal and that of the horrid McCarthy era, sixty years ago. Others liken today's political talk to a plague. Indeed, the same plague that spread through Nazi Germany in the 1930s.*
>
> *Never forget, my friends…Never forget that when prejudice and intolerance are tolerated, they are as well condoned and encouraged. We urge all of you, to continue to be a strong force to educate young people, and help counteract all the recent divisive rhetoric. Recognize the great danger.*
>
> *Let me close by also asking all of you to be the force that helps to build bridges, especially for our marginalized neighbors. So much more than bridges over rivers and highways, build bridges of love, bridges of hope, and bridges of understanding.*
>
> *Let there be bridges of opportunity, too. Let bridges such as these take us all where we otherwise could not go.*
>
> **W.S.C.**

Our comments were enthusiastically embraced at all four speaking events, but nowhere more loudly than during the foundation's annual grants presentation. There, we were again recognizing the efforts of 100 of the most deserving local nonprofits. These were the frontline organizations reaching out to help the neediest among us, so many of them targets in minority communities, singled out for ridicule and scorn in this year's tragic public propaganda. Throughout the summer, we were acutely mindful of these words of Elie Wiesel: "We must take sides. Neutrality helps the oppressor, never the victim. Silence encourages only the tormentor, never the tormented." Joyce and I first met Mr. Wiesel during a Remembrance Day celebration at the United States Holocaust Memorial Museum, where we were especially pleased to introduce him to Elie Ayalon during an inspiring private meeting.

> *"We must take sides. Neutrality helps the oppressor, never the victim. Silence encourages only the tormentor, never the tormented."*
> *Elie Wiesel*

A powerful recent major exhibit at the Holocaust museum depicted the enormous role Nazi propaganda played in acclimatizing war-ravaged Germans of the 1920s. Although much lesser known, the International Museum of World War II in Natick, Massachusetts, also has a highly impressive collection of Holocaust propaganda. The foundation has contributed a combined $500,000 to the Holocaust museum, the Museum of World War II, and Yad Vashem.

We have also pledged to help fund a new Holocaust Center in Guatemala and other Holocaust education work of Father Patrick Desbois. Jews and the free press were incessantly portrayed as the reason for Germany's devastating losses in the Great War. Then, with the decade of the Great Depression, this manufactured anti-Semitism created a catastrophe of unfathomable degree. Many Americans say that exhibits at each of these museums offer powerful portentous signals of things that could be to come from the current presidential administration.

Adolf Hitler finished the Great War as a corporal, but as he became political he developed great oratory skills, quickly learning the issues that would rouse his beleaguered audiences. While imprisoned for his activism in the mid-1920s, Hitler wrote *Mein Kampf* ("My Struggle"). In this book, he developed the plan and the basis for the monstrous Holocaust he would soon unleash. Through the early 1930s, however, most people had no idea of the threat Hitler posed.

Still suffering mightily from its ignominious defeat in World War I, compounded soon thereafter by the worldwide depression, Germany was ripe for a populist leader who would make everything right. A dominant theme in the Nazi propaganda barrage was *"Machen Deutschland wieder groß,"* which eerily translates as "Make Germany great again."

Thousands of miles to the south, and six decades later, Hitler's playbook emerged again. The forces behind the 1994 genocide against the Tutsi in Rwanda used many of Hitler's techniques in demonizing the country's population of "Tutsi cockroaches," "conditioning" the citizenry for the horrifying 800,000 murders there in just four months.

THE 2016 ELECTION of Donald Trump culminated an unprecedented primary season in which Trump overcame thirteen Republican rivals, while a supposedly "unbeatable" Hillary Clinton ultimately eked out only the Democratic nomination. Although Trump lost the popular vote by millions of votes, he was elected by the Electoral College. Many millions of Americans were first shocked and then gravely disappointed with the net result, including so many who reportedly voted for Trump because they could not bring themselves to vote for Secretary Clinton.

Most citizens who put Trump in office seemed to do so because they either believed in him or they believed he was the best option they had when they were casting their votes. Joyce and I have many friends who voted for Trump, and none of them are bad people. He is the President, and we feel duty-bound to respect the office, even if we find it impossible to become enthused about the man or his apocryphal and admittedly lying tactics.* The ongoing questions about Russian election interference remain under investigation in October 2018.

Underneath everything are millions of well-meaning Americans who are so fed up with Washington politics that they are willing to totally disregard, it seems, all of President Trump's intolerance and other possible shortcomings. This core of Trump supporters appears to condone even his most reckless and irresponsible behavior, just to bring about change. I am among those who would readily agree that the pendulum has, at times, swung too far to the left, but how President Trump can be tolerated any longer is just beyond me. We so much need a solid centrist leader from either party to come to the fore.

Many of Cummings Foundation's 2017 and 2018 grant winners have expressed great concern about possible significant rollbacks in funding of the social safety net upon which so many homeless, low-income, and underserved minority populations depend. More than ever before, our not-for-profit investments in a concentrated local area are intended to help build coalitions and help them weave together some vital goals to counter the extraordinary racist tones resonating so loudly, it seems, from Washington more than anywhere else.

It is possible that Trump's abuses of the office of the Presidency of the United

For anyone concerned about the mechanics behind the campaign of extreme candidates like Mr. Trump, I would strongly recommend the 2000 book Dark Money *by Jane Mayer of* New Yorker *fame. This riveting "Hidden History of the Billionaires Behind the Rise of the Radical Right" will open many eyes.*

States will become intolerable enough that opponents, including those in his own party, will eventually bring him under control. And if, at the same time, they can figure ways to legally help Middle America, our country should return to a more normal and rational situation, socially degraded though it may be.

IN ADDITION TO ASKING Ralph Nader for the blurb that appears on the back cover of this book, I asked him to comment on all the turmoil roiling America since Donald Trump's ascendency. Ralph did not disappoint: "A daily democracy requires daily citizenship engagement with the public affairs of our times. That starts with family upbringing and our educational civic experiences as youngsters in and outside of schools," he wrote. "If we the people are otherwise indifferent, distracted or fooled, we will get the politics of our times—unworthy of our better selves and trending toward ever more injustices, cruelly damaged lives and a battered, endangered posterity."

WITH SEVENTY YEARS of business experience to look back upon now, and a steadily shortening runway ahead, I am much more self-reflective, particularly regarding my career in business. It has been a productive one with a few exceedingly sad experiences to be sure, but with a preponderance of highly satisfying work and accomplishments. When Joyce and I celebrated our fiftieth wedding anniversary in Venice in August of 2016, she rather optimistically "signed up" for twenty-five more years together.

John Soares

| *Joyce and Bill Cummings, 2016*

By 2018, Cummings Foundation was close to or just over its second billion in net assets, and it is among the most prominent players in New England philanthropy. Joyce and I are among the oldest people we know now, but we are as determined as ever to preserve our active days until something stops us.

We publicly joined the Giving Pledge organization during its first year, but that membership does not in any way define us. We had long before donated the vast majority of our wealth for charitable purposes, and Joyce and I are still so much the same people we were when we married fifty-two years ago.

Someone asked me recently how it felt to have started out as a totally self-funded entrepreneur and to come as far as we have. My response was slow in coming. The question was a little "off," because by any measure I am still so much an entrepreneur that I can easily get in my own way. And while I was always self-funded, I have also always had enormous support of other types from colleagues, suppliers, teachers, and sometimes even competitors. Almost all of my "career" now involves the work of Cummings Foundation, where virtually all of our former assets now or will reside, but my business mindset remains entrepreneurial. And just as I clearly remember hearing in an industrial psychology class a full sixty years ago, it is so easy for me to get stuck in minutiae.

| *Dr. Anthony Monaco*

I continue to spend time working with or on behalf of various Tufts University interests in Medford certainly, as well as at the Cummings School. We have been particularly pleased to develop a close relationship with Tufts' current president and his wife, Drs. Anthony and Zoia Monaco, while working toward the proposed new Joyce Cummings Center. This new 120,000-square-foot Tufts structure is being built in conjunction with the soon-to-emerge Tufts College rail station at the corner of College Avenue and Boston Avenue, on the extended Green Line to Boston.

Additionally, as concerns "presidents," we felt a sense of quiet pride when Cummings Foundation's trustee *emeritus* Larry Bacow was inaugurated as the twenty-ninth president of Harvard University in October 2018. In the meantime, Foundation trustee David Harris, the former Provost of Tufts, assumed the

presidency of Union College, in Schenectady, New York. With Tufts President Monaco, there are now three sitting major college presidents among the trustees of the foundation. Cummings Foundation trustee Debroah Kochevar moved in 2018 from Dean of the Cummings School of Veterinary Medicine to Provost *ad interim* of Tufts, succeeding Dr. Harris.

In the long run, however, fifty years of running this business in an old-fashioned way has paid off so much more than I could ever have imagined. I never yearned to become a millionaire when that level was beyond my status, and never thought at all about

| *Dr. David Harris*

becoming a billionaire. Finding good ways to accomplish good tasks with our funds now is incredibly rewarding.

MEANWHILE AT CUMMINGS PROPERTIES we determined in 2017 to sell off parts of the 54-acre Dunham Ridge development we acquired in late 2011, rather than continue investing further in Beverly. We sold one prominent six-acre parcel near the center of that development in 2017 to Vitality Assisted Living, of California. We then closed on a second six-acre lot at the top of Dunham Ridge in a sale to Harmonic Drive, Inc., in August 2018. We actually created a six-unit land-only condominium of the heavily wooded site which consists of about 50 percent conservation land. We sold both parcels with no broker involvement.

As regards *Starting Small*, by the end of 2018 I have already spoken or am scheduled for more than one hundred author talks. We have more than 11,000 books sold, and just ordered an additional 10,000 copies in October 2018.

Included in the scheduled speaking engagements are schools as far away as University of Alabama in Tuscaloosa and University of Oxford, England. We are working on the likelihood of many "all-school" reading projects for next summer, and Harvard Business School has confirmed that it will produce an HBS case study on our Cummings story, prompted by the book.

JOYCE AND I are both extraordinarily grateful for the blessings of family, love, faith, and good health. Gifts of friends and trust are ever more meaningful as we begin to witness now dozens of good friends who ended their earthly journeys with so much left undone. We are grateful for the ability to open new doors and to sometimes connect others to help them make meaningful differences in this world. Despite any of our country's shortcomings, we are so appreciative and grateful for the blessings of living in the United States of America.

On June 5, 2017, in another front-page story, *Boston Globe* reporter Thomas Farragher offered an extremely supportive look at the work Joyce and I are doing at Cummings Foundation. The story resulted in an astounding number of notes, comments, and emails from old friends and new friends from all over. Prompted by a media release from the Giving Pledge about the latest group of members who had just joined, Tom first talked with us by phone while we happened to be attending the 2017 Giving Pledge meeting, and then in person in Woburn. He also included extensive comments from a telephone interview he conducted with our daughter Marilyn, in New York.

"It's a profound lesson," Farragher concluded, "one passed down from the people who once lived above that Medford liquor store—a mom and dad who taught their kids that generosity has an enduring and priceless dividend all its own."

[23]

Afterword

| Bill draws a standing-room-only crowd at his first book event, at Book Ends in Winchester

BENJAMIN FRANKLIN in his autobiography wrote: "Were it offered to my choice, I should have no objection to a repetition of my same life from its beginning, only asking the advantages that authors have in a second edition to correct some faults of the first."

By this edition of *Starting Small and Making it Big* I have, hopefully, snared most typos or other errors, and have made minor improvements, but have not made meaningful changes. We have, however, become increasingly disappointed by the ever-more-serious deterioration of our national discourse and national integrity, that I felt compelled to further protest the contrarious blatherskite from Washington.

Talking with literally thousands of New England-area readers and others during so many busy book presentations already, and at other civic and academic events, we have heard so much about the increasingly urgent needs of our deserving yet marginalized neighbors and the nonprofits that help them.

Among the great tragedies in our nation today are the growing inequities between the "haves" and the "have nots." And the current Administration and Congress insist on passing legislation that is still cutting funding for agencies, charitable organizations and other groups that so many average and low-income Americans depend upon for their daily survival. Even the recent tax changes provide the greatest benefits to the wealthiest few percent. Business interests must do more to help pick up the slack. We were delighted that Massachusetts' hugely popular (Republican) Governor Charlie Baker attended the Foundation's 2018 Awards Night in part to explain some of his major differences with the Trump Administration.

ONE MAJOR REASON I wrote this book has been to encourage the heads of corporations—many of whom are making more money and profits than ever before in history—as well as the most fortunate among us—to take the responsibility to give back to the less fortunate. Say "thank you" to a nation that has given us the opportunity to become as successful as we have been.

Anyone who reads this book should understand why we feel so grateful to be Americans… America does not need to be made "great again." America is already great. And I urge all those Democrats and Republicans who have been able to benefit the most from that greatness to find ways to help those who need our help.

Aside from correcting errata, this section is also a convenient place to provide some important late updates. One of the most obvious is the story of Cummings Properties which continues to provide the vast majority of all outside funding for Cummings Foundation, Inc. which now has its own endowment of $2 billion in commercial real estate and many other financial investments.

Eric S. Anderson became the fourth president of Cummings Properties on July 1, 2018. A Colby College graduate and a Connecticut native, Eric took over the key position from Dennis A. Clarke, who remains CEO and assumed the chairmanship

| *Eric S. Anderson*

from me.

A colleague since 1999, Eric has proven to be an outstanding leader with a strong knack for building and strengthening relationships with both clients and colleagues. His distinguished performance while serving as a sergeant in the U.S. Marine Corps early in his career prepared him well for many of the various roles he has filled with the company.

THE GREAT REAL ESTATE BUST following the Enron debacle and the financial collapse of 2001 have mostly passed us by, and the business of building and leasing space picked up greatly in Boston through all of 2018.

The large majority of Cummings Properties' one hundred or so commercial buildings display interior graphics informing visitors that "This Building Powers Charities." Other communications inform our clients that 100 percent of all net rent paid by some 2,000-plus client firms either goes directly or will ultimately be directed to support our rapidly developing charitable initiatives. Cummings Foundation is one of the largest, and certainly one of the most unique, private foundations in New England.

In round numbers, the $2 billion endowment of Cummings Foundation consists of about $1 billion of mostly domestic stocks and other securities, either currently owned by the foundation or pledged to it, and another $1 billion invested in a wide variety of mostly commercial real estate. These real properties primarily consist of about 11 million gross square feet of entirely debt-free office and research buildings, all in northeastern Massachusetts, which are (again) currently owned by or pledged to Cummings Foundation.

All of this real property is carefully managed, serviced, and maintained by about 350 full-time employees of our wholly owned Cummings management organization. There are another 500 full-time-equivalent employees of Cummings School of Veterinary Medicine, plus some 124 full-time-equivalent employees of New Horizons at Choate and New Horizons at Marlborough assisted and independent living communities. We are most proud that, as of January 1, 2018, the eighty longest-tenured Cummings colleagues have an average seniority of twenty-five years, with our longest-serving colleague (not counting me) having a tenure of forty-two years.

Client longevity rivals that of our staff, with L.H. Sisitzky Sales of Woburn, our longest seniority *client*, at forty-three years. As of 2019, more than one hundred and twenty client firms have twenty years or more of continuous support as cherished clients of Cummings Properties. For all of this collective loyalty, I shall be eternally proud and highly appreciative.

Although the Foundation never solicits contributions, it depends heavily on the rental income derived from its many leased commercial properties in eleven northern suburbs of Boston to fulfill its work. It uses these funds judiciously and, during recent years, it has distributed more than $200 million in cash grants to mostly small, low-profile charities in Essex, Middlesex, and Suffolk counties of Massachusetts.

The foundation is especially proud, however, to also have close working relationships with Boston-based Partners In Health, and with Bill and Melinda Gates Foundation in the construction and development of the brand-new University of Global Health Equity, in Butaro, Rwanda.

Referrals of prospective lessees from various sources are the

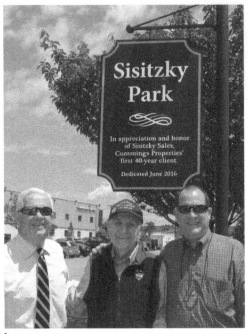

| *Bill Cummings with Leonard and Brian Sisitzky*

lifeblood from which we are able to continue to grow our support to benefit so many worthy charities. In the end, 100 percent of all rental profits are dedicated to Cummings Foundation, Inc., or they are directly donated to charitable causes in many cases. In addition to the foundation's philanthropy, each November, more than 350 Cummings Properties colleagues designate $1,000 or $2,000 each of *company* funds directly to local area charities of their choice. Called Employee Directed Giving, this program has proven to be hugely popular with staff at all levels, and often involves family members actually presenting the awards to their mostly small local charities.

[Acknowledgments]

The single most important acknowledgment is to my family, for all of their many sacrifices, for all the times that any number of issues or projects have kept me away from them. During the months before we were married, in 1966, Joyce and I spoke extensively about that probability, and Joyce graciously accepted those times as they occurred.

Though we now take extended annual vacations, I know that Joyce was expecting more time together in retirement and that surely would not include a serious writing project at age eighty. Yet, she has been immensely helpful with this book, especially in fact-checking, answering my endless questions, and all of the 2018 marketing efforts.

Our children, Daniel, Kevin, Marilyn, and Patricia, had no opportunity, of course, to make any kind of pre-conception deal. They just had to take what came along, but they, and now their spouses, have all made it possible for Joyce and me together to accomplish so much with Cummings Foundation and to do more good in this world than we might have ever otherwise thought possible. For this, I am so deeply grateful. I am even more grateful for the constant presence of our children and their respective families in our lives, and for their help in keeping our five terrific grandchildren—Sonia, Nate, Gus, Isabel, and Valerie—all so present to us and to each other.

The text of the book is completely my work, but since I have never before written a book, I am deeply appreciative of the great help provided by so many Cummings colleagues, too. I am also grateful to Tom Kelleher and Nils Shapiro for their generous guidance, and to Tom Campbell and his team from King Printing Company, in Lowell, Massachusetts, for their special attention and service in printing this writer's first book.

Special thanks go to Denise McKeown, Michael Pascavage, and Mark Herlihy for their generous written contributions to the book, and to the renowned author Bill Novak for carefully reading the first draft and appending so many helpful suggestions and comments to greatly improve my early efforts, and to Pulitzer Prize-winning author Tracy Kidder. To Boston photographer Richard Howard and The Boston Foundation for our cover photo, and to Michael Lamothe, for his many photos and especially for designing the great book cover, and to author and *Boston Globe* all-star Neil Swidey for his great interest and encouragement, and for his baker's dozen of "Themes to Consider," as well as for his generous blurb herein. There are so many other special Cummings colleagues whom I would have been honored to include in the book or in these acknowledgments, but most authors are limited by imperfect memories and by page counts.

The other most hands-on colleagues in Woburn, however, have been senior administrators Gloria Papile, Gail Goldman, Julie DeSilva, Kerry Crisley, Cindy Carey, MaryAnn Dickman, and most of all Lisa VanStry. Craig Ziady and Lucas Toffoli have been enormously helpful, too, as have Greg Ahearn, Bill Grant, Ernie Agresti, Eric Anderson, Dennis Clarke, Derek Russell, and Steve Drohosky. Assisting with the many important typesetting and design issues were Sarah Coelho-Rivera, Chloë Boyko, Abby Johnson and design chair Jim Trudeau. Others offering non-professional help and guidance include Steve Cusano, Rob Yacobian, Judith Muggia, Nancy Wunder, Martin O'Donnell, and Jamie's mom, Connie McKeown. Special thanks to Ellen Knight, who convinced me to write this book on my own, instead of a much different book focused on United Shoe Machinery Corporation that I originally envisioned many years ago. Our communications director, Joyce Vyriotes, has been abundantly helpful to me with managing so many early and ongoing aspects of this publication.

I am most grateful for the cover blurbs and other praise for *Starting Small and Making It Big* from Dean Deborah Kochevar of Cummings School of Veterinary Medicine; from my long-term friend attorney Ralph Nader, author of *Unsafe at Any Speed*; from Dr. Paul Farmer of Partners In Health; from Melinda Gates of Bill and Melinda Gates Foundation, and from Director Peter Drobac, M.D., of the Skoll Center for Social Entrepreneurship at Saïd Business School, University of Oxford. Although outside publications were used to reference work or accomplishments of Giving Pledge members, no information herein was gained during any Giving Pledge event.

The honor of the final pre-printing read-through for content went to Joyce Cummings, who so many times through the years this book was being written provided the perfect answer or information to keep the whole thing accurate and true. Special thanks also to Joe Halpern and Josh Resnek for some serious helpful thinking, and to Geraldine Sobkowicz for her two last-inning final reads. One hundred percent of all proceeds from the sale of this book will benefit the work of Cummings Foundation.

Instead of being a guide for entrepreneurs on the wave of brilliant revolutionary technologies, *Starting Small* pays more attention to some of the basic bedrock principles so necessary in any business: integrity, hard work, innovation, service, persistence, guts, and the other commonsense elements of building and running businesses. Thank you all!

[Index]